W9-BWG-689

Pastry Love

Pastry Love

JOANNE CHANG

PHOTOGRAPHY BY KRISTIN TEIG

HOUGHTON MIFFLIN HARCOURT

BOSTON NEW YORK 2019

For information about permission to reproduce selections from
this book, write to trade.permissions@hmhco.com or to
Permissions, Houghton Mifflin Harcourt Publishing Company,
3 Park Avenue, 19th Floor, New York, New York 10016.

hmhbooks.com

Library of Congress Cataloging-in-Publication Data

Names: Chang, Joanne, author. | Teig, Kristin, photographer.
Title: Pastry love : a baker's journal of favorite recipes / Joanne Chang ;
photography by Kristin Teig.
Description: Boston : Houghton Mifflin Harcourt, [2019] |
Includes index.
Identifiers: LCCN 2019004919 (print) | LCCN 2019010420 (ebook) |
ISBN 9780544836747 (ebook) | ISBN 9780544836488 (paper over board)
Subjects: LCSH: Baking. | Pastry. | Cookbooks. lcgft
Classification: LCC TX763 (ebook) | LCC TX763 .C4344 2019 (print) |
DDC641.86/5—dc23
LC record available at https://lccn.loc.gov/2019004919

Book design by Gary Tooth/Empire Design Studio

Printed in China

C&C 10 9 8 7 6 5 4 3 2 1

To Nicole,
the personification of
pastry love

and Christopher guide their staff taught me lifelong lessons on how to inspire and lead with passion and clarity. At the same time I was developing my spun sugar skills, I was learning from them the value of building a team that had your back, as you had theirs. I practiced piping cream puff after cream puff and then practiced the more important lesson of how to patiently train those around me so they could gain confidence in their abilities. Developing dessert menus allowed me to share my unbridled joy in creating pastries that would delight; sharing my vision of how to execute each dessert taught me the importance of painting as clear a picture as possible to everyone on my team.

Working at Rialto was the best job ever, not only because of all of the learning I gained, but most especially because it introduced me to Christopher, who immediately became a fast friend and mentor. Secret: I harbored a crush on him (no bueno since he was my boss!) and I dreamed from afar. It went unrequited for years and never in a million years did I think we would actually end up together. I remember going for a run with one of my closest friends, Jenn, shortly after leaving Rialto, pining for Christopher and bemoaning that we would never be together. "I'm going to be fifty and we're still going to be talking about Christopher Myers!" Well, sure enough, here we are. I still pinch myself in the morning when I wake up and he is there.

I eventually left Rialto to push myself to learn more—and what better place to do that than New York City, where some of the best pastry chefs in the country were practicing their craft. I was fortunate enough to be on the opening team of Payard Patisserie, run by world famous pastry chef François Payard. I spent a year with him, working from four in the morning to seven at night, six days a week. I'm not exaggerating. We all worked this hard—it was sort of like boot camp. Of course I learned so much! Not only did I immerse myself in traditional French pastry, but I also got a crash course in even more traditional French kitchen slang and swear words. Payard was a phenomenal experience, but I really missed home. Working in a patisserie reminded me of how happy I

was baking in a bakery (as opposed to in a fine-dining restaurant)—breakfast pastries, cakes, cookies, and tarts . . . these were my jam. During that year I started forming plans to return to Boston. I wanted to open a bakery, make all of the things I love, and share them with as many people as I could.

Christopher and I had kept in touch, and he was the one who named my dream bakery Flour. "You want a name that is simple and honest and easy to remember. Flour does all of those things." I moved back to Boston and got a job as pastry chef of Mistral restaurant while I started planning for Flour. I loved my time at Mistral. I baked for the restaurant and tested recipes for Flour on the side. Sometimes my tests made their way onto the dessert menu; more often, the cooks and servers and I just ate them for lunch. I was one of the most popular people in the kitchen because everyone knew that if I was working, there would likely be a mess of desserts to taste surrounding my station. My boss and chef, Jamie Mammano, taught me how to keep your message simple and stick to it no matter what. His motto, "Perfect will be just fine, thank you," runs through my head pretty much daily.

It took a few years to find the right location for Flour, and it was somewhat by chance. My friend Jenn (the one who patiently listened to me pine for Christopher during our daily runs) was getting married, and I made her wedding cake. One of the guests complimented me on the cake and suggested that I should do this professionally. I told him that I actually did and that I was looking for a space to open up my own place. He gave me his business card and assured me he had the perfect space for me in the South End neighborhood in Boston . . . and he is now our landlord at Flour. We opened in September 2000 to a line of eager Bostonians who craved what I was peddling: simple, classically executed French and American pastries. I lived upstairs and baked downstairs, and the bakery of my dreams was everything I had hoped and more. Around this time, Christopher and I started dating as well. Finally! He would visit the bakery in the morning before going off to work; we would have a coffee and pastry together, and he helped guide me as we were growing. He was in the middle of opening a few restaurants because he knew what I was starting to realize: if you have great people, you need to give them opportunities to grow.

My team was tremendous. I didn't want to lose any of them, so I started looking for a location for a second Flour bakery. Opening Flour 2 gave the key players at the original Flour new challenges and responsibilities. Eight of those team members are still with us today, including Nicole, our executive pastry chef, who is now a partner in the bakery.

We now number eight bakeries and counting. Every day my team and I are driven by an obsession to create pastries that make you moan, sigh, and lick your fingers . . . and that make your day better. Every day is a chance to make something new that will delight our guests. I'm always testing new recipes and improving old ones. Just when I think our sticky bun recipe is perfect, I discover another way to make someone say "wow" by making it with apples and apple cider "goo." That's what got me into baking in the first place—making people happy. It's that simple.

When Justin, my editor, and I were discussing this book, he kept referring to this as my "baking bible." And while I guess you could call this book a baking bible, that seems so very formal and even serious. This is anything but. Think of this book as my journal that I'm sharing with you. Jotting-in-the-sidelines, creasing-the-corners-of-my-favorites, sketching-what-I-want-it-to-look-like journal. Here are recipes that I've been developing since my first baking book, *Flour*, came out, such as Rhubarb Brown Sugar Pie, full of tart rhubarb and a creamy brown sugar custard, and Mushroom and Thyme Brioche, covered in melted fontina cheese. I share my notes from creating desserts after an inspiring travel adventure to Tokyo, like Alina's Milk Bread, and to Thailand, which resulted in one of my favorite desserts, Coconut Sticky Rice Pudding with Mango-Lime Curd and Mango Snow. I've updated some of my classics for you with whole grains, and I can't wait for you to try my new, improved Currant Oat Spelt Scones. My pastry team continues to inspire me with their baking, and you'll learn how to make Sarah's Adult Spice Cake with layers of apples and rum-soaked ginger cake and Jessi's Caramel Popcorn Cookies, sprinkled with a bit of salt to offset their buttery sweetness. I've continued my own education in pastry by delving into confections and candies; soon you too will be glowing with pride after making your own Vanilla-Mint Marshmallows (try them in hot chocolate) and wrapping gift bags of irresistible Chocolate–Peanut Butter Buttercrunch and chewy Almond Cherry Pistachio Nougat.

The chapters are arranged by pastry type, beginning with early morning breakfast and ending with end-of-the-day (really any-time-of-day) treats. Within each chapter, the recipes start from easiest to more challenging, and I also took into consideration how many subrecipes there were; sometimes you just want to make one recipe, and other times, the challenge of stringing together multiple recipes beckons. I want this book to sit open, dog-eared and splattered, on your kitchen counter like a friend (that's me!) who's hanging out with you, guiding you as you plan your next baking adventure. Let it inspire you and use it to bake magic for your family and friends. If you are not a baker yet, try a recipe and fall in love with baking; if you are already a baker, fall even deeper in love. I hope that you bake something so phenomenal that you can't wait to jump back into the kitchen to try another recipe, and then another. Share the pastry love with as many people as you can, because that is the reason we bake: to spread love and joy and deliciousness in the world.

A Baker's Dozen

TIPS TO BE A BETTER BAKER

—

1. Read the recipe, the whole recipe, and nothing but the recipe. I can't overemphasize how important this is. You would never leave the house for a road trip to an unknown destination without your GPS, would you? (Or maybe you are like me and you would, and then you end up in tears in a gas station trying to find your way to your destination. This was how I did it before Google Maps, which has changed my world.) Some of the recipes are multistepped, with components that can take up to two days to prepare. If you don't read the entire recipe before starting, you might think you can whip up the whole thing in a few hours. Thoroughly reading the recipe before you begin allows you to pace yourself, know what steps to be ready for, and avoid frustration. I am here to make baking fun for you, so please read the recipe first before you start.

2. Gather your mise en place. "Everything in its place" is the translation of this common French kitchen term. What it means is that before you start a recipe, you collect everything you need—your mise en place— and then, and only then, do you start the recipe. It's tempting to gather as you go, thinking you'll measure out that milk when you need it or cut those apples when you are ready for them. The trouble with that approach is that more often than not, you find yourself in the middle of a recipe trying to prep something that needs to be added immediately. Or you discover that those two eggs you thought you had were someone's breakfast earlier that day. The milk for the cake batter that is supposed to be at room temp is, instead, straight from the fridge. And so on. Get your mise en place together before you start, and you'll never have to worry about these baking predicaments.

3. Use a kitchen scale. Just do it! I wanted every copy of this book to come with a kitchen scale, like a power pack. That turned out to be logistically way too challenging, so instead I will implore you to go out and get a scale for baking. Baking is chemistry, and in order to ensure the ingredients all combine properly and bake well, you need everything to be measured in correct proportion. Volume measurements are wildly inaccurate and lead to unnecessary variations in your pastries. Switch to a scale and become a better baker pretty much immediately. If you bought this book, you either love to bake or want to learn to bake, so please shop for a scale!

4. Check your oven temperature. An easy way to make sure your baked goods bake properly is to get an oven thermometer and check the oven temp before baking. That means heat the oven before you start baking, then check the temperature. If you put a cake or cookie into an oven before it gets to the right temperature, your batter will slowly melt and die a slow death. It needs the heat of the oven to properly activate the baking powder, baking soda, yeast, and/or eggs that lighten your pastry. Home ovens are notorious for not being calibrated well, so don't skip this step if you want to bake successfully.

5. Confirm the temperature of ingredients. I've indicated everywhere you might need to have an ingredient at a certain temperature. With some understanding of why this is important, you can figure this out yourself for every recipe you encounter. I am always aware of the temperature of my butter, eggs, melted chocolate, and liquids. One ingredient at the wrong temperature can foil a recipe. For example, if you're making a flaky dough, it's important that the ingredients be as cold as possible. If they are warm, the fat will just combine into the dry ingredients, and you'll end up with a more cookie-like crust than a flaky one. For flaky crusts and scones, you need the fat to stay cold and not blend in completely with the dry ingredients. When the dough is in the oven, the fat melts and the steam created in the hot oven poufs up the dough and makes it flaky. Another example is beating butter and sugar together for a cake. The sugar crystals act like little shovels in the butter, carving out numerous microscopic air pockets that expand once in the oven and lighten the cake. If the butter is too warm, it won't hold the air pockets created by the sugar, and the cake will be dense. A third example is adding eggs or liquid to butter and sugar that have been beaten together (creamed). If the eggs or liquid are a lot colder than the butter and sugar, they won't blend in well, and you'll end up with lots of tunnels and tough spots in the cake. Cake batters and cookie doughs are all about the thorough emulsification of ingredients, and if you have ingredients that aren't around the same temperature, they can't emulsify. I could go on and on with more examples, such as mixing melted butter or melted chocolate into other ingredients at the right temperature, but the bottom line is this: Pay attention to the temperature of the ingredients specified in each recipe.

6. Use salt. It's second nature for me at this point to reach for the salt container when I'm tweaking a pastry recipe. Salt does for pastries the exact same thing it does for savory foods: It accentuates the flavor of whatever you are making. Try it yourself! Taste a bit of custard base or buttercream without salt, and then add it and taste again. Chocolate becomes richer, lemon becomes sharper, and vanilla becomes more fragrant and aromatic. It's an often-overlooked way to make your pastries really shine.

7. Make the recipe yours. Follow the recipe to a T the first time. It's been written with you in mind, and every precaution has been included to ensure a successful bake. However, once you've made a recipe, it becomes yours. You now have the recipe in your hands, and you can fiddle with it and adjust it to your liking. That might be something as simple as changing

the fruit in a tart or pie, or once you are more comfortable in baking, it might be substituting a different flour or using a different buttercream.

8. Test by touch and eye, not just by time. The times in any recipe are a guideline to give you a general idea of when a pastry is ready. But your oven is different from mine, which is different from your neighbor's, which means the times are a guesstimate. (I—and some of you—learned this lesson the hard way. My first book, *Flour*, often listed baking times that were sometimes very long for most home ovens, which at times led to burnt cookies and overbaked, dry cakes. I feel awful for misleading these bakers and hope to win you back here!) Instead, learn to judge the readiness of a pie or cookie or cake by using your fingers and your eyes. Most of the time you can tell if something is done by touching it. For cakes, muffins, and scones especially, you should be able to poke them in the middle and feel resistance. If your finger sinks, the batter or dough is still raw and needs more time in the oven. Use your eyes, too—when something starts to brown, it is getting close to ready. Check the oven every few minutes at this point and pull your pastry when it is browned according to the recipe. That doesn't mean don't use a timer when baking, but don't set the timer and trust it 100 percent. The time is a suggestion, not law.

9. Clean as you go. I remember my first week at Payard Patisserie; François assigned me to make a wedding cake for one of his employees. I was determined to impress my new boss and came in early three days in a row to bake, fill, and, finally, assemble the cake. On the last day, when I was finally finished with the cake, what I remember most was not how proud I was to have made a wonderful cake for such an important occasion, but instead how much flak I got from my fellow pastry cooks, all of whom were French and very well trained, for making such a mess of the kitchen while baking. They openly ribbed me for baking like a home baker, and I was aghast. I had never properly learned until that point the lesson of cleaning as you go, figuring it was fine to just clean up at the very end. I learned my lesson, and I want you to learn it, too: Clean as you go. Wipe your counters, put away ingredients after using them, keep your hands neat, and do everything you can to keep your work area tidy. It will ensure the greatest chance of baking success because your mind will be clear and you'll avoid making messy errors.

10. Be patient. That means reading the recipe through, gathering your mise en place, checking your oven temperature, everything listed above. It also means that at times when the pull of life makes you want to rush through a recipe, don't. Making a crêpe cake involves staying with every single crêpe that goes into the pan; you can't rush crêpe making or you'll mess up your crêpes and not have enough to build a gorgeous cake. You have to be patient when assembling the cake, or it will end up lopsided and wonky (still delicious, by the way, just not exactly as you planned). Learn to enjoy the step-by-step process involved in all baking, whether a simple muffin or an involved laminated dough.

11. Be present. You won't need to take a meditation class if you bake! Learn the ultimate test in calming your mind and slowing down to appreciate the moment by mixing the dough for a loaf of bread, watching it rise, and waiting for the right moment to put it in the oven. To be a good baker is to follow the directions through. To be a great baker is to fully experience and be thoughtful each step of the way. That's how you learn to improve: paying attention.

12. Don't give up. "Fall down seven times, get up eight" is one of my favorite mottos because it perfectly describes the journey of learning how to bake. Even if you mess up your first time making croissants (I did. And the second, and the third), you'll feel a rush of pride that you made a pastry with hundreds of layers—literally—all by hand. Jump back on that horse, learn from your mistakes, and try again. The more you practice, the stronger you'll be, and the more confidence you'll have. Walk around town knowing that you just made croissants! From scratch! How many people do you know who can do that?

13. Have fun! The most important rule of baking, even beyond buying a scale—which I can't preach enough—is to enjoy yourself and have fun baking. You can't bake a cake and be unhappy. The act of spreading frosting onto cake layers and nibbling on the scraps is a guaranteed formula for putting a smile on your face. Don't get caught up in failures and mistakes (which are often pretty darn delicious as well). Remember the reason we bake: to bring joy and delight to friends or family or even ourselves, with a mouthwatering, incredible, amazing pastry.

Master Techniques

When you travel to another country, you learn how to say hello and please and thank you and where is the bathroom. When baking, take the time to learn the basic language so you can get around easily in these recipes and in your kitchen.

Blind Baking Shells

Tart and pie shells often need to be partially baked before you fill them. This is called blind baking. If you don't bake the pie shell first, it can't fully bake once it is filled, and the result is an underbaked, gummy, doughy crust. Line the unbaked shell with parchment paper or a large coffee filter, and then place a generous amount of pie weights, unbaked dried beans, un-cooked rice, or even well-washed rocks on it to fill the shell fully. Press down slightly on the weights to make sure the shell is entirely filled, and place the whole thing in the oven. The pie weights will keep the shell from bubbling and puffing up. Check the shell for doneness by lifting the parchment and peeking at the color of the baked shell. It should be light golden and look matte; if it's shiny, it needs to bake longer. Be careful when peeking that the weights don't slip under the parchment and bake into the pie dough, especially if you are using rice. When the pie shell is done baking, remove it from the oven and let cool until you can remove the parchment and weights.

Buttering and Flouring Pans

Most cake recipes ask you to butter and flour the cake pans before using. This simple technique ensures that your cake will pop out of the pan easily rather than get stuck to the sides or bottom. Some recipes even suggest lining the bottom of the pan with a parchment circle (see page 23) and THEN buttering and flouring the pan's sides to absolutely, positively ensure the cake doesn't stick. The easiest way to do this is to put a little softened butter or a vegetable oil like canola on a paper towel and spread a very thin layer all over the inside of the pan. Once the entire inside is covered, toss a small handful of flour directly into the pan, then tap along the pan's sides and bottom so the flour coats it completely. Tap out any extra flour.

Some cakes require an unbuttered pan; in these recipes, the cake needs to stick to the pan while baking and cooling. Recipes for these cakes will specify NOT to butter and flour, so please pay attention.

Cooking Sugar

Cooking sugar to make caramel or buttercream can be intimidating. Don't do it long enough, and you won't get the right texture; do it too long, and the sugar will burn; don't do it quite right, and the whole pot may crystallize. Eek!

Let's start at the beginning. When cooking sugar, be sure that the sugar is completely moistened with water before putting it on the stove. (You can make caramel with only sugar, no water, but that is a tad trickier. If you know how to do that, then you probably don't need these words of wisdom.)

Make sure the sides of the pot are clean and there are no undissolved sugar crystals clinging to them. Lingering sugar crystals have a chance of messing with the sugar while it's cooking and starting a chain reaction within the syrup to crystallize the whole pot. It's easy to prevent: Simply brush the sides of the pot with a pastry brush dipped in water. Once the syrup is on the stove, cook it over high heat to bring it to a boil. I have found that if I cook sugar syrup on medium or low, there is a greater chance of it crystallizing, so I always cook it on the highest heat possible. As the syrup is coming to a boil, it's best not to jostle the pot, and definitely don't stir it until after it's been boiling for a while and starts to change color and turn golden. Either action too early could trigger crystallization of the sugar.

Once the sugar is boiling, you can check the temperature in one of two ways. The safest and easiest way is to use a candy thermometer—but this requires owning a candy thermometer. Simply clip the thermometer to the side of the pot or hold the thermometer in the syrup; watch the temperature gauge until it reaches the required temperature, and you're done. If you don't have a thermometer, you can test the syrup by dropping a tiny spoonful of it into a small cup of ice water, then using your fingers to feel how the syrup responds in the water. Many times recipes ask for you to cook syrup to soft ball stage (234° to 240°F)—this means that the syrup you gather in your fingers in the water will be pinchable into a soft ball that holds its shape and then slowly flattens when you take it out of the ice water. If the recipe asks for hard ball stage (250° to 265°F), then the syrup you gather in your fingers should form a ball that won't flatten when you remove it from the water and stays hard when you squeeze it. Once the syrup reaches the right temperature, work with it quickly, as the temperature will continue to rise even when it's off the stove.

But if you are making caramel, you don't need a thermometer or ice water, because you can use your eyes to see when the sugar reaches the right point. As the syrup is boiling, it will slowly get thicker and more viscous as the water evaporates out of it. Eventually, usually after 6 to 8 minutes or so, the sugar will start to color and become pale golden brown, like butterscotch candy. If the heat on your stove isn't even, most likely the syrup on one side of the pot will color first. At this point it's safe to move

the pot and swirl it around so the sugar caramelizes evenly. Don't walk away from it once the sugar starts to color as it doesn't take long for it to caramelize completely.

Remember that you need to watch the sugar mixture very carefully as it cooks and not leave its side once it has started to turn the lightest shade of brown. As soon as the sugar starts to take on color, gently swirl the pot until the sugar mixture is evenly golden brown, and then quickly move on to the next step. There is a fine line between beautifully cooked sugar and an inedible burnt mess—but as long as you don't turn your back on the sugar, you should be able to avoid the latter.

Now here's the trick: Many cooks think that once it's brown, caramel is good to go. But usually it needs to cook a tiny bit longer to really get that nice caramel taste that is much more interesting than just sweet sugar. How to test? Tilt the pot to look at the thin layer of caramel that clings to the bottom of the pot. The color of this layer is the true color of the caramel, and this is the layer that you want to be checking. Caramel in a small pot will look much darker than it really is simply because it's a deep layer. By tilting the pot and peeking at a shallow layer of caramel on the bottom, you see the actual color. Once that becomes lovely amber brown like the color of Samuel Adams lager, use the caramel immediately, as it will continue to darken even after you take it off the stove. Don't be afraid if it smokes just a bit; it is normal for some wisps of smoke to escape from the caramel right before you remove it from the stove. Whisk in any cream or butter, and it will immediately halt the caramelization.

To clean the pot after making caramel, when the residual sugar looks like an impenetrable mess, fill the pan with water and boil it until the caramel dissolves. Or if you don't need the pot again right away, simply soak it with water until the caramel eventually breaks down. It really will!

Creaming Butter and Sugar

Sugar crystals are magic. Think of them as thousands of little workers with shovels, burrowing into butter and creating zillions of tiny air pockets. When you cream butter and sugar together, the butter should be around 68°F, which is comfortable and slightly cool room temperature; you should be able to bend the stick of butter, but it shouldn't be so soft that you can poke your finger through it. If the butter is at the right temperature, then the sugar beats into the butter and makes lots and lots of air pockets, which then make the final product light and fluffy. If the butter is too cold, the sugar just isn't strong enough to dig those pockets; too warm, and the sugar just sloshes straight through the butter and doesn't create any pockets, either. Creaming is most important in cake and cookie recipes, which contain a hefty amount of both butter and sugar. It's best to beat the butter and sugar for longer than you would think: at least 6 to 8 minutes on medium speed with a stand mixer. Watch it, and you'll see the transformation from yellow sandy mixture to white and fluffy—and then you'll know you have a properly creamed mixture.

Crumb Coating a Cake

Once you've assembled a cake and you're ready to finish it off and make it fabulous with a luscious drape of frosting, it's important to give it a crumb coat first. This coat seals in any and all loose crumbs so that the final coat is spotless and crumb-free. Once the cake is assembled, take a little bit of the frosting or buttercream and spread it over the top. Spread as thin a layer as you can. Then take a bit more frosting and spread it along the sides of the cake, again keeping the layer very thin. Don't worry about how it looks—this crumb coat will eventually be entirely covered up with more frosting. The important thing is to make sure the whole cake gets covered with a thin layer of frosting. If time permits, place the cake in the refrigerator or freezer for 30 minutes or so to set the crumb coat. Then putting on the final coat of frosting will be a breeze.

Cutting a Parchment Circle

Often when making a cake, the easiest way to ensure you can remove it from the pan after baking is to line the bottom of the pan with a parchment paper circle. You can always trace a circle on the parchment and cut it out, but there's a nifty trick I've picked up that I use to make this a little simpler. Take a piece of parchment paper and fold it in half. Then fold that in half at a 90-degree angle. Fold in half again, then in half again, each time bringing the folded edges together, into a smaller and smaller square. Turn the cake pan upside down and place the folded point in the center of the pan. Use a pair of scissors to trim the edge of the parchment so that it follows the curve of the outside of the cake pan. When you unfold the parchment, you will have a circle that fits exactly in the pan.

Docking Dough

When baking pie and tart shells, you are often instructed to dock (poke holes into) the dough before baking. You can get a fancy docker that looks like a lint roller with spikes, or you can just use a fork. Docking the shell allows air to escape when you bake it. Tart and pie dough have a fair amount of liquid in them from the butter, eggs, and any other liquid you've mixed in. When the dough goes into the oven, the liquids turn to steam with the heat. This steam can cause big bubbles to form in the shell unless you give it a way to escape. Hence you dock pastry shells. If you are filling the tart with a liquid filling after you blind bake it, take care not to dock too aggressively. A few holes here and there will be enough to release the steam but not so much that the liquid filling leaks out.

Filling a Pastry Bag

Before you fill a pastry bag, first cut off the tip of the bag: Place a pastry tip in the bag and wedge it into the bottom so you can see where exactly to snip—you want to cut the hole large enough for the tip to stick out, but not so large that it falls out of the bag. Mark that spot. Then remove the tip and use scissors or a small knife to cut off the tip of the bag as marked. Place the pastry tip inside the bag and push it out of the cut bag until it's tightly wedged in the bottom of the bag. Give the bag a twist just above the tip and push the twisted part of the bag into the tip—this keeps the filling inside the bag when you start filling it. Cuff the bag at its halfway point around your hand (don't cheat and cup just the top of the bag or you'll have a mess on your hands later on—literally!). Open the bag with your other hand to create a nice big opening for the filling. Using a spatula or a bowl scraper, carefully fill the bag no more than halfway. Don't overfill it, or the filling will inevitably push out the top of the bag and you will spend your time cleaning up after yourself and making a mess on your cake or tart. Once the bag is half full, uncuff it and push the filling to the bottom of the bag. Twist the bag at the top of the filling a few times to keep the filling inside.

Flicking Flour

When rolling out tart shells or shaping bread, you want a well-floured work surface. Sure, you can just sprinkle flour over your work surface and you'll have achieved your purpose. But learning to flick flour across the counter is one of the more fun, easy skills to pick up when you are getting into bread and pies. Grab a small handful of flour and place your hand sideways, 3 or 4 inches above and parallel to the counter. Bend your wrist back and then quickly, as if you are skipping rocks, throw the flour across the work surface in a horizontal motion. The flour will shower the counter in an even, thin layer, allowing you to roll and shape to your heart's content. It doesn't matter what type of flour you flick, either—use any flour that is in the recipe (so you will need a little extra from what is listed).

Folding Ingredients

Folding—as opposed to stirring or whisking or mixing—is a controlled and gentle method of combining ingredients. Sometimes you want to keep ingredients light and airy (such as when adding ingredients to whipped egg whites or whipped cream), and sometimes you want to make sure not to overmix the ingredients, which would lead to toughness (such as when adding liquids to dry ingredients for cakes and muffins). Folding is perfect for these situations because it allows you to combine ingredients with the least amount of actual mixing and maintain as much air and lightness as you can. To fold properly, don't just sweep around the edge of the bowl—that creates a whirlpool of ingredients that don't really combine; they just get moved around in the vortex. Instead, use a rubber spatula to cut down through the center of the bowl, then sweep around the edge of the bowl.

Give the bowl a quarter-turn and keep repeating until you've rotated the bowl all the way around. Be sure to cut smack dab through the ingredients in the center of the bowl and go all the way down to the bottom and sweep up the sides, scraping up all the loose stuff along the way. Every few turns, scrape the sides of the bowl all the way around to catch any loose flour that accumulates there.

when I dump it out of the mixing bowl. Doing fraisage brings the shaggy mess together into a tidy dough that will have long striations of butter instead of little pieces. These long pieces will melt and turn to steam in the oven, separating the dough into a multitude of flaky layers and creating an incredibly tender pastry.

Fraisage

When making pie dough, to achieve perfect flaky pastry you need long, flat sheets of butter sandwiched between flour. When the dough goes into a hot oven, the liquid in the butter turns to steam and this steam instantly puffs up and leaves little flaky pockets within the dough. In order to get these long, flat layers of butter, I use the French technique called fraisage, in which I smear the dough with chunks of butter in it along the work surface with the heel of my hand, spreading and smooshing the butter into the long sheets I want. The trick is to first not mix the dough completely when I add the liquid to the dry ingredients. I want the dough to be shaggy and unkempt-looking

Making a Cornet

A cornet is a small parchment paper cone that you fill with melted chocolate, caramel, or piping icing that you use to write on cakes and cookies. To make a cornet, fold a piece of parchment paper on the diagonal and cut through the fold with a small paring knife so you have two triangles. Position one of the triangles so the longest edge is facing away from you on an angle from lower left to upper right, the shortest edge is on the right, and the middle-length edge is facing down (toward you). Now eyeball the mid-length edge to find the halfway point. Place your left hand at this point and hold it down with your forefinger and thumb. Bend down the top corner, then twist it under so that the point is approximately at the midpoint of the shortest edge and poking out about an inch. You will see the beginning of a cone forming. Slowly roll the parchment down with your right hand while anchoring the opposite tip with your left hand. After you've rolled the whole triangle into a cone, tuck the extended point of the open top inward to hold everything in place. Fill the cornet about halfway (don't overfill or you will end up with a mess) and roll the top of the cornet closed like a tube of toothpaste, making sure to roll the cornet with the seam on the bottom. Snip the point with scissors or cut it off with a small paring knife to make a tiny opening for the filling to come out.

Making Vanilla Sugar

When you split a fresh vanilla bean and scrape out the seeds, you are left with a vanilla pod that is most definitely not trash. Instead, use the pod to make vanilla sugar: Fill an empty container with a few cups of sugar and bury the pod in the sugar. Close the container; check back in a few days. The vanilla pod will perfume the sugar with its unmistakable scent, and you'll be left with vanilla sugar that you can use in baking and to sweeten drinks. The pod keeps indefinitely in the sugar, so keep adding pods and refilling the container with sugar regularly, and you'll always have vanilla sugar at the ready.

Melting Chocolate

This might seem like too basic a technique to describe, but I've seen too many bowls of scorched chocolate and marred cakes and brownies to omit it. The two ways to melt chocolate are either in the microwave or in a double boiler (bain-marie). When you microwave chocolate, it keeps its shape, as it is melting from the inside out; too often people think they need to continue microwaving it to fully melt. Not true! Use the medium power function, and stir every 20 to 30 seconds to prevent the chocolate from burning. Stirring the chocolate will mingle the melted chocolate on the inside with the unmelted parts on the outside. Once most of the chocolate is melted, you can remove it from the microwave and continue to stir. The residual heat will finish the melting.

To melt chocolate in a double boiler, place it in a metal or heatproof glass bowl (plastic doesn't conduct heat well, so it is not great for melting chocolate). Place the bowl on top of a pot of simmering water (make sure the bottom of the bowl doesn't touch the water, or it will scorch the chocolate) and stir the chocolate occasionally until it melts. The mistake I see here most often is having the water at a full rolling boil; the chocolate at the edge of the bowl burns. Once a little of the chocolate burns, it infuses its acrid scent into the whole bowl, so you don't want to let it get this far. Instead, keep the water at a gentle simmer, stirring the chocolate from time to time until it fully melts.

Piping with a Pastry Bag

So often I see people piping frosting on a cake and using both hands to hang on to the pastry bag as if their life depends on it. If there's one lesson I would love everyone to learn, it is how to properly pipe with a pastry bag. Assuming you are right handed, use your right hand to hold the filled bag at the top of the filling and pump the filling out of the bag with this hand. Your left hand and fingers hold and guide the tip so you can decorate the cake or fill the cream puffs. If you clench the filling with both hands and press it out that way, the heat of your hands warms up and melts the filling, and you won't have as much control over the decorating. So practice piping with just your dominant hand and use the other hand simply as a guide. As you are piping, pause from time to time to push the filling down toward the tip, and then continue piping.

Rolling Out Pastry Dough

Back and forth, back and forth—this is how many people roll out pie and tart doughs. However, if you go back and forth over the same piece of dough, you are essentially just moving it back and forth and not really rolling it out very effectively. Yes, eventually you'll get the dough rolled out, but doing it this way is a lot harder than it needs to be. This is why you should always roll starting from the center of the dough. Place

the rolling pin in the center and roll out, away from you. Lift up the pin and come back to center, and roll toward you. Center the pin again and roll to the left. Bring it back to center and roll to the right. Turn the dough every now and then to get a nice circle, but always use the center as your starting point.

Rotating Cake Pans, Baking Sheets, and Muffin Tins

Want to do a test to see how evenly (or not) your oven bakes? Empty a bag of shredded coconut onto a baking sheet and put it in a preheated 350°F oven for about 10 minutes. When the coconut starts to toast and brown (and makes your kitchen smell like you're in Hawaii), take a peek at the baking sheet. You'll see dark-brown toasted parts, pale-tan lightly toasted areas, snowy-white untoasted bits, and maybe even some burnt, blackened coconut if your oven runs hot. Oven heat is notoriously uneven, even in the best ovens, which is why you should always rotate your pans about midway through the baking time. The exact time is not critical: Pick a point around the middle of the estimated bak-ing time and carefully turn whatever is in the oven 180 degrees. If you are baking two pans, with one on the middle rack and one on the bottom, you should also swap their positions at this point, i. e., move the pan from the middle rack to the bottom rack and vice versa. This will give you a more evenly baked final product.

Scalding Milk and Cream

To scald is to heat a liquid to just under the boiling point, when small bubbles form around the edge of the pan and you can tell that the whole pot is just about to bubble. Scalding heats the liquid as hot as possible so it combines more smoothly with other ingredients, but without boiling, which would cause you to lose some liquid to evaporation and would throw off the proportions of ingredients.

Scoring and Slashing Bread

For the same reason you put on earrings or cufflinks, wear accessories, or button your coat, you slash and score bread dough before baking it: to make it look good—it's mainly an aesthetic technique. But if you don't slash, the bread will burst on its own every which way. Some bread bakers like that look, and you'll find that many rustic loaves don't have slashing and look more homestyle. Personally, I prefer a scored loaf, and I also really enjoy slashing a baguette before sliding it into the oven.

To slash bread, use a sharp paring knife or a razor blade. Dip it in water to keep it from dragging. Use the tip and length of the knife or blade and use quick, sure movements focusing most of the pressure on the tip of the blade. There's no wrong way to arrange your slashes, but here are a few suggestions: For baguettes and long loaves, the slashes should be evenly spaced

½ to ¾ inch apart, and parallel and offset so that you are slashing down the length of the baguette. For round loaves, either make four slashes in a square, so you'll end up with a little hat in the middle of the bread, or make one slash down the middle of the bread and a few slashes diagonally on either side, meeting the middle.

Splitting a Cake

To split a cake into layers, place it on a flat surface. If you have a cake stand or a lazy Susan, place the cake on it to make rotating the cake easier. Carefully and evenly score the cake with a long, thin serrated knife all the way around, about an inch deep, where you want to split it. Once the entire cake is scored, place the knife back into the groove you've made and slowly start cutting into the cake while rotating it. If you follow the groove and continue to rotate the whole time, the knife will cut through the cake evenly all the way through.

Splitting and Scraping Vanilla Beans

A fresh vanilla bean pod is plump and ready to be split to share its fragrant seeds in your baking. Lay the vanilla bean on a flat surface and flatten it with your fingers. Using a sharp paring knife, split the bean in half by poking it at one end, lay the knife parallel to the table, and fillet the bean open. Use the back of the knife to scrape the seeds out of the bean, collecting the seeds on the knife blade. If you are making custard or infusing a liquid with vanilla, throw the seeds and pod into the liquid. If you are adding vanilla to a batter, take a small bit of the

batter, smoosh the vanilla seeds into it until they are mixed in, and fold this concentrated vanilla batter into the rest of the batter. Save the pod and use it to make vanilla sugar (see page 26).

Spreading with an Offset Spatula

An offset spatula is my most valued and trusted implement in the pastry kitchen. I am at home when I am at a mixer with flour, sugar, butter, and eggs laid out in front of me and an offset spatula in my hand. The proper way to use an offset is to angle the long blade at a 30 to 45 degree angle to whatever it is you are spreading, whether it is brownie batter or frosting on a cake. Hold the handle firmly in your hand as if you are wagging your fingers at someone with the handle; your forefinger goes on the metal part of the offset (bend) and the rest of your hand grips the handle. Place the blade on its edge on the surface of the batter or frosting and slide it across firmly, going back and forth as needed to smooth the surface. Don't shift the blade upwards or hold it perpendicular to the surface, because you have less control over spreading that way; similarly, don't hold it flat and parallel to the surface, either. The magic spot is about halfway in between (an angle of 30 to 40 degrees) so the blade is slanted against the surface at all times.

Tempering Chocolate

Any chocolate you purchase is already tempered, which means the crystalline structure in the chocolate is all lined up, resulting in chocolate that snaps when you bite or break it, and it's shiny and glossy. Sometimes chocolate becomes untempered; if you ever see chocolates that are covered in what looks like white chalk, that means that the chocolate has come out of temper and has bloomed. Bloomed chocolate is still fine to eat; it just doesn't look great—it is not shiny—and it doesn't have good texture.

Why would you ever need to temper chocolate, since you buy it already tempered? If you want to dip candies or truffles in chocolate to give them a lovely thin chocolate coating, you need to melt the chocolate first. And guess what makes chocolate come out of temper? Melting it. Tempering chocolate is a way of melting the chocolate, then manipulating it, so that it is brought back to a tempered state even while melted, so you can use it for dipping and making chocolate decorations.

Tempering chocolate is a challenging skill that takes many years to learn. I've learned a quick shortcut method that is a lot easier than classic tempering and just as effective. It works best for small batches like I offer in this book. This method is called seeding. You melt most of the chocolate so it comes out of temper and then remove it from the heat. Finely chop some unmelted tempered chocolate (remember that all chocolate that you buy is already tempered) and add it to the melted chocolate. After stirring for a while (sometimes this takes up to 20 minutes) the tempered chocolate mixes and melts into the untempered chocolate and acts as a "seed" to bring all the chocolate into temper. It's truly magical. To test whether the chocolate has become tempered again, place a bit of chocolate right underneath your bottom lip. When it feels just barely cool, it is the right temperature (86° to 90°F for dark chocolate and 84° to 87°F for milk and white chocolates) and the chocolate is tempered. The chocolate does not stay in temper for long—usually you have 6 to 8 minutes to dip candies in it or spread it on toffee or nougat. Since it is in temper when you are dipping or spreading, it will firm up in a tempered state, meaning it will be snappy and glossy and shiny and not dull or streaky or soft. You can warm it up ever so slightly as you are using it, but never allow it to get so warm that it feels warm to the touch. At that point it will be out of temper again.

Tempering Ingredients

You know how some people like to dive headfirst into a pool and others like to inch their way into the water one toe at a time? If pastry were a swimmer, it would be in the latter group. Pastry is all about patience, and when combining two ingredients of different temperatures or textures, it's important to introduce one into the other gently via a method called tempering. This is when you whisk a little bit of hot liquid into a cold ingredient, then whisk in a little more and a little more, until the two are completely combined. This

is especially important when you are whisking a hot liquid into raw eggs. In this case, tempering ensures that the hot liquid doesn't cook the eggs—which would make the final product uncomfortably reminiscent of scrambled eggs. Tempering is also when you add a little bit of a light whipped mixture into a stiffer mixture and fold gently to lighten the stiffer mixture, then add the rest of the light mixture.

Speaking of eggs: When you combine them with sugar, don't just crack the eggs directly onto the sugar and let them sit. The sugar in effect "cooks" the eggs through a chemical reaction, and little hard lumps will form. Instead, crack the eggs into a bowl, whisk to break them up, then slowly whisk in the sugar. Once the sugar is mixed into the eggs completely, they are fine sitting with each other. It's when you dump one on top of the other without whisking that they don't play well together and things get lumpy.

Toasting Nuts

My baking team thinks I'm obsessed with nuts because whenever I see a tray of walnuts, pecans, or almonds, I grab a few and take a bite. I am in love with a lot of nuts, especially almonds, but my reason for trying them is to ensure they are toasted properly. Toasting nuts brings out their rich flavor and helps make their texture crunchier and snappier—it's one of the easiest ways to up your baking game. To toast nuts, preheat the oven to 350°F and spread the nuts in an even single layer on a baking sheet. Place the nuts in the oven for 6 to 8 minutes to start, then take out a nut, break it open (be careful, it will be hot!), and take a look. If the interior is a light pale brown, the nuts are ready; if it's lighter, continue baking for another minute or two and then check again. It typically takes about 10 minutes, but check earlier in case your oven runs hot. The nuts will get crunchier as they cool and become irresistible to snack on, so much so that if the bakers know I'll be in the kitchen, they purposely toast extra knowing I'll grab more than needed just for testing.

Whipping Egg Whites

There is so much water in eggs, especially egg whites, that they work beautifully as leaveners in recipes such as sponge cakes and angel food cakes. Problems arise (ha ha . . . arise . . .) when you don't know how much to beat the whites and end up overbeating them. Once they are overbeaten, the walls of the individual cells are stretched to the max. Then when you put the dessert in the oven, even if there is tons of steam being created by the water in the whites, the dessert won't rise because the egg cell walls have already been stretched to their limit. So the key is to whip the egg whites until right before they are completely whipped, so that they still have some stretch and give in the cell walls; then they can expand in the oven as the water in the whites turns to steam, leavening the dessert.

But how much is "right before they're completely whipped"? If the ratio of sugar to egg whites is low— that is, the dessert doesn't have a lot of sugar but does have a lot of egg whites—you want to beat the whites just until they hold a soft peak, but not beyond that point. To test for the soft-peak stage, lift the whip or whisk out of the whites and turn it upside down; the whites should peak and then droop. These whites are best gently folded into the batter; then when they get into the oven they will rise, rise, rise and expand the batter into a light and airy pastry. Whites with little sugar are the easiest to overwhip, since sugar adds stretchiness to the whites, allowing you to whip them much longer. But whites beaten with just a little sugar will never get stiff and glossy no matter how long you whip. As the ratio of sugar to whites goes up, you can whip longer and get a stiffer, shinier egg white mixture.

Also, when beating egg whites, be sure to use a spotlessly clean bowl, since any speck of egg yolk or oil or fat will weaken the walls of the whites, preventing them from being able to stretch and hold the air you are trying to beat into them. If you've been beating whites for a while—say, 5 minutes—and they are still sloshy and not stiffening at all, then unfortunately you are plumb out of luck and you'll have to start over. Once egg whites have been contaminated with fat, they are not good for much more than egg white omelets . . . so be sure to clean your bowls and whisks well!

Equipment

There's no need to stock your kitchen with every gadget for cooks on the market. In many cases you can get by with a few bowls, a whisk, a wooden spoon, a silicone spatula, and baking sheets and pans — all items that you may already own. But certain equipment does come in very handy for baking, making the process easier and the results better. Here are a few key items.

Bain-Marie

A bain-marie is a water bath. We use them all the time in pastry to melt things or gently cook things, and in ovens to bake custards. You can purchase a specifically designed set of nesting pots as a bain-marie, but you don't really need to. All you need is a pot and a metal or heatproof glass bowl that can rest on top of it. Pour at least 3 inches of water in the pot and bring it to a simmer. Place the bowl on top of that and voilà! Instant bain-marie. In the oven, you need a baking pan with high sides that is large enough to hold whatever you are baking. Place the item in the pan, place the pan in the oven, and add enough water to come halfway up the sides of the item. If you are baking in a springform pan, be sure to line it or wrap it with foil so the water from the bain-marie doesn't seep in.

Baking Pans

The best material for these is sturdy aluminum. Standard-size cake pans are round, 8 or 9 inches in diameter. They are somewhat interchangeable; if you go with 9-inch pans, the layers will be a little thinner; if you go with 8-inch pans, you'll have somewhat thicker cakes. Adjust the baking time accordingly; if a recipe calls for an 8-inch pan and you use a 9-inch one, check the cake 15 to 20 minutes earlier in case it bakes quicker. If you have other size pans, such as 6-inch, be sure not to fill the pans any more than two-thirds full (as with larger cakes) or the batter will overflow. You'll want at least two of whichever size you choose so that you can make layer cakes.

A 9 x 13-inch baking pan is standard for many cobblers and brownies, and an 8 x 8-inch pan is perfect for candies and caramels. A 9 x 5-inch loaf pan is great for making breakfast loaf breads, and you'll use it all the time when you want a simple cake. A 9- or 10-inch tube pan or angel food cake pan is necessary if you want to make angel food cake, but avoid nonstick angel food cake pans, since these cakes rely on gripping the sides of the pan to bake up light and fluffy. For tarts, I use a bottomless straight-edged 8- or 10-inch tart ring; you can substitute a standard two-piece fluted 9-inch tart pan.

A glass or ceramic pie plate is imperative for pies, although in a pinch you can use a disposable aluminum pie plate, which you can find in the baking section of most grocery stores.

Baking Sheets

One large baking sheet is plenty; two is nice but not necessary. I find the best to be aluminum half-sheet baking sheets that measure 13 x 18 inches and have a small rim all the way around. They are small enough to fit into home ovens but big enough to hold a decent number of cookies, sponge cakes, meringues, or whatever you are baking. It's also handy to have at least one quarter-sheet rimmed baking sheet that measures 9 x 13 inches, especially for making certain candies in this book.

Bench Scraper

A bench scraper—a small spatula-like metal rectangle with a wooden or plastic handle—is a handy tool for working with pie, tart, and bread doughs. Use it to pick up and move dough, to divide dough into smaller pieces, and to lift items off baking sheets. Clean your work surface by dragging and firmly scraping the bench scraper over the whole surface. If you live in a colder climate, it's not unlike scraping the snow off the windshield after a snowstorm; if you scrape frequently, it's a lot easier to keep the surface clean. I always have a scraper handy when I bake, and use it to clean and scrape every few minutes.

Bowls

Have at least one small metal or plastic bowl for holding cracked eggs and whisking together liquid ingredients; one medium-to-large metal bowl for folding cake batters and whipping cream and egg whites; and small and/or medium metal or heatproof glass bowls to use as a bain-marie (see page 31). A variety of other size bowls comes in handy as well.

Bowl Scraper

A half-moon-shaped plastic tool, a bowl scraper is handy for scraping out batters from mixing bowls and for folding in ingredients by hand if you have too much batter to use a rubber spatula. This is not essential, but they are really inexpensive, and if you have one you'll end up using it often because it can be used for so many other tasks, like cleaning your work surface and even cutting softer doughs.

Candy Thermometer

A candy thermometer is necessary if you are making something with a cooked sugar syrup and you are not comfortable testing the temperature of the sugar by hand. (I explain testing by hand on page 22.) For making buttercreams, I like the hand-testing method, but for candies, for which you need an exact temperature measurement, you should use a thermometer.

Knives

You'll want at least one long, thin serrated knife to cut through cakes and to slice bread. A small paring knife is perfect for trimming fruit and helping you pop cakes out of pans. A standard 8-inch chef's knife is necessary for chopping fruit and slicing candies and cakes.

Measuring Cups and Spoons

You need dry measuring cups for dry ingredients so you can level them off. Look for ones with straight-sided cylindrical walls. Use wet measuring cups (the ones that look like small pitchers) for liquids so they don't spill. If you get a scale (see page 33), though, you won't need any of these, as you can simply weigh the ingredients. But even with a scale, you will still need tablespoon, teaspoon, and teaspoon fraction measuring spoons.

Microplane Zester

These are the best and easiest tools to use to grate the zest of citrus fruits. They are also terrific for grating fresh ginger (which is much easier to do if the ginger is frozen first) and whole nutmeg.

Muffin Tins

Muffin tins come in all sizes, from mini to regular to jumbo to just muffin tops (an old craze that disappeared but has come back again). All the muffins in this book were tested with regular and jumbo 12-cup aluminum muffin tins. We line ours with muffin papers for easy removal after baking; you can also butter and flour the tins (see page 21) or spray them before using.

Parchment Paper

Parchment paper is a standby at the bakery because of its nonstick quality and because it's the perfect material to make piping cornets (see page 25) for decorating cakes. Use it to line baking sheets when baking cookies and pie shells for blind baking, and cut it into circles (see page 23) to line cake pans when making cakes. We reuse our parchment over and over until it basically falls apart.

Pastry Bags and Tips

Pastry bags are great for decorating cakes and for piping out soft doughs like pâte à choux for cream puffs. You can use cloth or disposable plastic. The advantage to cloth is that you can reuse a cloth pastry bag over and over; the disadvantages are that the bag will get smelly if you don't clean it with bleach every time, and the bulky material is sometimes challenging to pipe with. The advantage to disposables is that they are more flexible, so they are easier to pipe with; the disadvantage is that they are not environmentally friendly. However, you can—and we do—wash plastic pastry bags to reuse over and over. I like the larger 16- to 18-inch pastry bags, since smaller ones tend to get messy really quickly because there's a tendency to overfill them.

As for pastry tips, definitely get one small round tip (around ⅛ inch in diameter), one large round tip (between ¾ inch and 1 inch in diameter), and one small star tip (around ½ inch in diameter) as starters. The large round tip is exactly what you need when you're piping out pâte à choux into cream puffs or éclairs; the small round tip is what you'll use to fill them. A star tip is a basic decorating tip that can add pizzazz to any frosted cake.

Rolling Pins

I like using a tapered French pin—a long, simple tapered wooden rod—for rolling out pie and tart doughs. It allows me to feel the dough underneath the pin, and I can maneuver the dough with the tapered ends to roll it into the shape I want. For laminated doughs, a small pin that rotates around two handles is nice. You need more strength and leverage to roll out sheets of laminated dough; with a pin that rolls while you hold the handles, you can lean into it and push down and the pin will glide over the dough with the help of ball bearings.

Rotating Cake Stand

While not necessary, a rotating cake stand is something to consider if you decorate a lot of cakes. The task is much easier when you can place the cake on a spinning stand that lets you spread frosting evenly over a cake's sides and top.

Scale

This is the most important piece of equipment you can buy to become a good baker. Weighing ingredients ensures that your measurements are exact, which is really important in baking. Plus, it is easier to weigh ingredients rather than scoop and measure and level. Weighing takes out much of the unnecessary uncertainty in baking. You can find a decent digital scale at any kitchen store or online for $15 to $20, and it will be the best purchase you can make to improve your baking. Make sure you get one that goes easily from US weights (pounds and ounces) to metric, because if you are going to weigh, you should weigh in grams and kilos. Metric is more precise and allows for infinitely easier scaling up and down if you want to adjust the recipe; it is also much easier to understand because you don't have to toggle back and forth between pounds and ounces. Also make sure that it has a tare function, which allows you to zero out the scale for each new ingredient you add.

Sifter

This is essential for sifting flour and other dry ingredients to make sure they are as light and aerated as can be. When a recipe calls for sifting, be sure to sift! You don't know how long your dry ingredients have been sitting on a shelf, packing themselves into clumps and lumps; sifting allows them to air out and breathe. Once you sift, you should also give the dry ingredients a stir with a spoon, as sifting doesn't do a great job of evenly combining various dry ingredients. If you want to test this, sift some flour with a few tablespoons of cocoa powder and see for yourself how the flour and cocoa aerate, but don't combine. A sifter is also very handy for finishing off desserts that call for a dusting of confectioners' sugar to make them sparkle.

Silicone Baking Mats

Silicone baking mats (a common brand is Silpat) entered my baking world for the first time when I worked at Payard Patisserie in New York City. They were EXTREMELY expensive at the time and only used on special occasions. Now they are much more common and easy to come by, so I encourage you to purchase at least one. Silicone mats are used to line baking sheets; they are about as nonstick as it gets—no need for parchment, pan spray, or buttering and flouring. And since you can wash and reuse them over and over, they are also environmentally friendly. I especially like using them for making candies because cooked sugar can be a bear to remove from baking sheets and parchment.

Spatulas

Rubber and/or silicone spatulas are a must in a baking kitchen. Make sure you have one that is at least 12 inches long to give you enough leverage to fold and mix batters. When you don't have a bowl scraper handy, you can use a rubber spatula to scrape out batter from a bowl; the curved, somewhat flexible head will allow you to really clean out every last bit.

My absolute favorite piece of baking equipment is an offset spatula. This is a thin, flexible metal spatula with a wooden handle that has a bend at the handle, hence the name "offset." This tool is invaluable for frosting and decorating cakes and for spreading out jams and fillings on tarts.

Stand Mixer

I've used the exact same KitchenAid mixer at home ever since I started baking. I still have the original standard whisk, paddle, and dough hook attachments, and they are all very well worn. The whisk allows me to whip up eggs, egg whites, and heavy cream for items like mousses, egg-leavened cakes, and meringue-based buttercreams. (In fact, the first thing I made with the whisk attachment was meringues.) The paddle attachment is the workhorse: It creams butter and sugar until light and fluffy, which is the starting point for many cakes, cookies, and tart doughs. The dough hook is essential for bread. Kneading bread by hand is fun . . . once. After that, you'll learn to really

appreciate the dough hook, which does all the hard work for you. (I've also used Cuisinart and Krups stand mixers in other kitchens, but my heart belongs to KitchenAid.)

With a stand mixer, you can mix one item and have your hands free so that you can easily add another item to the mixing bowl. Using a mixer is also more thorough and even than mixing by hand. Many steps in baking—kneading bread dough, whipping eggs and cream, creaming butter and sugar—require a fair bit of muscle power. A mixer makes these actions easier.

If you don't have a stand mixer, a handheld electric mixer can do many of the same tasks, such as creaming butter and sugar together, cutting butter into dry ingredients, and whipping egg whites and cream. The one thing it doesn't do is knead bread.

If you don't have either mixer, don't despair! You can certainly make many of the pastries in this book by hand, but it's exponentially more efficient to use a machine. Mixing by hand takes longer and requires more patience and more muscle power; for some recipes, I find it difficult to keep the ingredients at the right temperature if mixing by hand.

Whisk

One 12-inch (from head to toe) whisk can serve multiple purposes. If possible, get a whisk that has thin, flexible wires, called a piano whisk. You'll use it to whisk sugar into eggs, whip cream by hand, and whisk pastry cream and other custards that require constant attention.

Wire Rack

A gridded wire rack is helpful when you are cooling items out of the oven, since it allows air to circulate around the baked goods, keeping them from getting soggy. A wire rack is also helpful when you are glazing cakes. Positioning the rack over a baking sheet allows any extra glaze to drip off rather than puddle at the bottom of the cake.

Ingredients

Rather than go into every single ingredient you'll encounter, here are specific points about certain ingredients that you need to bake successfully.

Brown Sugar

I used light brown sugar for all these recipes, unless otherwise specified. If you don't have brown sugar, you can easily make your own: In a food processor, blend together 1 cup granulated sugar and 2 tablespoons unsulfured molasses for every 1 cup brown sugar you need. That was easy!

Butter

Use unsalted grade AA butter when you bake. Always unsalted! Salt acts as a preservative, so salted butter is suspect—who knows how long it's actually been in the grocery store? Unsalted butter has a much shorter shelf life, so stores are forced to buy it in smaller quantities and therefore it's usually fresher. Plus, when you use salted butter you don't know how much salt is in there, and your final product might end up too salty. Start with unsalted butter and control the amount of salt you add. European-style butters, which have a higher butterfat content, tend to be too fatty for most of these recipes, so I don't bake with them.

Chocolate

Many recipes in this book call for chocolate—white, milk, semisweet, bittersweet, unsweetened—and each recipe was tested with a specific type of chocolate for flavor and texture. The best advice I can give you about choosing a chocolate is to taste it before you use it. If it's waxy, gritty, chalky, or harsh, then your pastry will be waxy, gritty, chalky, or harsh. Get the best chocolate you can, with the smoothest mouthfeel and the richest flavor. You will taste the difference in your final product.

Many different qualities and sweetness levels of chocolate are available. How can you tell how sweet it is? If you look at many packaged chocolates, they often list a percentage. For example, you might see "38% milk chocolate," which means that 38 percent of the chocolate is from actual cacao beans. (What's the rest? Sugar, and in the case of milk chocolate, milk.) Therefore, the higher the percentage of cacao listed on the label, the less sugar it contains. Milk chocolate can be anywhere as low as 10% cacao, but I prefer a richer milk chocolate in the range of 38 to 42%.

When I specify semisweet chocolate, the percentage I like best is 55 to 60% cacao. For bittersweet (my personal favorite—the more bitter, the better), I suggest a percentage of 70 to 75%. Bittersweet chocolate can go up to 85%, but that can be a little TOO bitter for many palates.

Unsweetened chocolate is always 99 to 100%. It's all cacao with no sugar added (and sometimes just a little vanilla).

Finally, white chocolate should always be made from real cocoa butter; avoid using the confectionery stuff made for decorating that's mostly just shortening and sugar.

Cocoa Powder

I use Dutch-processed cocoa, which means that the cocoa has been treated with an alkaline solution that makes it smoother, darker in color, and lower in acidity. It is the cocoa powder that is most readily available in the grocery store. It is not interchangeable with natural cocoa powder because the Dutch-processed will not react with acidic ingredients like natural will.

Crème Fraîche

If there's a "magic" ingredient in my baking arsenal, it's crème fraîche. Crème fraîche is quite common in France—I was introduced to it by French bakers—but in America, it hasn't swept the nation . . . yet. Crème fraîche is just heavy cream mixed with a little buttermilk and allowed to sit out overnight at room temperature until it thickens. It takes on a tangy, mellow flavor that is absolutely divine on its own as a topping for cobbler or pie. As a baking ingredient it adds a rich flavor that is impossible to replicate with sour cream, its closest substitute. So while sour cream will technically work in recipes that call for crème fraîche, in a side-by-side taste comparison of pastries made with crème fraîche and pastries made with sour cream, there is no contest. If you want pastries that will really impress, find or make crème fraîche. It's easy: Take a quart of heavy cream, stir in 3 to 4 tablespoons buttermilk, and let it sit out in a covered container at warm room temperature overnight, at least 10 hours, until it thickens. Stir it in the morning, and it should be thick and creamy; if it is still liquidy, place it back in a warm area and check it every hour or so until it thickens. Store crème fraîche in a covered container in the refrigerator for up to 2 weeks. To make more crème fraîche, you can just add a few tablespoons of old crème fraîche to heavy cream and proceed as directed. The old crème fraîche acts as a starter to get the new batch going, and you don't need to buy more buttermilk.

Eggs

Always use large eggs, and make sure they are at room temperature unless otherwise specified. A quick way to warm up eggs straight from the fridge is to place them in a bowl of warm water for about 10 minutes, or hold them under a stream of hot tap water for a minute or so. A large egg weighs about 50 grams without the shell, a large egg yolk is around 20 grams, and a large egg white is about 30 grams; use that as a guide if you end up with smaller or larger eggs. I've included the gram measurement for eggs in recipes in case you end up with other size eggs. If you need to weigh your eggs, whisk them lightly first so that you don't get too much white or yolk in your measurement. By volume, a large egg is about ¼ cup, and two large egg whites are about ¼ cup as well.

Flour

We tested all recipes that specify all-purpose flour with King Arthur unbleached all-purpose flour. All-purpose flour works well in many recipes, but when a recipe calls for cake flour or bread flour, it's important to use the specified flour. Cake flour is more finely milled than all-purpose flour, and it more readily absorbs fat and holds more sugar. It has a lower protein content, which means that it doesn't have a lot of gluten, which is what can make a cake tough. So cakes made with cake flour have a finer, more tender crumb. In a pinch you can substitute ¾ cup all-purpose flour and 2 tablespoons cornstarch for 1 cup cake flour.

On the other end of the spectrum is bread flour, which has a higher protein content, making it perfect for recipes in which you want a lot of gluten or chew, such as breads. The gluten that develops when you use bread flour in dough helps keep gases trapped inside the dough during baking, which makes for more rise.

We also bake with spelt flour, whole wheat flour, and light rye flour. Whole grains add a lot of flavor to your baking, with the added benefit of a bit of a nutritional boost as well. I've successfully made most recipes with whole grain flour by substituting half of the all-purpose with whole grain. It sucks up more moisture than all-purpose, so you might need to increase the fat or liquid a touch.

Fruits

Your fruit desserts will only be as good as your ingredients, so don't skimp and use underripe or out-of-season fruits. Use fresh, crisp apples. Pears should be firm but ripe. Stone fruits like peaches and plums should yield to gentle pressure and smell perfumey. Bananas should always be ripe; if they are tinged with green, WAIT! or go buy riper bananas. Berries should be ripe and delicious if eaten out of hand; even the best-made pastry won't disguise an underipe, whitish berry. All of these recipes were tested using fresh, in-season fruit except for the blueberry hand pies and cobbler, for which we used frozen berries (IQF, individually quick frozen). IQF blueberries allow me to bake with blueberries all year long and not just in July, when luscious berries are plentiful.

Milk

Always use whole milk in baking unless otherwise specified. Whole milk is rich and flavorful, and fat carries flavor, so using whole milk means your pastry will have more flavor carriers in it than if you were to use skim or low-fat milk. Buttermilk is always fat-free, and soy milk is always unflavored and plain. Coconut milk is not the same as coconut cream. Check the can carefully to be sure, and mix the contents thoroughly before measuring, as sometimes there can be some thickened coconut cream at the top of the can.

Salt

While many baking recipes call for table salt, I always bake with kosher salt. I tested all of these recipes with Diamond Crystal brand kosher salt. Perhaps it's my experience working in restaurants, where kosher is the salt of choice; it has a cleaner, milder flavor than table salt and its large, coarse grains allow you to control the amount you use more easily. In baking I find that table salt is so fine it is easy to mismeasure. Except for bread recipes, in which salt is a key ingredient that reacts with the yeast to alter the dough chemically, salt in pastries is used solely for flavoring,

so you certainly could use table salt if you don't have kosher. However, since kosher salt comes in nice big grains, you'll have to use less table salt than called for in the recipe. Use about half the amount of table salt as kosher salt.

Sugar

The recipes in this book will be delicious if you use regular granulated sugar, but I love baking with superfine sugar. Superfine sugar is granulated sugar that has been pulverized to a finer texture. In baking it results in lighter and fluffier creamed butter-sugar mixtures, it dissolves better in meringues, and it generally leads to a finer-crumbed product. You can buy superfine sugar, or make it by pulsing regular granulated sugar in a food processor for 5 to 10 seconds to make it finer.

Vanilla Beans and Vanilla Extract

Did you know that vanilla beans are actually the pod of a climbing orchid plant native to southern Mexico that only flowers for one day each year? Each flower must be hand-pollinated on this day to ensure that it bears its fruit, the vanilla bean—hence the beans' hefty price! But it's worth it. Nothing compares to the fragrant, mellow essence of real vanilla. Store beans tightly wrapped in plastic in a cool dark area or in your refrigerator. The real essence of the bean is stored within the pod in the form of millions of tiny black specks. Pure vanilla extract is a more cost-effective way to add vanilla flavor to baked goods. It's also more readily available, and it mixes easily into batters. If you can't find vanilla beans, substitute 1 tablespoon pure vanilla extract for the seeds of 1 vanilla bean.

My favorite meal

Country Feta Pies / 40

Gorgonzola and Bacon Drop Biscuits / 43

Parmesan-Chive Scones / 45

Gluten-Free Ham and Cheese Puffs / 47

Mushroom and Thyme Brioches / 49

Vegan Chocolate-Banana Muffins / 52

Vegan Carrot-Ginger Muffins / 55

Gluten-Free Lemon Raspberry Chia Muffins / 56

Gluten-Free Apple Spice Pecan Muffins / 58

Blackberry-Buttermilk Muffin Cakes / 61

Apple-Vanilla Pound Cake / 62

Currant Spelt Oat Scones / 64

Irish Soda Bread / 66

Whole Wheat Maple-Blueberry Scones / 69

Ricotta-Cherry Scones / 73

Rhubarb-Strawberry Jam-n-Butter Biscuits / 75

Nutty Seedy Breakfast Cookies / 78

Spelt Croissants / 81

Almond Croissants / 86

Fresh Fig Danish / 89

Apple Cider Sticky Buns / 93

Brown Butter Cinnamon Rolls
with Cream Cheese Frosting / 97

Sticky Bun Kouigns Amann / 99

Choux Donuts with Mascarpone Cream / 103

CHAPTER 1

What's for
Breakfast

Country Feta Pies

MAKES 8 INDIVIDUAL PIES

1 recipe Master Single-Crust Pâte Brisée (page 438)

1 cup/**250 grams** whole milk ricotta cheese

1 cup/**140 grams** crumbled feta cheese

2 large eggs (about **100 grams**)

2 cups packed/about **60 grams** baby spinach leaves, roughly chopped

½ cup/**120 grams** half-and-half

2 scallions, minced (about ¼ cup)

¼ teaspoon freshly grated nutmeg

¼ teaspoon kosher salt, plus more for the tomato

¼ teaspoon freshly ground black pepper, plus more for the tomato

1 medium tomato, sliced into eight ¼-inch-thick slices

When Flour first opened, I didn't think much about savory breakfast options. I can't remember the last time I started the day with an omelet or bacon and eggs—probably because that was never. I wake up craving sweet and only sweet. It took the nudging of Nicole, one of our pastry cooks at the time and now our executive pastry chef and partner, to add a few nonsweet options to our morning menu. She wanted something sort of but not quite like a quiche since we already offered slices of quiche. She found a recipe for a farmhouse torte in one of the La Brea Bakery cookbooks that piqued her interest, and from there she made savory turnovers and scrambled egg roll-ups until she figured out this little pie. Simple to make, it is a little flaky pie shell filled with creamy cheese and spinach, topped with a slice of tomato, and baked until golden brown. It is a great little breakfast on the run.

Make the pâte brisée. Remove it from the fridge about 15 minutes before using it, to soften slightly.

Spray 8 cups of a 12-cup regular muffin tin with pan spray, or use a paper towel dipped in softened butter or oil to coat the cups. Generously flick flour over the work surface, place the pâte brisée on it, then flour the pâte brisée. (You want enough flour so the pâte brisée does not stick to either the rolling pin or the work surface.) Use the rolling pin first to press the dough down into a flat disk, pressing the pin with an up-and-down motion into the pâte brisée. Flour the pâte brisée again and roll it out into a rough circle about ¼ inch thick and 15 inches across. Cut circles out of the dough that are about an inch larger than the diameter of the muffin tin cups and press them firmly into the prepared cups. You will need to pleat them inside the cups a bit to get them to fit. Smush all the scraps together and reroll them, then cut more circles until you have lined all 8 muffin tin cups. Place the lined tins in the fridge for at least 1 hour or up to 2 days; wrap the tin lightly with plastic wrap if refrigerating it for more than a few hours.

Preheat the oven to 350°F and place a rack in the center of the oven.

In a large bowl, combine the ricotta, feta, and eggs. Stir them together with a wooden spoon until the eggs are completely mixed into the cheeses. Add the spinach, half-and-half, scallions, nutmeg, salt, and pepper. Stir until all of the ingredients are well mixed. Remove the muffin tins from the fridge. With a large spoon, fill the cups evenly with the cheese mixture, using it all up. The filling should come up all the way to the tops of the dough. Top each pie with 1 slice of tomato, to cover the top. (The tomato will shrink a bit when baked, so it's okay if a slice is a little larger than the top of the cup; if it's a lot larger, cut the slice in half or trim it to fit.) Sprinkle the tomato slices with a pinch each of salt and pepper.

Bake the pies for 45 to 55 minutes, rotating the muffin tin midway through baking, until the pastry is golden brown, the bottoms are totally baked through (gently pop out a pastry from the tin to take a peek), and the centers of the pies are firm when you press them. Remove from the oven and let cool for 15 minutes.

Country feta pies are best served within an hour or so after baking. But you can store them, well wrapped in plastic, in the fridge for 1 day. Warm them up before serving by placing them in a 300°F oven for 10 to 12 minutes.

Gorgonzola and *Bacon Drop Biscuits*

MAKES 8 TO 10 BISCUITS

Caramelized Onions
(page 44)

5 slices thick-cut applewood-smoked bacon (about **75 grams**)

2¾ cups/**385 grams** all-purpose flour

1½ teaspoons baking powder

1½ teaspoons kosher salt

½ teaspoon baking soda

½ cup/1 stick/**115 grams** unsalted butter, cold

1½ cups/6 ounces/**170 grams** crumbled Gorgonzola or any other strong blue cheese

½ cup/**120 grams** fat-free buttermilk

¼ cup/**60 grams** heavy cream

1 large egg (about **50 grams**)

1 large egg yolk (about **20 grams**), for egg wash

¼ teaspoon coarsely ground black pepper

Sometimes the best ideas come at the end of a long day when you are hungry and trying to figure out what to eat. (Sometimes the worst ideas come at this time, too—I've had my fair share of tuna-sandwich-leftover-Chinese-chicken-noodle salad when I've been too tired to cook.) I got this idea watching one of our bakers pull apart a warm buttermilk biscuit right out of the oven and stuff it with some blue cheese and crumbled-up bacon as she was heading out after a busy day. What a great quick snack! I save you a step and add these all directly to the dough so the bacon and cheese and onion bake into the buttery biscuit for an excellent breakfast/snack on the go. Caramelizing the onions is the most time-consuming step, with cooking the bacon second—make them both ahead of time and these biscuits will come together easily for you.

Make the caramelized onions and set aside.

Preheat the oven to 325°F. Lay out the bacon on a small rimmed baking sheet and bake until fully crispy, 25 to 35 minutes. Drain the bacon on paper towels, then chop into ¼-inch pieces. Set aside.

Turn the oven up to 350°F and place a rack in the center of the oven. Line a baking sheet with parchment paper or butter it lightly, and set it aside.

In the bowl of a stand mixer fitted with a paddle attachment, mix the flour, bacon, baking powder, salt, and baking soda on low speed until combined, 10 to 15 seconds. Cut the butter into 8 to 10 pieces and add it to the flour mixture; paddle for 20 to 30 seconds on medium-low, until the butter is somewhat broken down and the mixture resembles coarse crumbs. Add the Gorgonzola and pulse the mixer a few times to start to incorporate the cheese.

Whisk together the buttermilk, cream, and egg until thoroughly mixed. Stir in the onions. With the mixer on low, pour in the buttermilk mixture and paddle for another 10 to 15 seconds, until the dough just comes together. There will probably still be a little loose flour at the bottom of the bowl.

Remove the bowl from the mixer. Gather and lift the dough with your

Caramelized Onions

MAKES ABOUT 1 CUP

1 tablespoon vegetable oil
(such as canola)

2 medium yellow onions,
peeled, cut in half, and sliced as
thin as possible (about 5 cups)

1 teaspoon kosher salt

½ teaspoon freshly ground
black pepper

—

In a medium skillet, heat the
oil over medium heat. Add the
onions and cook, stirring
occasionally, until softened,
5 to 10 minutes. Reduce the
heat to low and continue
cooking, stirring occasionally,
until the onions are completely
soft, caramelized, and dark
brown, another 30 to 40
minutes. Remove from the
heat. Season with the salt and
pepper. Store in airtight
container in the refrigerator
for up to 2 weeks.

hands and turn it over in the bowl so
that it picks up any loose flour at the
bottom; turn the dough over several
times until all of the loose flour is
mixed in.

Using a ½-cup ice cream scoop or
large serving spoon, scoop out
mounded rounds of dough, about
½ cup each, and place them evenly
spaced on the prepared baking sheet.
You should get 8 to 10 biscuits.
(At this point the biscuits can be
frozen on the baking sheet, transferred to a plastic freezer bag, and
frozen for up to 1 week. Add 5 to 10
minutes to the baking time.)

Whisk the egg yolk for the egg wash
in a small bowl with a fork. Use a
pastry brush to lightly brush the egg

wash all over the biscuits. Sprinkle
evenly with the pepper. Bake for
35 to 40 minutes, rotating the
baking sheet midway through the
baking time, until the biscuits are
entirely golden brown. Remove the
biscuits from the oven and let them
cool on the baking sheet on a wire
rack.

These biscuits are best served the
day they are baked, but you can store
them, tightly wrapped in plastic, in
the refrigerator for 1 day and refresh
them in a 300°F oven for 10 to 12
minutes before serving.

Parmesan-Chive Scones

MAKES 8 SCONES

2¼ cups/**315 grams** all-purpose flour

1 cup/**100 grams** shredded parmesan cheese

½ cup/**25 grams** chopped chives (about ½ bunch)

2 teaspoons baking powder

1½ teaspoons kosher salt

½ teaspoon baking soda

½ cup/1 stick/**115 grams** unsalted butter, cold

1 cup plus 2 tablespoons/ **270 grams** crème fraîche

¼ cup/**60 grams** fat-free buttermilk

1 large egg (about **50 grams**), at room temperature

1 large egg yolk (about **20 grams**), for egg wash

¼ teaspoon freshly ground black pepper, for garnish

Salty and savory, these scones are so rich and flaky that they shouldn't be reserved just for breakfast. In fact we use this dough to make an excellent potpie topping, and we've been known to build our famous egg sandwiches with these instead of our standard focaccia roll. Be sure to use fresh parmesan that you shred yourself; don't cheat and buy preshredded cheese, which can be dry. And don't even look at the green cans of "parmesan cheese" that have about as much flavor as salty sawdust. You'll be rewarded with mouthwatering scones that you'll love to make again and again.

Preheat the oven to 350°F and place a rack in the center of the oven. Line a baking sheet with parchment paper or butter it lightly, and set it aside.

In a stand mixer fitted with a paddle attachment, briefly mix the flour, ¾ cup/75 grams of the parmesan, the chives, baking powder, salt, and baking soda on low speed until combined. Cut the butter into 8 to 10 pieces and add it to the flour mix-ture; paddle for 20 to 30 seconds on low until the butter is somewhat broken down but there are still pieces about the size of lima beans.

In a small bowl, whisk together the crème fraîche, buttermilk, and whole egg until thoroughly mixed. With the mixer running on low, pour the crème fraîche mixture into the flour mixture and paddle for another 10 to 15 sec-onds, until the dough just comes

together. There will probably still be a little loose flour at the bottom of the bowl.

Remove the bowl from the mixer. Gather and lift the dough with your hands and turn it over in the bowl so that it starts to pick up the loose flour at the bottom. Turn the dough several times until all the loose flour is mixed in.

Dump the dough out onto the prepared baking sheet and pat it into an 8-inch circle, about 1 inch thick. Whisk the egg yolk for the egg wash in a small bowl with a fork. Use a pastry brush to brush the egg wash evenly over the entire top of the dough. Sprinkle the dough evenly with the remaining ¼ cup/25 grams parmesan and the pepper. Score the dough into 8 wedges with a knife. (At this point the scones can be tightly wrapped in plastic wrap and frozen

for up to 1 week. Add 5 to 10 minutes to the baking time and proceed as directed.)

Bake for 35 to 45 minutes, rotating the baking sheet midway through the baking time, until the entire circle of scones is golden brown. Let cool on a wire rack for 30 minutes, cut the scones at the scores into 8 wedges, and serve.

Scones are best enjoyed the same day you bake them but they can be stored in an airtight container at room temperature for 2 to 3 days. If you keep them for longer than 1 day, refresh them in a 300°F oven for 4 to 5 minutes before serving. Or freeze them, tightly wrapped in plastic, for up to 1 week and reheat them in a 300°F oven for 10 to 12 minutes.

Gluten-Free
Ham and Cheese Puffs

MAKES 12 PUFFS

1 cup/**240 grams** whole milk

½ cup/1 stick/**115 grams** unsalted butter

1 teaspoon kosher salt

2 cups/**240 grams** tapioca flour (sometimes labeled tapioca starch)

4 large eggs (about **200 grams**), at room temperature

1¼ cups/**125 grams** freshly grated parmesan cheese

4 ounces/**110 grams** sliced country ham, chopped into ¼-inch pieces

A home baker who made gougères—cheesy, rich pastry puffs— out of my book *Flour Too* tagged me on Instagram and asked if I had ever heard of *pão de queijo*, a similar pastry popular in Brazil and Portugal. I had never heard of them, and after doing some research I was eager to try this popular national bread. The first time I made these, my parents were visiting and they ate the whole batch. The second time, I shared them with Rita, a long-time steward at Flour who is everyone's favorite person. She comes from Brazil, and after trying these she launched into an excited monologue in Portuguese. They are crispy outside, wonderfully soft and chewy inside, and oddly addictive. I add chopped ham to make them a bit more substantial for breakfast but you can omit the ham for a vegetarian option.

Preheat the oven to 350°F and place a rack in the center of the oven. Lightly butter a baking sheet or line it with parchment paper, and set aside.

In a medium saucepan, heat the milk, butter, and salt over medium heat until the butter is melted; do not let the mixture come to a boil or the liquid will evaporate. Add the tapioca flour all at once; use a wooden spoon to stir the flour into the liquid until it is fully incorporated. It will glob up immediately and start to get stretchy and chewy. Remove from the stove once the flour is fully incorporated into the liquid.

Place the dough in a stand mixer fitted with a paddle attachment.

Crack the eggs into a small pitcher or liquid measuring cup and whisk to break up the yolks. With the mixer on low speed, gradually add the eggs to the dough. It will look a bit like scrambled eggs when the eggs are all added. Add the parmesan and ham. Turn the mixer up to medium and paddle for about 20 seconds to incorporate the cheese and ensure the dough is fully mixed.

Using a ¼-cup measure or ice cream scoop, scoop out balls of dough and place them about 2 inches apart on the prepared baking sheet. You should get about 12 balls. Bake for 30 to 35 minutes, rotating the baking sheet midway through the baking time, until the puffs are entirely brown. Remove

from the oven and let cool for about 15 minutes on a wire rack. Serve immediately.

Baked puffs can be stored in an airtight container in the freezer for up to 2 weeks. Remove from the freezer and refresh them in a 300°F oven for 8 to 10 minutes, until warmed through. You can also store them in an airtight container at room temperature for up to 2 days. Refresh in a 300°F oven for 3 to 4 minutes, until warmed through.

Mushroom and Thyme Brioches

MAKES 6 BRIOCHES

½ recipe/21 ounces/**600 grams** Master Brioche Dough (page 444) or ⅔ recipe/ 22 ounces/**620 grams** Whole Wheat Brioche (page 119)

1 pound/**455 grams** cremini mushrooms

1 small red onion, peeled and roughly chopped

1 medium garlic clove, peeled and finely chopped

1 teaspoon dried thyme

½ teaspoon kosher salt

¼ teaspoon freshly ground black pepper

3 tablespoons/**45 grams** unsalted butter

2 tablespoons heavy cream

2 tablespoons white wine vinegar

½ cup/**120 grams** crème fraîche

1 cup/**100 grams** shredded fontina or provolone cheese

6 large eggs, poached, for serving (optional)

Once you've mastered making the dough for brioche, a rich buttery bread from France, you'll want to start experimenting with all of the different breakfast treats you can make. It's a remarkably versatile and straightforward dough that lends itself well to both sweet and savory variations. Here we make mushroom duxelles (a finely chopped mushroom mixture) and use it to fill pizzalike rounds of fluffy brioche dough. Top it all off with salty, creamy fontina and bake until golden brown. You can also make mini versions of these for a fantastic cocktail party treat.

——

Mix and proof the brioche dough.

Preheat the oven to 325°F and place a rack in the center of the oven. Line a baking sheet with parchment paper or butter it lightly, and set it aside.

Stem and wipe the mushrooms clean. Chop them roughly and mix together with the red onion, garlic, ½ teaspoon of the thyme, the salt, and pepper until thoroughly combined. Spread the mushroom mixture on an unlined baking sheet. Cut the butter into small pieces and dot it evenly on top of the mushrooms. Bake for 40 to 50 minutes, until the moisture has cooked off, rotating the baking sheet and stirring the mushrooms every 10 to 15 minutes. Remove from the oven and scrape into a bowl or storage container. Mix in the cream and vinegar until completely mixed together. (The mushroom duxelles

can be made in advance and stored in an airtight container in the fridge for up to 4 days.)

Shape the brioche dough into a rectangle about 12 inches long, 2 inches wide, and 1 inch thick. Divide the dough into 6 equal squares about 2 x 2 inches and 3½ ounces/100 grams each. Stretch a dough square into a circle about 5 inches in diameter, as if you are making a mini pizza. Stretch out the inner part of the circle so it is thin while leaving a rim of dough around the edge of the circle. Place the dough circle on the prepared baking sheet and repeat with rest of the dough squares, spacing them a few inches apart.

Using the back of a spoon, spread a scant 2 tablespoons of the crème fraîche over each dough circle as if you are spreading the sauce on a mini pizza, leaving the rim

untouched. Place 3 tablespoons of the mushroom mixture evenly on top of the crème fraîche. Evenly sprinkle the fontina and the remaining ½ teaspoon thyme over the rims and filled centers of the dough circles.

Bake for 30 to 35 minutes, rotating the baking sheet midway through the baking time, until the brioches are medium golden brown along the edge. Remove from the oven and place on a wire rack to cool and set for 10 to 15 minutes before serving.

The brioches can be stored in an airtight container in the fridge for up to 2 days; reheat in a 300°F oven for 6 to 8 minutes, until warmed through.

VARIATION: *For an awesome variation, place a poached egg on top of each brioche before serving.*

Vegan Chocolate-Banana Muffins

MAKES 8 JUMBO OR 12 REGULAR MUFFINS

1 cup/**240 grams**
plain soy milk

¾ cup/**150 grams**
superfine sugar

½ cup/**110 grams** vegetable oil
(such as canola)

1 tablespoon white or
cider vinegar

1 teaspoon pure vanilla extract

2 cups/**280 grams**
all-purpose flour

2 tablespoons Dutch-
processed cocoa powder

1 teaspoon baking powder

½ teaspoon baking soda

½ teaspoon kosher salt

3 very ripe medium bananas,
mashed (about 1 cup/
300 grams)

3 ounces/**85 grams**
vegan bittersweet chocolate
chunks, finely chopped, or
vegan chocolate chips (about
½ cup/**85 grams**)

2 tablespoons sanding or
pearl sugar, for garnish

Chocolate and banana are a natural pairing and in this I-can't-believe-it's-vegan muffin they join together to make a tender soft breakfast treat that has become a Flour favorite. It tastes a little bit like Cocoa Puffs cereal in a really good way. We rotate our vegan muffin offerings bimonthly and when this one leaves the menu I always receive a slew of email requests for the recipe. I'm so happy to be able to share it with you here. Make sure the bananas are super ripe; otherwise they will bake off starchy and not very pleasant.

Preheat the oven to 350°F and place a rack in the center of the oven. Line a 12-cup regular muffin tin or 8 cups of a 12-cup jumbo muffin tin with muffin papers, or generously butter the cups. If using muffin papers, spray them with pan spray or the muffins will stick to the paper. Set aside.

In a medium bowl, whisk together the soy milk, superfine sugar, oil, vinegar, and vanilla. In a large bowl, stir together the flour, cocoa powder, baking powder, baking soda, and salt. Make a well in the center and pour in the soy milk mixture. Fold until almost entirely mixed together. Add the bananas and chocolate and fold until thoroughly combined. Scoop evenly into the prepared muffin tin cups, filling them all the way to the top and even a bit over (these muffins don't rise very much). Sprinkle them evenly with the sanding sugar. Bake for 25 to 30 minutes, rotating the muffin tin midway through the baking time, until the centers spring back when you press them and a cake tester inserted into the middle of a muffin comes out clean.

Remove from the oven and let cool in the tin on a wire rack. Remove from the muffin tin and serve.

The muffins can be stored in an airtight container at room temperature for up to 2 days; refresh them for 6 to 8 minutes in a 300°F oven if not serving the same day.

Vegan Carrot-Ginger Muffins

MAKES 8 JUMBO OR 12 REGULAR MUFFINS

½ cup/**60 grams** walnuts, roughly chopped

1 cup/**240 grams** plain soy milk

¾ cup firmly packed/**165 grams** light brown sugar

7 tablespoons/**95 grams** vegetable oil (such as canola)

1 tablespoon grated fresh ginger

1 tablespoon white or cider vinegar

1 teaspoon pure vanilla extract

2 cups/**290 grams** whole wheat flour

1 teaspoon baking powder

1 teaspoon ground cinnamon

½ teaspoon ground ginger

½ teaspoon baking soda

½ teaspoon kosher salt

1¾ cups/**190 grams** peeled and coarsely shredded carrots (about 3 medium carrots)

½ cup/**80 grams** golden raisins

2 tablespoons confectioners' sugar, for dusting the muffins

My husband's favorite pastry at Flour is our carrot cake (or maybe it's our vanilla cream–filled donuts . . . or the chocolate cupcakes . . . or the lemon meringue pie . . .). This muffin is my answer to his desire to eat cake every single day. It's got the same sweet, spicy flavors as carrot cake and is made with whole grains and raisins and nuts and carrots. I love these split in half and toasted so they get crunchy.

Preheat the oven to 350°F and place a rack in the center of the oven. Line a 12-cup regular muffin tin or 8 cups of a 12-cup jumbo muffin tin with muffin papers, or generously spray the cups with pan spray. If using muffin papers, spray them with pan spray or the muffins will stick to the paper. Set aside.

Place the walnuts on a baking sheet and toast for 8 to 10 minutes, until they start to smell nutty and turn pale golden inside. Set aside. Leave the oven on.

In a medium bowl, whisk together the soy milk, brown sugar, oil, fresh ginger, vinegar, and vanilla. In a large bowl, stir together the flour, baking powder, cinnamon, ground ginger, baking soda, and salt. Make a well in the center and pour in the soy milk mixture. Using a rubber spatula, fold the flour mixture into the soy milk mixture until almost entirely mixed together. Add the carrots, raisins, and walnuts and fold until thoroughly combined.

Scoop the batter evenly into the prepared muffin tin cups, filling them all the way to the top and even overfilling a bit. Bake for 30 to 35 minutes, rotating the muffin tin midway through the baking time, until the centers spring back when you press them and a cake tester inserted into the middle of a muffin comes out clean.

Remove from the oven and let cool in the muffin tin on a wire rack. Remove the muffins from the tin and use a sifter to lightly dust with confectioners' sugar.

The muffins can be stored in an airtight container at room temperature for up to 2 days; refresh them for 6 to 8 minutes in a 300°F oven if not serving the same day.

Gluten-Free
Lemon Raspberry Chia Muffins

MAKES 12 JUMBO OR 16 REGULAR MUFFINS

10 tablespoons/1¼ sticks/**140 grams** unsalted butter, melted and cooled

1⅓ cups/**270 grams** sugar

2 tablespoons grated lemon zest (about 2 large lemons)

2 large eggs (about **100 grams**), at room temperature

1 large egg yolk (about **20 grams**), at room temperature

1¼ cups/**300 grams** whole milk, at room temperature

1 cup/**240 grams** crème fraîche, at room temperature

1 teaspoon pure vanilla extract

3¼ cups/**455 grams** gluten-free flour (we love Cup-4-Cup)

2 tablespoons chia seeds

1 tablespoon baking powder

½ teaspoon baking soda

½ teaspoon kosher salt

2 cups/**250 grams** fresh raspberries

This gluten-free muffin is so good that we once had a guest order it, take one bite, and return to the bakery to demand a refund. She wanted her money back because she was certain that we had made a mistake; she said it was so good we must have inadvertently given her a regular muffin chock-full of gluten. That was the happiest non-complaint I think I've ever fielded— the look on her face when she realized she could enjoy the muffin was awesome. Lemon and raspberry are a natural pairing and adding chia seeds to this muffin gives it great crunch.

Preheat the oven to 350°F and place a rack in the center of the oven. Line a 12-cup jumbo muffin tin or 16 cups of two 12-cup regular muffin tins with muffin papers, or butter the cups and flour them with gluten-free flour. Set aside.

In a medium bowl, whisk together the melted butter, sugar, and lemon zest. Whisk in the eggs and egg yolk until thoroughly combined. Slowly whisk in the milk, crème fraîche, and vanilla.

In a large bowl, stir together the flour, chia seeds, baking powder, baking soda, and salt until well mixed. Make a well in the center and pour in the butter mixture. Using a rubber spatula, gently fold them together until almost all the way combined. Add the raspberries and fold gently until combined and there are no more dry patches of flour. Scoop the batter evenly into the prepared muffin tin cups, filling them all the way to the brim.

Bake for 35 to 45 minutes, rotating the muffin tin(s) midway through the baking time, until the centers spring back when you press them and a cake tester inserted into the middle of a muffin comes out clean. Remove from the oven and let cool in the tin(s) on a wire rack. Remove from the tin(s) and serve.

Muffins can be stored in an airtight container at room temperature for up to 2 days; refresh them for 6 to 8 minutes in a 300°F oven if not serving the same day.

Gluten-Free
Apple Spice Pecan Muffins

MAKES 12 REGULAR MUFFINS

½ cup/**50 grams** pecan halves, roughly chopped

1 cup/**100 grams** almond flour

¾ cup/**90 grams** confectioners' sugar

½ cup/**60 grams** buckwheat flour

1 teaspoon ground cinnamon

1 teaspoon kosher salt

½ teaspoon baking powder

¼ teaspoon freshly grated nutmeg

⅛ teaspoon ground cloves

½ cup/**110 grams** vegetable oil (such as canola)

3 large eggs (about **150 grams**), separated, at room temperature

1 teaspoon pure almond extract

1 medium apple, peeled, cored, and coarsely chopped (about 1 cup/**120 grams**)

Apple Glaze (opposite)

When we first opened, I was always surprised at how many people would walk into a bakery named Flour and ask if we had gluten-free offerings. Mind you, this was almost twenty years ago, when I had never heard the term *celiac* and the idea of gluten-free pastry seemed like a cruel joke. And in some ways it was—I managed to choke down a few gluten-free pastries that were around at the time and was shocked at how awful they were. I was determined to create a gluten-free pastry that was delicious all on its own. I had no knowledge of gluten-free flours, which now populate the grocery aisles. Instead I took what we had in-house—almond flour for our dacquoise and buckwheat flour for our multigrain bread—and created a muffin that was moist, tender, rich, and delicious. This became one of our more popular seasonal muffins, enjoyed by celiacs and gluten lovers alike.

—

Preheat the oven to 350°F and place a rack in the middle of the oven. Line a 12-cup regular muffin tin with muffin papers, or butter the cups and flour them with almond or buckwheat flour, or spray the cups generously with pan spray. Set aside.

Place the pecans on a baking sheet and toast for 8 to 10 minutes, until they start to smell nutty and turn pale golden inside. Set aside. Leave the oven on.

In a medium bowl, stir together the almond flour, confectioners' sugar, buckwheat flour, cinnamon, salt, baking powder, nutmeg, and cloves until well combined. In a small bowl, whisk together the oil, egg yolks, and almond extract. Make a well in the almond flour mixture, pour in the oil mixture, and use a rubber spatula to fold them together.

In a small, clean bowl, use a clean whisk to vigorously whip the egg whites until they get foamy like seafoam and can hold a very soft peak, about 1 minute. Add about one-third of the whipped whites, one-third of the apple, and one-third of the pecans to the batter and gently fold them in. Fold in the remaining egg whites, apple, and pecans. Scoop the batter evenly into the prepared muffin tin cups, filling them all the way to the top.

Bake for 25 to 35 minutes, rotating the muffin tin midway through the baking time, until the muffins are entirely golden brown on top and spring back lightly when you press them in the middle, and a cake tester inserted into the middle of a muffin comes out clean. Let cool in the muffin tin on a wire rack for 20 minutes.

While the muffins are cooling, make the apple glaze.

While the muffins are still warm, remove them from the tin and remove the muffin papers, if you used them. Using a pastry brush, brush the glaze evenly onto the muffins.

Muffins are best enjoyed the same day you bake them, but they can be stored in an airtight container at room temperature for 2 to 3 days. If you keep them for longer than 1 day, refresh them in a 300°F oven for 4 to 5 minutes. Or you can freeze them, tightly wrapped in plastic wrap, for up to 1 week and reheat them in a 300°F oven for 8 to 10 minutes.

Apple Glaze

MAKES ABOUT ⅓ CUP

½ cup/60 grams confectioners' sugar

1 to 2 tablespoons apple cider or apple juice

In a small bowl, whisk together the confectioners' sugar and enough cider to make a smooth, thick, pourable glaze. The glaze can be stored in an airtight container at room temperature for up to 1 week.

Blackberry-Buttermilk
Muffin Cakes

MAKES 12 JUMBO OR 16 REGULAR MUFFINS

1 cup plus 2 tablespoons/
225 grams sugar

3 large eggs (about **150 grams**),
at room temperature

1½ cups/**360 grams**
fat-free buttermilk, at room
temperature

¾ cup/1½ sticks/**170 grams**
unsalted butter, melted
and cooled until just barely
warm so it is still liquid

1 tablespoon pure
vanilla extract

1½ cups/**210 grams**
all-purpose flour

1½ cups/**180 grams** cake flour,
sifted after measuring

1½ teaspoons baking powder

¾ teaspoon baking soda

¾ teaspoon kosher salt

3 cups/**330 grams**
fresh blackberries

Any time you bake with buttermilk you are rewarded with a pastry that boasts an uber-tender crumb and unmistakable mellow tang. These muffins balance velvety, buttery cake with buttermilk richness and tart blackberries. They are so rich I call them muffin cakes; they are a decadent way to start the morning. Feel free to use raspberries or blueberries or a mixture of all three when you have them.

Preheat the oven to 350°F and place a rack in the center of the oven. Line a 12-cup jumbo muffin tin or 16 cups of two 12-cup regular muffin tins with muffin papers, or butter and flour the cups. Set aside.

In a medium bowl, whisk together the sugar and eggs. Slowly whisk in the buttermilk, melted butter, and vanilla. In a large bowl, stir together the all-purpose flour, cake flour, baking powder, baking soda, and salt. Make a well in the center and pour in the buttermilk mixture. Use a rubber spatula to fold gently just until the ingredients are combined. Fold in the blackberries until the fruit is well distributed.

Using a ½-cup ice cream scoop or a large spoon, scoop about ½ cup of the batter into each muffin tin cup (spoon in ¾ cup if using jumbo muffin tins), filling the cups to the brim — almost to overflowing — and making sure the cups are evenly filled.

Bake for 30 to 40 minutes, rotating the muffin tin(s) midway through the baking time, until the muffin cakes are entirely golden brown on top and spring back lightly when you press them in the middle, and a cake tester inserted into the middle of a muffin cake comes out clean. Let the muffin cakes cool in the tin(s) on a wire rack for 20 minutes, then remove the muffin cakes from the tin(s).

Muffin cakes are best enjoyed the same day you bake them, but they can be stored in an airtight container at room temperature for 2 to 3 days. If you keep them for longer than 1 day, refresh them in a 300°F oven for 4 to 5 minutes. Or you can freeze them, tightly wrapped in plastic wrap, for up to 1 week and reheat them in a 300°F oven for 8 to 10 minutes.

Apple-Vanilla Pound Cake

MAKES 1 LOAF

½ cup/1 stick/**115 grams**
unsalted butter

Seeds scraped from ½ vanilla
bean (see page 28)

3 tablespoons/**45 grams**
heavy cream

½ teaspoon pure
vanilla extract

3 large eggs (about **150 grams**),
at room temperature

¾ cup/**150 grams**
superfine sugar

1¼ cups/**165 grams** cake flour,
sifted after measuring

½ teaspoon baking powder

¼ teaspoon kosher salt

1 medium Granny Smith
apple, peeled, cored, and
thinly sliced

1 tablespoon confectioners'
sugar, for garnish

On special Sundays when I was growing up, my mom would serve us toasted slices of Sara Lee pound cake. I savored every tender, buttery bite, sometimes slicing my piece even thinner and running it through the toaster again to get more crunchy bits. When I started working for François Payard, one of the top pastry chefs in America, at his eponymous Payard Patisserie, one of the first recipes I learned was French-style pound cake. He instructed me to whip the eggs and sugar together until light and voluminous and gently fold in melted butter and a touch of heavy cream. Dry ingredients were even more gently folded in after that to preserve the airy foam, and the cake baked off soft and tender with a much lighter crumb than what I was used to. As fond as my memories of my Sundays with Sara are, this light-as-a-cloud cake has become my preferred way to make and eat pound cake.

Preheat the oven to 350°F and place a rack in the center of the oven. Line a 9 x 5-inch loaf pan with parchment paper or butter and flour the pan. Set aside.

In a medium saucepan, melt the butter. Add the vanilla seeds and whisk in the cream and vanilla extract. Let the mixture cool to room temperature.

In a stand mixer fitted with a whisk attachment, whip the eggs and superfine sugar until thick and lemony colored, 4 to 5 minutes on medium-high speed. While the eggs and sugar are whipping, sift and stir together the cake flour, baking powder, and salt. When the egg-sugar mixture is thick, add the flour mixture and gently fold it in by hand using a rubber spatula. Scoop a few large spoonfuls of the batter into the butter mixture and stir to combine well. Once the butter mixture is lightened, add it to the batter and fold until completely combined. Scoop the batter into the prepared loaf pan. Layer and shingle the apple across the top in two rows. Bake for 50 to 60 minutes, rotating the pan midway through the baking time, until the cake peeking out around the apple on top is golden brown and firm when you press it in the middle, and a cake tester inserted into the middle of the cake comes out clean.

Remove the cake from the oven and let cool in the pan on a wire rack until cool enough to handle, about 20 minutes, then remove it from the pan and sift a bit of confectioners' sugar on top. Using a very sharp serrated knife, gently slice through the apple and cake and serve.

Pound cake can be stored in an airtight container at room temperature for up to 2 days.

Currant Spelt Oat Scones

MAKES 8 SCONES

1¼ cups/**175 grams**
all-purpose flour

1 cup/**140 grams** spelt flour

1 cup/**160 grams** dried
currants

⅔ cup/**70 grams** rolled oats,
plus about ¼ cup/**25 grams**
for sprinkling on top

⅓ cup/**70 grams** sugar

1½ teaspoons baking powder

½ teaspoon baking soda

½ teaspoon kosher salt

1 cup/2 sticks/**225 grams**
unsalted butter, cold

½ cup/**120 grams**
crème fraîche

⅓ cup/**80 grams**
fat-free buttermilk

1 large egg (about **50 grams**),
at room temperature

1 large egg yolk (about
20 grams), for egg wash

I always like simple. My favorite flavor for pastries is vanilla, I eat multigrain toast every morning, and my pizza of choice is cheese. To me, simple is best, so I was hesitant to fiddle with our classic currant scone. Why mess with something so perfect? If I could make it more delicious and also a bit healthier, that's why. I've been bitten by the whole grain bug and I love trying to make every pastry possible with whole grains, not only for the health benefits they add but also because they lend wonderful flavor to our pastries. We took the original currant scone recipe and added heartiness and earthiness by mixing in oats and spelt flour. This new-and-improved scone wins over even classic diehards like me.

Preheat the oven to 350°F and position a rack in the center of the oven. Line a baking sheet with parchment paper or butter it lightly, and set it aside.

In a stand mixer fitted with a paddle attachment, briefly mix the all-purpose flour, spelt flour, currants, oats, sugar, baking powder, baking soda, and salt on low speed until combined. Cut the butter into 8 to 10 pieces and add it to the flour mixture; paddle for 20 to 30 seconds on low, until the butter is somewhat broken down but there are still pieces about the size of grapes.

In a small bowl, whisk together the crème fraîche, buttermilk, and whole egg until thoroughly mixed. With the mixer running on low, pour the crème

fraîche mixture into the flour mixture and paddle for another 10 to 15 seconds, until the dough just comes together. There will probably still be a little loose flour at the bottom of the bowl.

Remove the bowl from the mixer. Gather and lift the dough with your hands and turn it over in the bowl so that it starts to pick up the loose flour at the bottom. Turn the dough over several times until all the loose flour is mixed in.

Dump the dough out onto the prepared baking sheet and pat it into an 8-inch circle about 1 inch thick. Whisk the egg yolk for the egg wash in a small bowl with a fork. Use a pastry brush to brush the egg wash evenly over the entire top of the dough. Sprinkle the surface with

about ¼ cup/25 grams rolled oats and score the dough into 8 wedges as you would cut a pizza. (At this point the scones can be tightly wrapped in plastic wrap and frozen for up to 1 week. Add 5 to 10 minutes to the baking time.)

Bake for 30 to 40 minutes, rotating the baking sheet midway through the baking time, until the entire circle of scones is golden brown. Let the

scones cool on the baking sheet on a wire rack for 30 minutes, then cut into wedges along the scored lines and serve.

Scones are best enjoyed the same day you bake them, but they can be stored in an airtight container at room temperature for 2 to 3 days. If you keep them for longer than 1 day, refresh them in a 300°F oven for 3 to 4 minutes. Or you can freeze

them, tightly wrapped in plastic, for up to 1 week and reheat them in a 300°F oven for 10 to 12 minutes.

Irish Soda Bread

MAKES 1 LARGE LOAF, CUT IN 8 WEDGES

2 teaspoons caraway seeds

2 cups/**280 grams** rye flour

⅓ cup/**70 grams** sugar

⅓ cup/**50 grams**
dried currants

2 teaspoons baking powder

½ teaspoon baking soda

½ teaspoon kosher salt

½ cup/1 stick/**115 grams**
unsalted butter, cold,
plus 1 teaspoon at room
temperature, for finishing
the soda bread

⅓ cup/**80 grams**
fat-free buttermilk

⅓ cup/**80 grams** crème fraîche

1 large egg (about **50 grams**),
at room temperature

1 large egg yolk (about
20 grams)

St. Patrick's Day is as big a holiday in Boston as Thanksgiving and Christmas and New Year's Eve. Some businesses even close for the day to allow the city's many Irish and friends-of-the-Irish to celebrate in the annual daylong parade. At Flour we commemorate the special occasion for the whole month of March by offering this quick bread as a popular breakfast treat. Traditionally Irish soda bread can be a bit dry and is meant to be toasted and served with a lot of butter. We make ours with the butter mixed directly into the dough to create a tender crumb, and we flavor it with 100 percent rye flour, caraway seeds, currants, and even more butter. It's richer than the classic—but don't let that stop you from serving it as is tradition, with a side of soft butter.

Preheat the oven to 350°F and place a rack in the center of the oven. Line a baking sheet with parchment paper or butter it lightly, and set it aside.

Place the caraway seeds on a cutting board and sprinkle with a few drops of water to keep them from sliding around. Use a chef's knife to roughly chop the caraway seeds a bit so that they are not all whole seeds. Place the seeds in a stand mixer fitted with a paddle attachment. Add the rye flour, sugar, currants, baking powder, baking soda, and salt and mix on low speed for a few seconds until combined. Cut the butter into 8 to 10 pieces and add it to the flour mixture; paddle for 20 to 30 seconds on low until the butter is somewhat broken down but there are still pieces about the size of grapes.

In a small bowl, whisk together the buttermilk, crème fraîche, and whole egg until thoroughly mixed. With the mixer running on low, pour the buttermilk mixture into the flour mixture and paddle for another 10 to 15 seconds, until the dough just comes together. There will probably still be a little loose flour at the bottom of the bowl.

Remove the bowl from the mixer. Gather and lift the dough with your hands and turn it over in the bowl so that it starts to pick up the loose flour at the bottom. Turn the dough over several times until all the loose flour is mixed in.

Dump the dough out onto the prepared baking sheet and pat it into an 8-inch circle about 1 inch thick. Whisk the egg yolk lightly in a small bowl with a fork. Use a pastry brush to brush the egg wash evenly over the entire top of the dough. Score the dough into 8 wedges as you would cut a pizza. (At this point the soda bread can be tightly wrapped in plastic wrap and frozen for up to 1 week. Add 5 to 10 minutes to the baking time.)

Bake for 30 to 40 minutes, rotating the baking sheet midway through the baking time, until the entire circle of soda bread is golden brown and firm when pressed in the center.

Remove from the oven and immediately smear the butter evenly over the entire top surface. Let cool on the baking sheet on a wire rack for 30 minutes, then slice the soda bread along the scored lines into wedges and serve.

Soda bread is best enjoyed the same day you bake it, but it can be stored in an airtight container at room temperature for 2 to 3 days. If you keep it for longer than 1 day, refresh it in a 300°F oven for 4 to 5 minutes. Or you can freeze it, tightly wrapped in plastic, for up to 1 week and reheat it in a 300°F oven for 10 to 12 minutes.

Whole Wheat
Maple-Blueberry Scones

MAKES 8 SCONES

1⅔ cups/**240 grams**
whole wheat flour

1 cup/**140 grams**
all-purpose flour

1½ teaspoons baking powder

½ teaspoon baking soda

½ teaspoon kosher salt

¾ cup/1½ sticks/**170 grams**
unsalted butter, cold

½ cup/**120 grams**
crème fraîche

½ cup/**170 grams** maple syrup

⅓ cup/**80 grams**
fat-free buttermilk

1 large egg yolk (about
20 grams), at room
temperature

1 cup/**125 grams** fresh
blueberries

Maple Glaze (page 70)

The earthiness of whole wheat flour is a natural partner with buttery maple syrup and juicy blueberries. Whole wheat flour absorbs a lot of liquid, so instead of being flaky, these scones are a bit softer and cake-like. I can't stop eating them. Neither can my bakers. At one point I was tasting a batch with one of our pastry chefs, Joe, and we were trying to decide if we should add maybe some chopped fresh apples, or dried apricots, or dried apples. During the discussion we both ate an entire scone each. That's when we realized that this scone is pretty perfect as it is. The buttermilk adds a slight tang that reminds me of pancakes, which is always a good thing.

—

Preheat the oven to 350°F and position a rack in the center of the oven. Line a baking sheet with parchment paper or butter it lightly, and set it aside.

In a stand mixer fitted with a paddle attachment, briefly mix both flours, the baking powder, baking soda, and salt on low speed until combined. Add half of the butter to the flour mixture and paddle for 2 to 3 minutes, until the butter is fully mixed into the flour. (This will coat the flour with butter so the scones are tender.) Cut the remaining butter into ¼- to ½-inch pieces and add them to the flour mixture. Pulse the mixer 3 or 4 times to mix the butter pieces into the dough while keeping them whole. (This step will give you small pieces of butter in the dough, which will help the scones be a bit flaky.)

In a small bowl, whisk together the crème fraîche, maple syrup, buttermilk, and egg yolk until thoroughly mixed. Stir in the blueberries. With the mixer running on low, pour the crème fraîche mixture into the flour mixture and paddle on low for about 10 seconds to get some of the liquid mixed into the flour. Stop the mixer and mix the rest of the loose flour into the batter by hand: Gather and lift the dough with your hands and turn it over in the bowl several times until all the loose flour is mixed in.

Using a ½-cup measuring cup or ice cream scoop, scoop out mounds of dough and place them on the prepared baking sheet a few inches apart. (At this point the scones can be frozen on the baking sheet, transferred to a plastic freezer bag, and frozen for up to 1 week. Add

Maple Glaze

MAKES ABOUT ⅓ CUP

½ cup/**60 grams**
confectioners' sugar

2 to 3 tablespoons maple syrup

—

In a small bowl, whisk together the confectioners' sugar and enough of the maple syrup to make a thick, spreadable glaze. Use immediately or store the glaze in an airtight container at room temperature for up to 1 week. Rewhisk before using.

5 to 10 minutes to the baking time.) Cover the scones loosely with plastic wrap and place them in the fridge for at least 1 hour or up to 1 day — this gives the flour time to fully absorb the liquid.

Bake for 35 to 45 minutes, rotating the baking sheet midway through the baking time, until the scones are evenly golden brown and firm when you press them.

While the scones are baking, make the maple glaze. Remove the scones from the oven and use a pastry brush to brush them with the glaze while warm. Let cool on the baking sheet on a wire rack for 30 minutes, then serve.

Scones are best enjoyed the same day you bake them, but they can be stored in an airtight container at room temperature for 2 to 3 days. If you keep them for longer than 1 day, refresh them in a 300°F oven for 4 to 5 minutes. Or you can freeze them, tightly wrapped in plastic, for up to 1 week and reheat them in a 300°F oven for 8 to 10 minutes.

Ricotta-Cherry Scones

MAKES 8 SCONES

2¾ cups/**385 grams**
all-purpose flour

1 cup/**200 grams**
dried cherries

⅓ cup/**70 grams**
superfine sugar

1½ teaspoons baking powder

½ teaspoon baking soda

½ teaspoon kosher salt

½ cup/1 stick/**115 grams**
unsalted butter, cold

½ cup/**120 grams** fat-free
buttermilk

½ cup/**120 grams**
crème fraîche

½ cup/**120 grams** whole milk
ricotta cheese

1 large egg (about **50 grams**),
at room temperature

2 teaspoons grated lemon zest
(about 1 medium lemon)

1 teaspoon pure vanilla extract

8 ounces/**225 grams** whole
fresh sweet dark cherries,
pitted (about 1 cup/
125 grams pitted)

1 large egg yolk (about
20 grams), for egg wash

2 tablespoons sanding sugar,
pearl sugar, or granulated
sugar, for garnish

Scones are typically flaky and buttery but sometimes a scone can be soft and tender like this one. Instead of relying on pockets of butter to add rich flavor and crispy texture, we fold a generous amount of creamy ricotta into this scone dough. Two types of cherries—fresh (or frozen) and dried—along with bright lemon zest make this breakfast treat extra special. The scone bakes off with a creamy tenderness that is just as irresistible as a traditional flaky scone.

—

Preheat the oven to 350°F and place a rack in the center of the oven. Line a baking sheet with parchment paper or butter it lightly, and set it aside.

In a stand mixer fitted with a paddle attachment, briefly mix the flour, dried cherries, superfine sugar, baking powder, baking soda, and salt on low speed until combined. Cut the butter into 8 to 10 pieces and add it to the flour mixture; paddle for 20 to 30 seconds on low until the butter is somewhat broken down but there are still pieces about the size of grapes.

In a medium bowl, whisk together the buttermilk, crème fraîche, ricotta, whole egg, lemon zest, and vanilla until thoroughly mixed. With the mixer running on low, pour the buttermilk mixture into the flour mixture and paddle for another 10 to 15 seconds, until the dough just comes together. There will probably still be a little loose flour at the bottom of the bowl.

Remove the bowl from the mixer. Add the fresh cherries. Gather and lift the dough with your hands and turn it over in the bowl so that it starts to pick up the loose flour at the bottom and the cherries mix in. Turn the dough over several times until all the loose flour is mixed in.

Using a large spoon, scoop out baseball-size balls of dough and place them on the prepared baking sheet. You should have about eight scones total. Whisk the egg yolk for the egg wash in a small bowl with a fork. Use a pastry brush to brush the egg wash evenly over the entire top of the scones. Sprinkle the surface with the sanding sugar. (At this point the scones can be frozen on the baking sheet, transferred to a plastic freezer bag, and frozen for up to 1 week. Add 5 to 10 minutes to the baking time.)

Bake for 30 to 40 minutes, rotating the baking sheet midway through the baking time, until the scones are golden brown all over and firm when you press them in the middle; don't underbake these or they will be gummy inside. Let the scones cool on the baking sheet on a wire rack for 30 minutes and serve.

Scones are best enjoyed the same day you bake them, but they can be stored in an airtight container at room temperature for 2 to 3 days. If you keep them for longer than 1 day, refresh them in a 300°F oven for 4 to 5 minutes. Or freeze them, tightly wrapped in plastic, for up to 1 week and reheat them in a 300°F oven for 10 to 12 minutes.

Rhubarb-Strawberry
Jam-n-Butter Biscuits

MAKES 8 TO 10 BISCUITS

Salted Butter (page 76)

Homemade Rhubarb-
Strawberry Spoon Jam
(page 76)

2¾ cups/**385 grams**
all-purpose flour

1½ teaspoons baking powder

½ teaspoon baking soda

½ teaspoon kosher salt

½ cup/1 stick/**115 grams**
unsalted butter, cold

½ cup/**120 grams**
fat-free buttermilk

½ cup/**120 grams** heavy cream

1 large egg (about **50 grams**),
at room temperature

1 teaspoon pure vanilla extract

Seeds scraped from 1 vanilla
bean (see page 28)

There is a whole category of pastries we wish we could put on the counter at Flour but don't—maybe it is something that has to be assembled to order (like the amazing Passion Fruit and Raspberry Pavlova on page 383) or perhaps it's a dessert that relies on being served fresh from the oven to be at its best (molten chocolate cakes fall into this group). This biscuit is one of those pastries that I thought wouldn't work because I didn't think they could sit on the counter for long before falling apart and getting soggy. We tried anyway, and our guests bought them so quickly I needn't have worried. We now offer them each year for the few months when rhubarb and strawberries are at their finest. When we inevitably take them off the menu, I am inundated with requests begging to put them back on; when we announce their return in the spring, our social media feed is filled with every happy-dance/heart/smiling-face/celebration/clapping-hand emoji out there. The spoon jam lasts for quite a while, so you can certainly extend the summer season and enjoy these well into the cooler months.

Make the salted butter and jam and set them aside.

Preheat the oven to 350°F and place a rack in the center of the oven. Line a baking sheet with parchment paper or butter it lightly, and set it aside.

In the bowl of a stand mixer fitted with a paddle attachment, mix the flour, baking powder, baking soda, and salt on low speed until combined, 10 to 15 seconds. Cut the butter into 8 to 10 pieces and add it to the flour mixture; paddle for about 45 seconds on medium-low until the butter is somewhat broken down and the mixture resembles coarse crumbs.

In a small bowl, whisk together the buttermilk, cream, egg, and vanilla extract until thoroughly mixed. Place the vanilla seeds in a separate small bowl, add a little bit of the buttermilk mixture, and mix with a rubber spatula or spoon until the seeds loosen and mix into the liquid. Scrape this into the rest of the buttermilk mixture and whisk until the seeds are evenly dispersed. With

Salted Butter

MAKES ½ CUP

½ cup/1 stick/**115 grams**
unsalted butter, at room
temperature

¾ teaspoon kosher salt

—

In a small bowl, beat the
butter and salt together with a
wooden spoon until the butter
is fluffy and the salt is entirely
incorporated.

Salted butter can be stored in
an airtight container in the
refrigerator for up to 1 month.
Bring to room temperature
and beat with a wooden spoon
before using.

Homemade Rhubarb-Strawberry Spoon Jam

MAKES ABOUT 1¾ CUPS

This makes a bit more than you really need for the biscuits, but you'll
also use it on toast or eat it straight from the container.

—

8 ounces/**225 grams** chopped rhubarb
(about 4 small stalks/2 cups chopped)

1 pint/**230 grams** strawberries, trimmed and halved

1 cup/**200 grams** sugar

2 tablespoons fresh lemon juice (about ½ large lemon)

⅛ teaspoon kosher salt

—

Place the rhubarb, strawberries, sugar, lemon juice, and salt in a
medium saucepan. Cook over medium heat, stirring occasionally,
until the fruit starts to soften and let off juice, about 5 minutes. Turn
the heat up to high and bring the jam to a rapid boil. Reduce heat back
to medium and let the jam simmer, stirring occasionally, for about
30 minutes, until the fruit is mostly broken down and the jam is thick.
Remove from the heat and let cool.

Spoon jam can be stored in an airtight container in the fridge for up to
3 weeks, or the freezer for up to 3 months.

the mixer on low, pour the buttermilk
mixture into the flour mixture and
paddle for another 10 to 15 seconds,
until the dough just comes together.
There will probably still be a little
loose flour mixture at the bottom of
the bowl.

Remove the bowl from the mixer.
Gather and lift the dough with your
hands and turn it over in the bowl
so that it picks up the loose flour at
the bottom. Turn the dough over
in the bowl several times until all
the loose flour is mixed in.

Flick flour over the work surface
then dump the dough out onto it.
Pat it into a layer about 1 inch thick.
Using a 3-inch round cookie cutter,
cut out biscuits; place them on the
prepared baking sheet. Gently bring
the dough scraps together, pat
them into a 1-inch layer again, and

continue cutting biscuits until all the
dough is used up. You should get
about 8 biscuits. (At this point the
biscuits can be frozen on the baking
sheet, transferred to a plastic freezer
bag, and frozen for up to 1 week. Add
5 to 10 minutes to the baking time.)

Bake for 40 to 45 minutes, rotating
the baking sheet midway through
the baking time, until the biscuits
are entirely golden brown on top.
Remove the biscuits from the oven
and let them cool on the baking
sheet on a wire rack.

While the biscuits are cooling,
let the salted butter come to room
temperature, then beat it with a
wooden spoon. Split the biscuits in
half and smear about 1 tablespoon
of the salted butter on each bottom
half; top with about 2 tablespoons
of the jam, cover with the top halves,
and serve.

These biscuits are best served the
day they are baked; you can store
the unfilled biscuits, tightly wrapped
in plastic, at room temperature for
1 day; refresh them in a 300°F oven
for 6 to 8 minutes before filling and
serving.

Nutty Seedy Breakfast Cookies

MAKES 18 TO 20 COOKIES

¾ cup/**90 grams** walnuts, roughly chopped

1 cup/2 sticks/**225 grams** unsalted butter

½ cup/**170 grams** maple syrup

1 teaspoon pure vanilla extract

3 large eggs (about **150 grams**), at room temperature

1 ripe banana, thoroughly mashed (about ⅓ cup/**100 grams**)

¾ cup/**100 grams** raw unsalted pepitas (shelled pumpkin seeds)

¾ cup/**40 grams** unsweetened flaked coconut

½ cup/**45 grams** raw shelled sunflower seeds

½ cup/**50 grams** flaxseeds

¼ cup/**50 grams** millet

1½ cups/**150 grams** rolled oats

1 cup/**120 grams** dried cranberries

⅔ cup/**100 grams** whole wheat flour

½ cup/**100 grams** dried cherries

1 teaspoon baking soda

1 teaspoon kosher salt

½ teaspoon ground cinnamon

¼ teaspoon freshly grated nutmeg

Eating cookies for breakfast might seem like a ruse your kids try to pull on you to get out of eating their Wheaties. But when we created this recipe, we made sure it was full of whole grains and seeds and fruits and nuts and that it was wholesome enough for you to feel good about how you were starting off your morning. Don't be daunted by the number of ingredients. While it most likely will require a trip to the grocery store, you'll end up with a pantry nicely stocked with useful staples to encourage your whole grain baking even further. This cookie has become one of my favorite ways to start the morning, and I think it will become one of yours, too.

—

Preheat the oven to 350°F and place a rack in the center of the oven. Place the walnuts on a baking sheet and toast for 6 to 8 minutes, until they are light golden brown and fragrant. Remove from the oven and set aside to cool.

Melt the butter, then place it in a medium bowl. Whisk in the maple syrup and vanilla until well combined. Whisk in the eggs and banana until the mixture is totally homogeneous. (The banana needs to be completely mashed so it whisks in smoothly.)

In a large bowl, stir together the pepitas, coconut, sunflower seeds, flaxseeds, and millet. Remove ½ cup/about 50 grams of the mixture and set it aside for topping the cookies. Add the walnuts, oats, cranberries, flour, cherries, baking soda, salt, cinnamon, and nutmeg to the bowl

and stir well to combine. Make a well in the center and pour in the butter mixture. Stir well to combine — the dough will be more like a soft batter than a stiff cookie dough. Cover the bowl and refrigerate for at least 30 minutes or up to overnight, to allow the grains to absorb the liquid and firm up the batter.

When ready to bake the cookies, preheat the oven to 350°F. Line a baking sheet with parchment paper or butter it.

Wet your hands and use them to scoop about ¼ cup of the dough from the bowl. Roll the dough into a rough ball, dip the top of the ball into the reserved seed mixture, and plop it seed side up on the prepared baking sheet. Repeat to form the remaining dough. Press the cookies down with the palm of your hand to make them flat. Bake for 20 to 22 minutes, rotating the baking sheet midway through the baking time, until the cookies are golden brown on the edges and firm when you press them in the middle.

Remove from the oven and let cool on the baking sheet on a wire rack.

Cookies can be stored in an airtight container at room temperature for up to 2 days.

Spelt Croissants

MAKES 11 CROISSANTS

1¼ cups/**300 grams** whole milk, at room temperature

2¼ teaspoons/**7 grams** / 1 (¼-ounce) packet active dry yeast, or 2 tablespoons plus 1 teaspoon/**18 grams** fresh cake yeast

1½ cups/**210 grams** spelt flour

1½ cups/**210 grams** high-gluten bread flour

¼ cup/**50 grams** sugar

2 teaspoons kosher salt

18 tablespoons/2¼ sticks/ **255 grams** unsalted butter, cold

2 large egg yolks (about **40 grams**), for egg wash

If there's one pastry I'm particularly obsessed with, it is croissants. I'm awed by the web of flaky layers of dough-butter-dough-butter-dough which seem to go on to infinity. The care and precision that go into making an excellent croissant are not hard, necessarily, but they do require a level of patience that in this world of GO GO GO is hard to come by naturally (at least for me). Making croissants and making them well forces you to stop and, well, smell the butter. You can't rush the lamination or folding, and the temperature of the dough and butter has to be just so. It takes your full concentration to keep the layers intact by finding that fine balance of rolling out the dough both gently enough and firmly enough. I truly love the whole process.

A perfectly made and baked croissant is glossy and golden brown, shatters when you bite into it, is so tender it practically dissolves in your mouth, and tastes of pure sweet butter. In this spelt flour version, the nuttiness of the whole grain flour adds robust flavor to the traditional white flour croissant. Read the recipe through several times, carefully, before starting; the whole process takes at least 2 days. Then get ready for that rush of pride when you bite into a flaky warm buttery croissant that you made from start to finish.

—

In a medium bowl, stir together the milk and yeast for a few seconds to combine; if using cake yeast, mash it well. Add the spelt flour, bread flour, sugar, and salt and stir it all together to make a shaggy mess. Dump it out onto a work surface and knead it by hand by bringing the outer parts of the dough into the center and then pushing outward with the palm of your hand; every now and then, turn the whole thing over. (It will be very sticky at first, but it will smooth out.) Keep kneading until it forms a smoothish ball, about 2 minutes. Place the dough in a bowl and cover it lightly with plastic wrap or a lint-free towel and refrigerate for at least 8 hours or up to overnight.

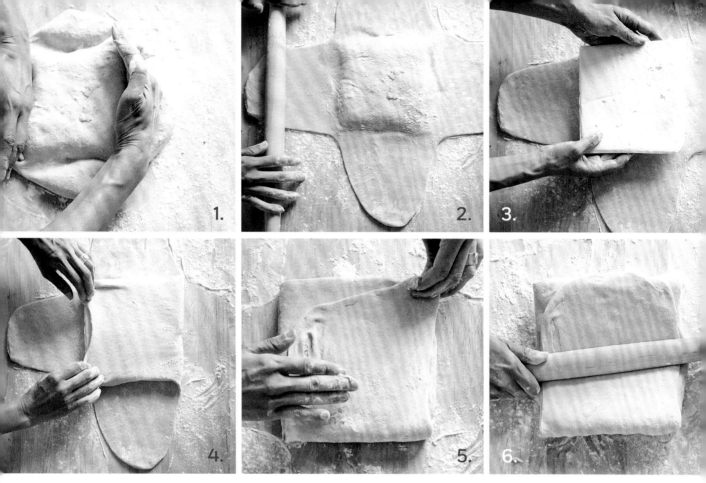

The next day, in a stand mixer fitted with a paddle attachment, beat the butter on medium-high speed until it softens and all lumps are removed, about 1 minute. Scrape the sides of the bowl and the paddle to make sure you beat all the butter. Set aside. You can also beat the butter by hand by pounding it with a rolling pin until it mashes and softens but is still cool to the touch.

Generously flick flour over the work surface. Remove the dough from the fridge, unwrap it, and press it down firmly on the work surface into a square roughly 9 x 9 inches. Rotate the square 45 degrees so that as you face it, it looks like a baseball diamond. Use the sides of your palms to mark a 7 x 7-inch square in the middle of the

diamond, creating triangular flaps at each corner.

Roll out these triangular flaps as best as you can into about 4 x 4-inch squares; you will have to tug a bit at the edges to pull them square as you are rolling. When you are done the entire piece of dough will be about 15 x 15 inches, with a 7 x 7-inch square lump in the middle and four squarish flaps, one on each side of that lump. The 7-inch square lump will be about 1 inch thick, and the four squarish flaps will be roughly ¼ inch thick.

Scrape the butter from the bowl onto a piece of parchment and top it with another piece of parchment. Using your hands, smush and spread the butter into a 7-inch square, then remove it from the parchment and

place it on the square lump in the center of the dough. The butter and dough should be about the same consistency.

Lift up one of the flaps and stretch it over the butter square to cover it entirely. Tug at the flap to keep it in a square. (The dough is quite stretchy, so it will stretch to cover the butter completely.) Fold and stretch a second flap over that in the same way; repeat with the third and fourth flaps. You will now have a butter square that is entirely encased in dough. Using the palms of both hands, firmly press down on the dough package to flatten it into a square roughly 9 x 9 inches.

Switch to a rolling pin and continue to flatten the dough. To preserve the

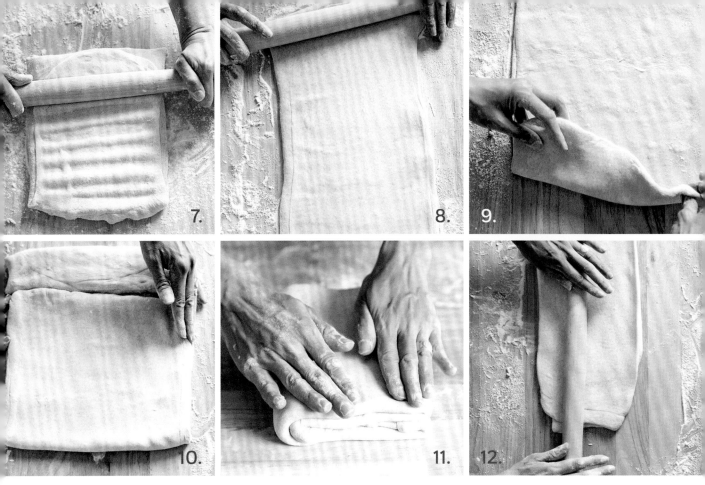

7.

8.

9.

10.

11.

12.

layers of dough and butter (which makes for a flakier end product), you want to firmly press down on the dough and then move the rolling pin up and down along the length of the dough, using the pin to create ridges as it compacts the dough. Once the dough is pressed down all over, use the pin to roll back and forth, smoothing out the ridges while flattening the dough. (When rolling out laminated dough, your goal is to keep the layers directly on top of one another and even, to preserve the layering. Using this technique to compress the dough first helps to keep the layers even.)

Roll the dough into a rectangle about 18 inches wide from side to side and 10 inches long from top to

bottom. Flour the dough and work surface generously as needed to prevent the rolling pin from sticking to the dough and the dough from sticking to the work surface. Take the left side of the dough and fold it inward about 3 inches to make a small lip. Take the right side of the dough and fold it all the way over to meet the lip. Press down on the folds with your hands so the dough adheres to itself; you will have a nice package about 9 inches wide. Now fold it exactly in half by folding the right half onto the left half so it is about 4½ inches wide.

Press the rolling pin up and down the dough package, compressing the folds together. Rotate the whole package clockwise 90 degrees

(a quarter-turn) so that it is now longer than it is wide. Roll out the dough out into a large rectangle, again about 18 inches long and 10 inches wide.

Repeat the folding process, making the lip, bringing the right edge to it, and folding it all in half.

Place the dough on a baking sheet and cover it completely with plastic wrap, tucking the plastic under the dough as if you're tucking it into bed. Refrigerate the dough for at least 1½ hours but no more than 3 hours.

Line a baking sheet with parchment paper and set it aside. Generously flick flour over the work surface. Remove the dough from the refrigerator, unwrap it, and place it on the

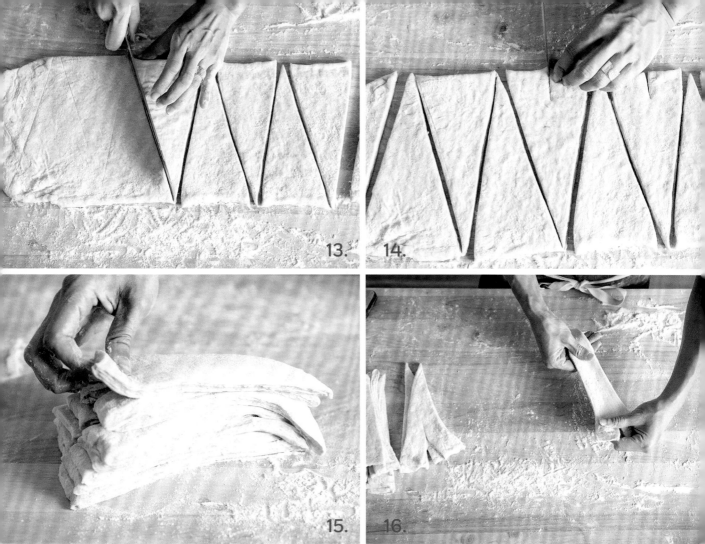

13.

14.

15.

16.

work surface with the long side of the rectangle facing you. This time roll the dough into a rectangle about 24 inches wide and 6 inches long.

Starting at the bottom left corner, mark along the bottom edge of the rectangle every 4 inches until you get to right side of the dough. Then starting at the top left corner, mark along the top edge exactly midway between the notches on the bottom edge — so your first notch will be about 2 inches from the left and then you'll notch every 4 inches. Use a sharp chef's knife to cut the dough into triangles by cutting diagonally

from notch to notch. You will end up with 11 triangles and a few scrap edge pieces.

Cut a 1-inch slit in the center of the base of each triangle. Rotate all the triangles so they are oriented with the base on top and the point pointing down toward you. Pick up a triangle, hold it by its base with one hand, and gently stretch and stroke it lengthwise with your other hand to elongate it to 10 to 12 inches.

Place the lengthened triangle on the work surface with the point toward you, fan open the base at the 1-inch slit into a Y, and then roll the

dough down to the point to form the classic croissant shape. Place the croissant on the parchment-lined baking sheet with the point side down, touching the parchment. Repeat with the remaining dough triangles, spacing the croissants 2 to 3 inches apart on the baking sheet.

Cover the croissants with plastic wrap and leave them in a warm place for 2 to 2½ hours, until they are somewhat poufy and airy.

Whisk the egg yolks for the egg wash in a small bowl with a fork. Use a pastry brush to brush the egg wash lightly over all the croissants. Cover

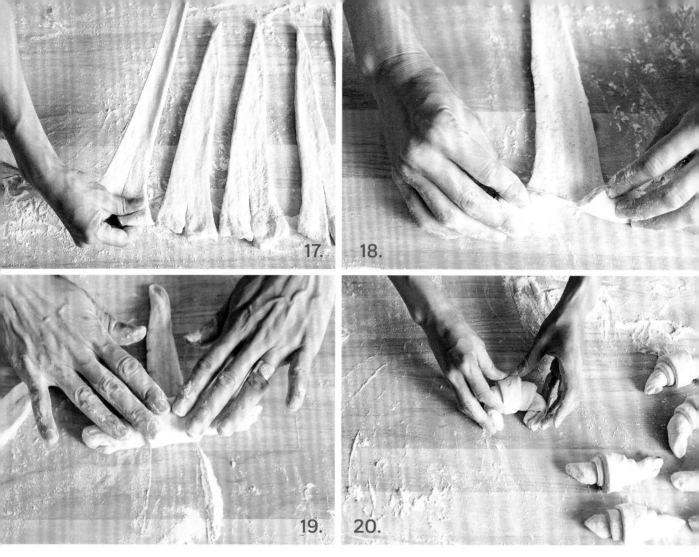

17.

18.

19.

20.

and refrigerate any remaining egg wash.

If you are baking the croissants the same day, cover them again with plastic and let them finish proofing for another 30 minutes to 1 hour. They will get even more poufy and jiggly when you nudge them. If you are baking the croissants the next day, wrap the baking sheet in plastic and place it in the refrigerator. The next morning, remove the croissants from the fridge and let them sit at room temperature for 30 to 40 minutes.

While the croissants are proofing, preheat the oven to 400°F and place a rack in the center of the oven.

When the croissants are done proofing, egg wash them again. Bake for 5 minutes, then turn the oven down to 350°F and bake for another 25 to 35 minutes, rotating the baking sheet midway through the baking time, until they are completely golden brown all over, even in the layers and crevices.

Let the croissants cool for 20 minutes before serving so you don't burn your mouth on the hot dough.

Croissants are best enjoyed the same day. If you want to store them overnight, store them in an airtight container at room temperature and refresh them in a 300°F oven for 5 to 6 minutes before serving.

Almond Croissants

1 recipe Master Frangipane (page 433), at spreadable room temperature

¾ cup/**150 grams** superfine sugar

¼ teaspoon pure almond extract

8 day-old Spelt Croissants (page 81) or regular croissants

½ cup/**55 grams** sliced raw almonds

2 tablespoons confectioners' sugar, for garnish

When you have leftover croissants, the best way to enjoy them is by making these decadent almond croissants. There are a few key points to making a great almond croissant. First, make sure you dip and soak the day-old croissant thoroughly. After a day or so croissants get pretty dry, and soaking them in almond syrup gives them much-needed moisture as well as a bit of sweetness. Second, don't be shy with the fragrant almond cream filling since it is what makes the almond croissant so rich and delicious. Finally, don't overbake the almond croissant: Remember that the croissant itself is already baked and you are baking the whole thing again just long enough to set the almond cream. Our almond croissants are so popular that we purposely make way more regular croissants than we could ever sell in a day so that we know we will have leftovers to make these.

Make the frangipane.

Preheat the oven to 350°F and place a rack in the center of the oven. Line a baking sheet with parchment paper or butter it lightly, and set aside.

In a small saucepan, combine the superfine sugar and ¾ cup/180 grams water and bring to a boil. Remove from the heat and add the almond extract. Pour into a shallow container and let cool for 15 to 20 minutes, until it's no longer piping hot.

Split each of the croissants in half horizontally. Quickly submerge each croissant half cut side down in the sugar syrup, giving each a slight squeeze as you remove it to keep it from being too soggy. Use an offset spatula or the back of a spoon to spread about 3 tablespoons of the frangipane evenly over each bottom croissant half, using up almost all the frangipane but reserving a few tablespoons for garnish. Top each croissant bottom with a top croissant half and press down gently to adhere.

Place the croissants on the prepared baking sheet, spacing them evenly apart. Dab the top of each croissant with a smear of the reserved frangipane. Sprinkle about 1 tablespoon of the sliced almonds on top of the frangipane, pressing them into

the frangipane so they stick. (At this point the croissants can be covered in plastic wrap and stored in the fridge overnight.)

Bake for 25 to 30 minutes, rotating the baking sheet midway through the baking time, until the almonds and frangipane are golden brown on the top and edges. Remove from the oven and let cool on the baking sheet on a wire rack for about 15 minutes, until cool enough to handle. Sprinkle with confectioners' sugar and serve warm.

Almond croissants can be stored in an airtight container at room temperature for up to 2 days; refresh in a 300°F oven for 6 to 8 minutes before serving.

What's for Breakfast

Fresh Fig Danish

MAKES 16 DANISH

4⅔ cups/**655 grams** all-purpose flour

⅓ cup/**70 grams** superfine sugar

2 teaspoons kosher salt

10 tablespoons/1¼ sticks/ **140 grams** unsalted butter, at room temperature

1 cup/**240 grams** whole milk, heated until warm but not hot

2 large eggs (about **100 grams**)

2¼ teaspoons/**7 grams**/ 1 (¼-ounce) packet active dry yeast

30 tablespoons/3¾ sticks/ **425 grams** unsalted butter, cold

Cream Cheese Filling (page 90)

3 large egg yolks (about **60 grams**), for egg wash

2 pints ripe fresh figs

3 tablespoons confectioners' sugar, for garnish

My very first baking job was at a small scratch bakery called Bentonwood Bakery, in Newton Center, Massachusetts, a tony suburb of Boston. While I had dabbled—A LOT—in baking at home, I had never stepped foot in a professional bakery kitchen before. I learned how to use a 60-quart mixer that was big enough for me to sit inside, and a six-deck rotating oven that was larger than my first car. I made homemade vanilla extract for the first time, whacked open my first fresh coconut, learned the invaluable skill of fraisaging pie dough so it was flaky as can be. What I was most proud of was learning how to make traditional danish. I had only had danish as most of us have had danish—from an Entenmann's box, with either red or yellow filling and an even striping of white frosting that somehow looked homemade even though you knew a machine had zigged and zagged it. I had doubts I could ever learn to make something as perfect as Entenmann's. When I baked off my first test danish (for every batch of everything we made, we made a test to ensure it was made properly and to reward us for our hard work—a practice I continue at Flour), it hit me that what I'd originally thought was the holy grail of danish was a far cry from the real thing. THIS danish filled my mouth and tasted of sweet butter. It was flaky and tender and rich rich rich. It redefined *danish* in my mind (pretty much everything I learned to make in this formative job redefined itself for me) and I immediately went to work on perfecting my lamination skills to make the best danish I could each time. I don't make danish regularly anymore, but when I can get my hands on ripe fresh figs, there are few better ways to enjoy their jammy honeyed sweetness than in this classic breakfast treat. Of course, don't let the fleeting season of figs stop you from trying these; you can use fresh blueberries, raspberries, cherries, peaches—pretty much any fruit you would bake in a pie will make a spectacular danish.

Cream Cheese Filling

MAKES ABOUT 1½ CUPS

1 cup/8 ounces/**225 grams** cream cheese

⅓ cup/**70 grams** sugar

1 large egg yolk (about **20 grams**), at room temperature

½ teaspoon pure vanilla extract

⅛ teaspoon kosher salt

In a stand mixer fitted with a paddle attachment, beat the cream cheese until it is soft and fluffy. Slowly add the sugar, egg yolk, vanilla, and salt. Scrape the sides of the bowl and the paddle with a rubber spatula occasionally and mix until well combined.

Cream cheese filling can be made in advance and stored in an airtight container in the fridge for up to 1 week.

Place the flour, superfine sugar, and salt in a stand mixer fitted with a paddle attachment. Add the room temperature butter and mix on medium speed for 2 to 3 minutes, until the butter is completely mixed in and the mixture is crumbly. Change the attachment to a dough hook. In a medium bowl, whisk together the milk, whole eggs, and yeast until the yeast is dissolved. Add the milk mixture to the flour mixture all at once and mix until the dough comes together, about 30 seconds. It will be soft and mushy.

Remove the dough from the bowl and place it on a large piece of plastic wrap. Press it into a square about 8 x 8 inches. Wrap it lightly in the plastic and refrigerate for at least 30 minutes or up to 2 hours.

Right before you take the dough out of the fridge, place the cold butter in the stand mixer fitted with the paddle attachment and beat on high until the butter is softened and malleable but still cold, about 1 minute.

Generously flick flour over the work surface. Remove the dough from the fridge, unwrap it, and press it down firmly on the work surface into a square roughly 9 x 9 inches. Rotate the square 45 degrees so that as you face it, it looks like a baseball diamond. Use the sides of your palms to mark a 7 x 7-inch square in the middle of the diamond, creating triangular flaps at each corner.

Roll out these triangular flaps as best as you can into about 4 x 4-inch squares; you will have to tug a bit at the edges to pull them square as you are rolling. When you are done the entire piece of dough will be about 15 x 15 inches, with a 7 x 7-inch

square lump in the middle and four squarish flaps, one on each side of that lump. The 7-inch square lump will be about 1 inch thick, and the four squarish flaps will be roughly ¼ inch thick.

Scrape the butter from the bowl and, using your hands, pat it directly onto the 7-inch square lump in the center of the dough, patting it with your fingers to shape the butter into a square that covers the center dough square. The butter should be about the same consistency as the dough.

Lift up one of the flaps and stretch it over the butter square to cover it entirely. Tug at the flap to keep it in a square. (The dough is quite stretchy, so it will stretch to cover the butter completely.) Fold and stretch a second flap over that in the same way; repeat with the third and fourth flaps. You will now have a butter square that is entirely encased in dough. Using the palms of both hands, firmly press down on the dough package to flatten it into a square roughly 9 x 9 inches.

Switch to a rolling pin and continue to flatten the dough. To preserve the layers of dough and butter (which makes for a flakier end product), you want to firmly press down on the dough and then move the rolling pin up and down along the length of the dough, using the pin to create ridges as it compacts the dough. Once the dough is pressed down all over, use the pin to roll back and forth, smoothing out the ridges while flattening the dough. (When rolling out laminated dough, your goal is to keep the layers directly on top of one another and even, to preserve the layering. Using this technique to compress the dough first helps to keep the layers even.)

Continues...

CHAPTER 2

I Knead Bread

Gluten-Free Focaccia

MAKES ONE 13 X 18-INCH LOAF

2 cups/**480 grams** water, at body temperature (when you stick your finger in it, it does not register as either warm or cold)

3 tablespoons/**40 grams** sugar

2 tablespoons plus ¾ teaspoon/**21 grams** active dry yeast (3 packets)

3 large eggs (about **150 grams**), at room temperature

3 egg whites (about ⅓ cup/ **90 grams**), at room temperature

6 tablespoons/**80 grams** vegetable oil (such as canola)

4 teaspoons kosher salt

4¼ cups/**510 grams** gluten-free flour (such as Cup-4-Cup)

3 tablespoons/**45 grams** extra-virgin olive oil

½ teaspoon freshly ground black pepper, for garnish

As someone who could not live without bread, I wanted to create a bread for those who eat gluten-free that did not feel like a punishment. It needed to be tender but still a bit chewy, with a soft crumb. It could not taste or feel like sawdust. It had to be so good that if I did not tell you it was gluten-free, you would not notice. This focaccia checks all the boxes. I use a gluten-free flour blend as the base and then add richness and texture with eggs and oil. It's tremendously satisfying and it makes terrific sandwiches.

Preheat the oven to 350°F and place a rack in the center of the oven. Spray a 13 x 18-inch rimmed baking sheet with cooking spray (without flour) or line it with parchment paper. Set aside.

In a large bowl, whisk together the water, sugar, and yeast. In a small bowl, whisk together the whole eggs, egg whites, vegetable oil, and 3½ teaspoons of the salt. Add the egg mixture to the yeast mixture and whisk until well combined. Add the flour and stir with a wooden spoon until combined; the dough will be soupy and loose like pancake batter. Pour the dough into the prepared pan and gently push it to the edges of the pan to fill it. Lightly drape plastic wrap over the pan and let it sit at warm room temperature for 30 to 35 minutes, until the dough is a little jiggly and tall and coming up the edge of the pan.

Drizzle the dough with the olive oil and sprinkle with the remaining ½ teaspoon salt and the pepper. Bake for 20 to 25 minutes, rotating the pan midway through the baking time, until the focaccia is thoroughly golden brown all over and firm when you touch the center. Remove from the oven and let cool in the pan on a wire rack.

Cut the focaccia into squares and split for sandwiches, or serve as is.

Focaccia can be stored in an airtight container or well wrapped in plastic at room temperature for up to 2 days.

Challah

MAKES 1 BRAIDED LOAF

½ cup/**120 grams** water, at body temperature (when you stick your finger in it, it does not register as either warm or cold)

2 large eggs (about **100 grams**), at room temperature

3 tablespoons/**45 grams** vegetable oil (such as canola)

2¼ teaspoons/**7 grams**/ 1 (¼-ounce) packet active dry yeast

2½ cups/**350 grams** all-purpose flour

3 tablespoons/**40 grams** sugar

2 teaspoons kosher salt

Challah is a traditional and symbolic egg bread made to celebrate the Jewish sabbath and other holidays. Ours is barely sweet, light but firm, tender, and a dream to work with. Learning how to braid challah is one of the more fun baking challenges I know. There are all different kinds of braids and we've had a number of bakers at Flour come through our doors and show us various ways. Three-braids, four-braids, knots, loops, turbans. Here you learn a simple—but not the simplest—six-braid technique, which yields a dramatic, gorgeous loaf.

In a small bowl, whisk together the water, 1 egg, the oil, and the yeast. Pour into a stand mixer fitted with a dough hook attachment and mix on low speed for a few seconds, until mixed together. Add the flour and sugar and mix on low for about 5 minutes, until a shaggy dough forms and when you pull at the dough gently it stretches thin and you can see light through it. Cover the dough with plastic wrap or a lint-free towel and let rest for 10 minutes.

Add the salt and mix on medium for about 8 minutes; the dough will be soft and still a bit shaggy.

Remove the dough from the mixer, place it in a lightly oiled bowl, and cover it again with the plastic wrap or a towel. Let the dough proof for 3 hours at warm room temperature, punching it down once at the 1½-hour mark. (To punch down the dough, literally punch it down in the center and fold the sides into the center, then turn the dough over. This expels some of the gas that has built up and redistributes the yeast, allowing the yeast to keep feeding and working its magic.) After 3 hours the dough should be super smooth and supple, and when you stretch it it will be nicely elastic and feel like a baby's bottom. Weird but true.

Divide the dough equally into 6 pieces. Use a scale if you can to ensure each piece is the same weight, which will give you the prettiest, most even loaf. Fold the pieces into short cylinders and let them rest for a few minutes to relax a bit. Roll each piece back and forth against the work surface with both hands to stretch it out into a skinny, even rope about 12 inches long. When all 6 ropes are rolled, line them up next to each other, with the ends facing you. Gather them at the top

Start here →

and pinch the ends all together. Now comes the fun part! Starting with the far right rope, you are going to weave the rope into the 5 ropes to its left with the following pattern: over two, under one, over two, so that it ends up being the far left rope. Start again with the rope that is now to the far right: lift it over the two ropes to its left, weave it under the next rope, and lift it over the far two left ropes. Keep up this weaving, always starting with the far right rope, until you have gotten to the ends of the ropes. Tuck the bottom ends of the ropes into each other and pinch them together.

Line a baking sheet with parchment paper. Carefully lift up the braided loaf and place it on the baking sheet. Whisk the remaining egg in a small bowl with a fork. Use a pastry brush to lightly brush the loaf evenly with the egg wash. Be careful that the egg wash doesn't pool in the crevices of

the braid or it will bake into bits of hardened egg. Cover and refrigerate the remaining egg wash. Lightly cover the loaf with plastic wrap or a lint-free towel and let it rest in a warm place in your kitchen for 1½ to 2 hours, until the loaf has loosened and relaxed and is a bit jiggly when you poke it gently.

Preheat the oven to 350°F and place a rack in the center of the oven. Brush the loaf again lightly with the remaining egg wash. Bake the challah for 30 to 35 minutes, rotating the baking sheet midway through the baking time, until the challah is golden brown with a little paleness in between the ropes and sounds hollow when you thump it on the bottom. Remove from the oven and let cool on the baking sheet on a wire rack.

Challah can be stored at room temperature in a paper bag for up to 3 days.

2.

3.

4.

6.

8.

When the braiding is done,
brush with egg wash
and rest it for 2 hours.

9.

MG Rye Bread

MAKES 2 LOAVES

1¾ cups/**420 grams** water, at body temperature (when you stick your finger in it, it does not register as either warm or cold)

⅓ cup/**110 grams** unsulfured molasses

2 tablespoons vegetable oil (such as canola)

2¼ teaspoons/**7 grams**/ 1 (¼-ounce) packet active dry yeast

3 cups/**450 grams** high-gluten bread flour

1 cup/**140 grams** rye flour

¾ cup/**110 grams** whole wheat flour

½ cup/**90 grams** fine cornmeal, plus more for sprinkling

2 tablespoons Dutch-processed cocoa powder

1 tablespoon caraway seeds

1 tablespoon kosher salt

All-purpose flour, for flicking

MG is short for Mike G, our production kitchen manager, who is also a bread whisperer. He's been baking bread around Boston for over twenty years, and when he joined our team I immediately challenged him to come up with some great new breads we could put on our sandwich menu. A chewy, hearty bread with a fine, tight crumb, this rye bread is perfect for homemade Reubens and grilled cheese sandwiches. It is subtly flavored with cocoa powder, molasses, and caraway seeds, which bring out the slightly nutty flavor of the rye flour. It's a great starter bread: If you are unsure about your bread-baking skills, this dough is easy to work with, and the resulting loaves are sure to impress everyone (including you).

In a large bowl with a wooden spoon, or a stand mixer fitted with a dough hook attachment, combine the water, molasses, oil, and yeast. Mix together until the yeast has dissolved. Add the bread flour, rye flour, whole wheat flour, cornmeal, cocoa powder, caraway seeds, and salt. Mix until the dough comes together and is shaggy but all the loose flour is incorporated. Cover the bowl with plastic wrap or a lint-free towel and let sit for about 10 minutes in a warm spot in the kitchen. (This will hydrate the flour more fully and make for a finer texture.)

Mix the dough on low speed for about 3 minutes, until the dough comes together into a ball but is still soft and somewhat tacky. (Alternatively, flick flour over the work surface, turn out the dough, and knead it by hand for 5 to 7 minutes. It will still look rough but will smooth out after proofing for several hours, so don't worry. If you're kneading by hand, the work surface may become sticky; use a bench scraper to scrape the dough from the surface, and dip your hands lightly in flour as you work and knead the dough. Place the dough in a mixing bowl.) Cover the dough again with the plastic wrap or a towel and let sit in a warm place for about 1 hour.

Lift up the edges of the dough and fold them into the center, then flip the dough over and cover again. Let sit at warm room temperature for another hour. At this point the dough should be pillowy and doubled in bulk.

Split the dough into 2 equal pieces. Shape each piece by bringing the edges of the dough into the center, flipping the dough over so the seam faces down, and rounding the dough against the table to create a beautiful round boule. Use the friction of the work surface to your advantage to round the boule by cupping the boule in your hands and pressing down slightly as you push the boule outward counterclockwise. (As you push round and round, the dough will start to gather and smooth out.) Sprinkle about 2 tablespoons cornmeal evenly over a baking sheet and place the boules on it, 3 to 4 inches apart, as you shape them.

Flick a small handful of all-purpose flour on top of the boules to keep the plastic or towel from sticking and cover one last time.

Let the boules proof at warm room temperature for 1 to 1½ hours. The boules will be relaxed and full and they will jiggle like water balloons when you shake the baking sheet a bit.

In the meantime, preheat the oven to 400°F and place a rack in the center of the oven. Score the boules decoratively (see page 27) with a sharp paring knife, lame, or razor blade. Bake the boules for 35 to 45 minutes, rotating the baking sheet midway through the baking time,

until the boules are burnished brown on top and sound hollow when you thump them on the bottom.

Remove from the oven and let cool completely, directly on a wire rack, before you cut into the loaves.

Rye loaves can be stored at room temperature in a paper bag for up to 3 days. If serving day-old bread, toast it first to refresh it.

Whole Grain
Pull-Apart Rolls

MAKES 1 DOZEN ROLLS

1 recipe Sponge
(page 118)

1 cup/**150 grams**
whole wheat flour

⅓ cup/**45 grams**
all-purpose flour

3 tablespoons/**40 grams** sugar

2½ teaspoons kosher salt

1 large egg yolk (about
20 grams), at room
temperature

5 tablespoons/**70 grams**
unsalted butter, at warm
room temperature

1 tablespoon/**15 grams**
unsalted butter, melted, for
finishing

Every year at Thanksgiving and Christmas we used to sell hundreds and hundreds (or was that thousands and thousands?) of our signature country sourdough rolls. Slightly tangy with a hearty chew, these rolls were great for toasting and making sandwiches with all your holiday leftovers. A few years ago Nicole and I realized that not everyone wants to give their jaws a work-out when they eat a roll. Many of us grew up with soft, buttery Pepperidge Farm rolls that were great for soaking up gravy. We decided to offer our spin on these rolls by making a whole wheat version that had the same familiar texture but way more flavor. These are lovely, tender, and moist with a gorgeous crust. Try them for your next holiday feast—you'll never go back to the packaged kind again.

Make the sponge and let it rest for 2 hours.

If you would like to make this in a mixer, use a stand mixer fitted with a dough hook. Otherwise you can make this by hand with a wooden spoon. Place the sponge in the bowl and add the whole wheat flour, all-purpose flour, sugar, 2 teaspoons of the salt, and the egg yolk. Mix on low speed or with your hands until it comes together, 1 to 2 minutes using the mixer and 3 to 5 minutes by hand. Add the room temperature butter and mix until the butter is fully incorporated. With a mixer this will take about 2 minutes; by hand you will knead the butter in for about 5 minutes. When the dough is

pliable, smooth, stretchy, and still a tad sticky and all the butter is entirely incorporated, it is ready to proof. Cover the dough with plastic wrap or a lint-free towel and let it sit in a warm place for about 1½ hours, until it has doubled in size.

Line a 13 x 18-inch baking sheet with parchment paper or lightly flick flour over it. Divide the dough evenly into 12 balls, each about 2⅔ ounces/ 75 grams. To shape the rolls, bring the edges of a ball into the center to make a tight pouch, then turn it upside down on a clean work surface. Cup it with the palm of your hand. Using a circular motion and pushing the ball into the table, round the ball into a tight roll. Place on the

Sponge

**MAKES ENOUGH FOR
1 RECIPE WHOLE GRAIN
PULL-APART ROLLS**

2¼ cups/**315 grams**
all-purpose flour

1⅓ cups/**320 grams** whole
milk, at body temperature
(when you stick your finger in
it, it does not register as either
warm or cold)

1 teaspoon active dry yeast

In a small bowl, mix together
the flour, milk, and yeast with
a wooden spoon. Keep mixing
until the mixture becomes a
doughy paste — a little sludgy
and wet. Cover the sponge
with plastic wrap or a lint-free
towel draped across the bowl
and let sit at warm room
temperature for about 2 hours,
until the sponge is aerated and
a bit frothy.

prepared baking sheet. Continue
with the rest of the balls, spacing
them in three rows of four, about
2 inches apart.

Lightly flick flour over the tops of
the rolls and cover with plastic wrap
or a lint-free towel. Let proof in a
warm place in the kitchen for about
1 hour, until the rolls have become
soft and round and are almost
touching.

Preheat the oven to 400°F and
place a rack in the center of the oven.
Bake the rolls for 25 to 30 minutes,
rotating the baking pan midway
through the baking time, until the

rolls are entirely golden brown on top
and sound hollow when you thump
them on the bottom.

Remove from the oven, brush
the tops with the melted butter,
and sprinkle with the remaining
½ teaspoon salt. Let the rolls cool
before serving.

Rolls can be stored in a paper bag
at room temperature for 2 days.
Refresh in a 300°F oven for 6 to
8 minutes before serving.

Whole Wheat Brioches à Tête

MAKES JUST OVER 2 POUNDS/950 GRAMS DOUGH, 9 BRIOCHES

3 large eggs (about **150 grams**), at room temperature, for the dough, plus 1 large egg (about **20 grams**) for egg wash

½ cup/**120 grams** ice-cold water

2¼ teaspoons/**7 grams**/ 1 (¼-ounce) packet active dry yeast

1½ cups/**210 grams** all-purpose flour

¼ cup/**50 grams** sugar

2 teaspoons kosher salt

1½ cups/**225 grams** whole wheat flour

13 tablespoons/**185 grams** unsalted butter, cut into 10 to 12 pieces, at room temperature

Learning how to make *brioche à tête* ("brioche with a head") was when I finally felt I could hold my own while working at one of the top French patisseries in New York City in the late 1990s. Bruno, the pastry chef who took me under his wing when I worked in his viennoiserie department, counseled me every day in a mix of vigorous French and English on how to make the perfect little tête to perch on top of the round brioche body. "You must press *comme ça ici* very hard *avec* your fingers!! Otherwise *la tête* falls off and *tout le monde* can see you are not professionalllll!" I lived in fear of being deemed not worthy to work in this very French kitchen, so I learned to dig my fingers deep into the brioche. There was no way my têtes were going to fall off. Once I made my first perfect set of brioches à tête you could have heard my squeal across the room. This whole wheat version of our classic Master Brioche Dough recipe is wheaty and buttery and a delicious way to introduce whole grains into your baking.

Nothing this delicious comes quickly; note that the entire recipe takes two days, at minimum, to make.

In a stand mixer fitted with a dough hook attachment, combine the 3 eggs for the dough, the water, and the yeast and stir to dissolve the yeast. Add the flour, sugar, and salt and mix on low speed until all the ingredients have come together, 3 to 4 minutes. Scrape the bowl if necessary to make sure all the flour is incorporated. Mix on low for another 3 to 4 minutes, until the dough is smooth and wet and resembles pancake batter. Cover the dough with plastic wrap or a lint-free towel and let sit at room temperature for at least 1 hour or up to 2 hours.

Add the whole wheat flour and mix on low until completely incorporated. Add the butter to the dough piece by piece and mix on low until the butter is completely incorporated into the dough, stopping the mixer occasionally to scrape the sides of the bowl and breaking up the dough with your hands if necessary to help the butter mix in.

Garlicky Cheesy Monkey Bread

MAKES 6 BREADS

½ recipe/21 ounces/**600 grams**
Master Brioche Dough
(page 444), or ⅔ recipe/
21 ounces/**600 grams** Whole
Wheat Brioche dough
(see page 119)

4 tablespoons/½ stick/
60 grams unsalted butter

1 medium garlic clove

½ teaspoon kosher salt

1¼ cups/**95 grams** shredded
fontina cheese

½ teaspoon dried thyme

The first thing to know about this recipe is that it is easily doubled. You want to know that because these monkey breads are so delicious you will want to make a double batch. Marina, one of our pastry chefs at Flour, created this as a monthly special out of the little brioche nuggets she uses when making our sugar brioche buns, a sweet pull-apart roll. Instead of sugar, she tosses the nuggets in garlic-flavored butter and layers them with nutty fontina cheese. Try these gooey monkey breads at your next brunch.

—

Mix the brioche dough and let it proof for 6 hours or up to overnight in the fridge, as directed.

Line 6 cups of a 12-cup regular muffin tin with muffin papers; spray the papers generously with pan spray or butter them generously. Alternatively, use six disposable 4-ounce aluminum ramekins; spray or butter them generously. (The dough is very sticky, so you want to spray or butter a lot.) Set aside.

Melt the butter in a small saucepan on the stove, or in the microwave. Smash the garlic clove, add it to the butter, and stir it around to flavor the butter. Mix in the salt.

Remove the brioche dough from the fridge. Using a sharp chef's knife or a bench scraper, divide it into 6 equal pieces, each about 3½ ounces/100 grams. On a clean work surface, shape each piece into a rough

rectangle. Cut each piece into 6 equal nuggets by cutting the rectangle in half, then cutting each half in thirds. Remove and discard the garlic from the butter and place about three-quarters of the butter in a large bowl (set the remaining butter aside). Add all the nuggets and toss lightly to coat them with the butter. Add the fontina and thyme and toss to mix evenly. Distribute the nuggets evenly into the muffin tin cups, making sure to evenly distribute the cheese in between the nuggets as well. (Each cup should hold 6 nuggets, and they will peek out over the tops of the muffin cups.) Cover lightly with plastic wrap and let proof in a warm place in your kitchen for 1½ to 2 hours, until the dough is pillowy and soft.

Preheat the oven to 350°F and place a rack in the center of the oven. Bake the monkey breads for 25 to 28

minutes, rotating the muffin tin midway through the baking time, until the breads are evenly golden brown on top. Remove from the oven and let cool in the muffin tin on a wire rack for a few minutes.

As soon as you can, pop the monkey breads out of the tin and remove the muffin papers, if you used them.

(This will be much easier to do while the breads are still warm.) Brush them generously with the remaining garlic butter. Serve warm.

The monkey breads can be stored in an airtight container at room temperature for up to 1 day; refresh in a 300°F oven for 4 to 6 minutes before serving.

I Knead Bread

127

Alina's Milk Bread

MAKES 2 LOAVES

Tangzhong (page 134)

½ cup/**120 grams** heavy cream, at room temperature

½ cup/**120 grams** whole milk, at room temperature

2 large eggs (about **100 grams**), at room temperature

4½ teaspoons/**14 grams**/ 2 (¼-ounce) packets active dry yeast

4¾ cups/**710 grams** high-gluten bread flour

½ cup/**100 grams** sugar

2 teaspoons kosher salt

½ cup/1 stick/**115 grams** unsalted butter, cut into pieces, at warm room temperature

1 large egg yolk (about **20 grams**), for egg wash

Our dear friend Alina, who is the brilliant designer who works with Christopher to design our bakeries, is obsessed with food. I don't have a design bone in my body but she and I bonded over our mutual love for all food, especially Asian. She grew up in Japan and is always texting me pictures of a cool breakfast pastry or cookie or bread that she's dying for us to try. Recently when Christopher and I traveled to Tokyo, she gave us the firm directive to eat milk bread (and also bring some back for her). She described it as soft and sweet and fluffy and unlike anything you can find in the States. We searched everywhere we went but couldn't find it, so when I returned home I was determined to make it for her. I loved learning about using *tangzhong*, which is a technique that mixes a cooked flour mixture into bread dough to keep the bread tender and fresher for longer. We often think of great bread as hailing from Old World Europe, but making this reminded me that amazing bread is made in Asia as well. This is a beautiful bread and, as Alina promised, worth the long hunt.

In a stand mixer fitted with a dough hook attachment, place the tang-zhong, cream, milk, whole eggs, and yeast and mix on low speed for about 2 minutes, until combined. Add the bread flour, sugar, and salt and mix on medium-low for another 4 to 6 minutes, until the dough has come together and is starting to feel a bit elastic. Add the butter bit by bit and mix on medium-low for another 8 minutes. The dough should be supple and smooth and a little tacky. Cover the bowl with plastic wrap or a lint-free towel and let the dough

proof for about 1 hour at warm room temperature.

Punch the dough down by literally punching it in the middle and bringing up all of the edges into the center. Scoop the dough up and turn it over. Re-cover and let proof for another 30 minutes at warm room temperature.

Generously flick flour over the work surface. Generously butter two 9 x 5-inch loaf pans or spray with pan spray. Scrape the dough out of the bowl and divide it in half. Divide

Tangzhong

MAKES ABOUT 1¼ CUPS

⅓ cup/**45 grams** high-gluten
bread flour

½ cup/**120 grams** whole milk

Whisk together the bread
flour, milk, and ½ cup/
120 grams water in a small
saucepan. Place over medium-
high heat and bring to a boil.
Whisk for 6 to 8 minutes,
until the mixture comes
together and forms a smooth,
doughy paste. It will start out
completely liquid; after it
comes to a boil it will get
thicker and thicker until it
finally leaves a trail in the pan
and is more like a soft paste.
Remove from the heat and let
cool to room temperature.

Tangzhong can be stored in
an airtight container in the
fridge for up to 1 day.

each half into 4 equal pieces. Use a
rolling pin to roll each piece into a
rough oval about 5 inches wide from
side to side and 8 inches long from
top to bottom, with the narrow end
facing you. Fold the right side of the
dough into the center and the left
side of the dough into the center so it
meets the right side. Press down so
you now have a long skinny piece of
dough. Starting from the bottom, roll
the dough upward away from you so
you have a little jelly-roll piece of
dough. Place it seam side down in
one of the prepared pans. Repeat
this with 3 other pieces of dough so
the rolls are lined up crosswise in the
loaf pan, nestled next to one another.
Repeat with the other 4 pieces of
dough and the second loaf pan.
Cover the loaves with plastic wrap or
a lint-free towel and let proof at
warm room temperature for 60 to
70 minutes, until the loaves are puffy
and jiggly when you poke them.

Preheat the oven to 350°F and
place a rack in the center of the oven.
Whisk the egg yolk for the egg wash
in a small bowl with a fork. Use a
pastry brush to brush the egg wash
evenly on the tops of each loaf. Bake
the loaves for 35 to 40 minutes,
rotating the pans midway through
the baking time, until the breads are
golden brown on top and sound
hollow when you thump them on top.

Remove from the oven and let the
loaves cool in the pans on a wire rack
until they are cool enough to remove
from the pans, about 15 minutes. Tip
them out, place them directly on the
wire rack, and let cool until room
temperature.

Milk bread is best served the day it
is baked, but you can store it at room
temperature in a paper bag for up to
2 days, or well wrapped in plastic
wrap in the freezer for up to 3 weeks.
If frozen, milk bread is best sliced
and toasted to freshen it up.

1.

2.

3.

4.

5.

6.

Use a pastry brush to brush the egg wash evenly on the tops of each loaf.

Ciabatta

MAKES 2 LONG LOAVES

Poolish for Ciabatta (page 138)

1¼ cups/**300 grams** water, at body temperature (when you stick your finger in it, it does not register as either warm or cold)

1 tablespoon vegetable oil (such as canola)

½ teaspoon active dry yeast

3⅓ cups/**470 grams** high-gluten bread flour

2 tablespoons kosher salt

About 2 tablespoons cornmeal, for the baking sheet

Every day we make dozens of these long ciabatta loaves for our roast beef sandwich with horseradish mayo and crispy onions. The sandwich team cuts each loaf into four large pieces; the ends are trimmed off and put in a bowl for snacking. Spread with a little butter, these chewy, airy ends are my breakfast and lunch as I travel from bakery to bakery. I can't get enough of them. Ciabatta, which means "slipper" in Italian, is a rustic white bread that gets its name from its long, flat, slipper-like shape. It's become such a mainstay in bakeries and sandwich shops that you'd think it has a long history in bread baking; however, it turns out that it was created in the early 1980s in Verona, Italy, for sandwiches. We created our ciabatta recipe after testing about half a dozen variations. Some were light and airy, others dense and chewy. Ours is right in the middle, just right. It's a great starter bread recipe if you're nervous about bread shaping, proofing, or baking. The hardest part is remembering to make the poolish the day prior. A poolish is a very loose mixture of flour and water and a bit of yeast that you mix together and let sit at room temperature for some period of time to capture the natural yeasts in the air; it adds flavor and improves the longevity of bread, a very easy way to make your bread more flavorful.

Note that this recipe takes two days to make, so you'll need to start it the day before you plan on baking.

—

At least 12 hours and up to 16 hours before you'll be baking the ciabatta, make the poolish and set it aside.

In a large bowl, combine the water, oil, and yeast. Whisk until the yeast dissolves. Add the poolish, bread flour, and salt. Mix with your hands until thoroughly combined. It will seem very soupy and loose. (This is the magic of bread — soon this will become a lovely, supple bread dough.) Cover the dough lightly with plastic wrap or a lint-free towel and let it sit at room temperature for about 40 minutes, until it looks a bit more billowy and airy.

After 40 minutes, fold the dough on itself: Take the edges of the dough from the top, bottom, left, and right of the bowl and fold them into the center. Repeat. Turn the whole dough mass over. Cover again and let sit for another 40 minutes.

Repeat the folding of the dough again. Cover again and let sit for another 40 minutes. In all, the dough will sit for about 2 hours and you'll fold it onto itself three times.

At this point the dough should be very loose but soft and silky and floppy. Lightly flick flour over the work surface and stretch out the dough on it so it is about 6 inches wide from side to side and 12 inches long from top to bottom. Pick up the top third of the dough and flip it down over onto the middle third. Then take the bottom third of the dough and flip it on top of the middle third. (This is like folding a business letter.) Repeat folding, working in from the shorter ends. Turn the whole thing over, then gently pick it up and stretch it over and over a few times until it elongates back to 12 x 6 inches. Use a knife or bench scraper and cut the dough down the middle the long way so you end up with 2 loaves, each 12 x 3 inches.

Preheat the oven to 450°F and place a rack in the center of the oven. Sprinkle a baking sheet lightly and evenly with the cornmeal. Gently transfer the loaves to the baking sheet, placing them a few inches apart. Lightly cover the loaves with plastic or a lint-free towel and let sit for 30 minutes at warm room temperature to allow the dough to relax and proof a bit.

Bake the ciabatta loaves for 30 to 35 minutes, rotating the baking sheet midway through the baking time, until the loaves are deep golden brown and sound hollow when you thump them in the middle.

Remove from the oven and let cool directly on a wire rack. Slice into quarters for sandwiches.

Ciabatta can be stored in a paper bag at room temperature for up to 2 days. It is best either toasted or grilled or refreshed in a 300°F oven for 5 to 8 minutes if not eaten fresh.

Poolish for Ciabatta

MAKES ABOUT 2 CUPS

2 cups/**280 grams** high-gluten bread flour

Pinch of active dry yeast

—

In a large storage container with a lid, combine the flour with 1¼ cups/300 grams room temperature water and the yeast. Mix together with a wooden spoon or your hands until the flour is totally combined with the water. It will look like a very, very soupy dough. Cover the container with a loose-fitting lid or drape a piece of plastic wrap or a towel over the top and let it sit at room temperature for at least 12 hours or up to 16 hours.

Panettone

MAKES 2 LARGE LOAVES

Overnight Starter (page 140)

1 cup/**100 grams**
slivered almonds

⅓ cup/**80 grams** whole milk

1 teaspoon active dry yeast

2½ cups/**375 grams**
high-gluten bread flour

2 large eggs (about **100 grams**),
at room temperature

⅓ cup/**70 grams** sugar

1 tablespoon grated orange
zest (about 1 large orange)

2 teaspoons kosher salt

Seeds scraped from 1 vanilla
bean (see page 28)

½ cup/1 stick/**115 grams**
unsalted butter,
at room temperature

¾ cup/**120 grams**
golden raisins

¾ cup/**75 grams** dried cherries

Panettone Topping
(page 140)

Christmas Eve is the second busiest day at Flour (with Thanksgiving Eve taking the honors as the busiest day of the year). At the end of the very long and tiring but extremely fulfilling workday, I always go to Flour on Washington Street, our original location, to bid the team happy holidays and pat them (and myself) on the back for crushing another holiday season. The spoils of working all the way until we close that particular day are that anything that did not sell is up for grabs to take home. I usually get a bûche de Noël or two and some cranberry-orange scones and maybe a pear crostata. But what I always cross my fingers for is a panettone. A towering soft, tender bread, panettone is a dramatic Italian celebratory sweet bread studded with fruits and nuts. I eat this all vacation break, as is or toasted with butter, but my very favorite way to enjoy it is as French toast. I slice the loaf the long way so I get fat round pieces of bread and I fry them off as quickly as Christopher and I can eat them.

Plan ahead when making this up-to-three-day recipe because it not only requires an overnight starter for the dough, but also needs another day or two of proofing before the panettones are ready to bake.

—

The day before you will be making the panettones, make the overnight starter.

Preheat the oven to 350°F and place a rack in the center of the oven. Place the slivered almonds on a baking sheet and toast for 6 to 8 minutes, until light golden brown. Remove from the oven, set aside, and turn off the oven.

In a stand mixer fitted with a dough hook attachment, combine the overnight starter, milk, and yeast. Mix on low speed for a few seconds. Add the flour, eggs, sugar, orange zest, salt, and vanilla seeds and mix on medium for 8 to 10 minutes, until the dough is smooth and stretchy and more supple. You may need to stop the mixer from time to time to pull the dough away from the dough hook and loosen it up. (Sometimes the dough likes to climb up the hook.) The dough will seem wet, but resist the urge to add flour; given time, the dough will develop structure. With the mixer running, add the softened butter a tablespoon at a time, allowing each piece of butter to mix into the dough before adding more. Mix on medium for another 5 minutes. At this point the dough should look smooth and satiny. Add the raisins, cherries, and almonds. Mix on low until the fruits and nuts are evenly dispersed. (You may want to knead and fold the soft dough by hand to fully incorporate these ingredients.) Lightly oil a large bowl, place the dough in it, and cover lightly with plastic wrap or a lint-free towel. Let the dough proof and double in size in a warm place in the kitchen for about 2 hours.

Line two 6 x 3-inch round cake pans with parchment paper collars so that the parchment extends beyond the top edge of the pan by 4 inches. Use a bit of butter or oil or even water to help the parchment adhere to the sides of the pans. Spray the inside of the pans and the parchment with pan spray. Divide the dough in half. Shape both halves into tight balls (see page 150) and place carefully in the prepared pans with the taut, rounded parts of the dough facing up. Cover the panettones loosely with plastic wrap and let proof again at warm room temperature for 1 hour.

Place the panettones in the fridge and let continue to proof and develop flavor for at least 10 hours or up to overnight.

When you're ready to bake, preheat the oven to 350°F and place a rack in the bottom third of the oven. Spread the panettone topping evenly over the panettones. Bake for 1 hour 10 minutes to 1 hour 20 minutes, rotating the pans and switching their positions midway through the baking time, until the panettones are golden brown and sound hollow when you thump them along the sides. Remove from the oven and let cool completely in the pans on a wire rack.

Remove from the pans, remove the collars, and serve.

Panetones can be stored in a paper bag at room temperature for up to 3 days; toast slices before serving to refresh. You may also store them well wrapped in the freezer for up to 1 week; be sure to toast slices before serving.

Overnight Starter

MAKES ABOUT 1¼ CUPS/380 GRAMS

1 cup/**140 grams** all-purpose flour, plus more if needed for storing the starter

Large pinch of active dry yeast

—

In a small plastic container, stir together 1 cup/240 grams water, the flour, and the yeast until well combined. Cover loosely with plastic wrap and let it sit out at room temperature in your kitchen for at least 18 hours or as long as 36 hours. The yeasts in the air will combine with the yeast in the starter and they will feed on the flour and continue to grow and become active. It should be bubbly and smell fragrant.

If you are not going to use the starter within 36 hours, place it in the fridge. The day before using it, remove and discard about ½ cup. Add another ¼ cup/60 grams water and ¼ cup/35 grams flour and mix well. Let the starter come back to life by letting it sit at room temperature for at least 12 hours.

Panettone Topping

MAKES 1¼ CUPS/350 GRAMS

1 cup/**200 grams** sugar

1 cup/**100 grams** slivered almonds

1 large egg (about **50 grams**)

—

In a small bowl, combine the sugar, almonds, and egg to make a thick slurry. The topping can be stored in an airtight container in the fridge for up to 1 week. Stir before using so it spreads more easily.

Multigrain English Muffins

MAKES 10 ENGLISH MUFFINS

Poolish for English
Muffins (page 144), at room
temperature

¾ cup/**180 grams**
fat-free buttermilk,
at room temperature

1½ cups/**210 grams**
high-gluten bread flour

1 cup/**145 grams**
whole wheat flour

1 cup/**140 grams** spelt flour

½ cup/**50 grams** rolled oats

3 tablespoons/**40 grams** sugar

1 tablespoon/**9 grams**
active dry yeast

4 teaspoons kosher salt

4 tablespoons/½ stick/
60 grams unsalted butter, at
warm room temperature

Cornmeal, for the
baking sheet

At the very first bakery I worked at, my pastry chef, Rick, quickly recognized how eager I was to add something, anything, to our menu. I had been testing and baking at home for years and now that I was working as a professional pastry cook, I was dying to see if one of my creations could make it in the "real" world. "Write a list of everything you think might work and we'll see," Rick offered. I came back the next day with a single-spaced front-and-back sheet of legal-size yellow paper filled with ideas. I still remember Rick explaining that one of my favorite ideas, English muffins, was not feasible due to space constraints in our kitchen. *Someday!* I thought.

Years later, after opening my own bakery where I can put any idea I want on the menu, I still pine for English muffins. Those same space constraints exist at Flour. It took one of our top pastry chefs, Sarah Murphy, who left to start her own bakery, Vinal Bakery in Somerville, Massachusetts, to give me the chance to learn how to make these chewy, begging-for-butter muffins.

In her own words: "Vinal Bakery is a New England bakery, focused on local flavors and traditions. The name comes from the street I live on and is a nod to older New England bakeries. New Englanders by nature are simple and straightforward, and bakeries were often named for the town or street where they were located.

"These multigrain English muffins are nutty, soft, and hearty. We source the spelt flour and rolled oats from Maine Grains, a local grain company. Seek out local grains for this recipe. The flavor will be unmatched, you will be supporting your local community and farmers, and the muffins will become your own. While it's tempting to split open a muffin straight from the griddle, for best results let them rest overnight. The center dries out just a touch and makes for perfect toasting and eating."

Thank you, Sarah, for sharing your recipe with all of us!

Continues...

Poolish for English Muffins

MAKES 1¼ CUPS/260 GRAMS

1 cup/**140 grams**
all-purpose flour

Large pinch of active dry yeast

—

Combine the flour, ½ cup/ 120 grams room temperature water, and the yeast in a bowl with enough room for the mixture to double in size. Stir to combine well. Cover and leave at room temperature overnight. The poolish is ready to use when it has approximately doubled in size and gas bubbles cover the top. You can refrigerate it at this point for up to but no longer than 1 day. If you refrigerate it, bring it to room temperature before using.

Make sure you plan ahead because you will need a few days to make the poolish and dough for the most flavorful English muffins you've ever tasted.

—

At least 16 hours before mixing the dough, make the poolish.

In a stand mixer fitted with a dough hook attachment, combine the poolish, ¾ cup/180 grams room temperature water, and the buttermilk. Turn the mixer on low speed to mix together for a few seconds. Add the bread flour, whole wheat flour, spelt flour, oats, sugar, yeast, and salt. Mix on medium for 4 to 5 minutes, scraping once or twice to make sure no flour or oats remain in the bottom of the bowl. When the dough is smooth and slightly pulling away from the sides of the bowl, add the butter 1 tablespoon at a time. Continue mixing for 1 to 2 minutes, until the butter is fully incorporated into the dough.

Coat a large bowl with butter, oil, or pan spray and place the dough in it. Cover with a lint-free towel or plastic wrap and place in a warm spot in your kitchen to rest for 45 minutes.

Fold the dough by pulling up the far edge of the dough and folding it into the center. Repeat with the bottom, right, and left edges of the dough. Flip the dough over in the bowl. It should be a smooth, round ball. Re-cover and let rest for another 45 minutes.

Repeat the dough folding and flip the dough over again. Re-cover and let rest for another 30 minutes.

Sprinkle a baking sheet with cornmeal. To shape the muffins, cut the dough into 10 equal pieces, approximately 5 ounces/140 grams each. The dough will be quite sticky. If it is too difficult to handle, refrigerate for 10 to 15 minutes before shaping. Flour your hands to prevent sticking and shape each piece into a smooth ball; place on the prepared baking sheet, leaving 2 to 3 inches between the balls. Sprinkle the top of each dough ball with cornmeal and press firmly to flatten and stretch each ball into a 1-inch-thick disk. Cover with plastic wrap or a lint-free towel and let sit at warm room temperature for about 1 hour or refrigerate for 4 hours.

Uncover the muffins and test that they are fully proofed: They should be double in size, and when you press the dough with your finger, the indentation should fill in slowly. If they are not fully proofed, leave them at room temperature to finish proofing for up to another hour.

Heat a cast-iron griddle on the stove over medium-low heat or an electric fry pan to 350°F. Preheat the oven to 350°F and place a rack in the center of the oven.

When the muffins are fully proofed, carefully place them on the griddle or in the fry pan using a spatula, leaving 2 to 3 inches between them. (Work in batches if necessary.) Griddle for 4 to 5 minutes per side, until golden brown. Transfer the griddled muffins to a baking sheet and bake for 10 to 15 minutes, rotating the baking sheet halfway through the baking time, until the muffins are medium golden brown on top and feel hollow when you thump them. To double-check that the muffins are baked through, insert an instant-read thermometer — the muffins are done when the center reaches 205°F.

Transfer the muffins to a wire rack and allow them to cool, ideally overnight. Try not to eat them fresh because they can be doughy that way; have patience and eat them a day old. Split, toast, top, and enjoy!

The muffins can be stored in a paper bag at room temperature for up to 3 days, or well wrapped in plastic wrap in the freezer for up to 2 weeks. Thaw, split, and toast before serving.

Cranberry-Pecan Bread

MAKES 2 LOAVES

Sponge for Cranberry-Pecan
Bread (page 148),
at room temperature

1 cup plus 2 tablespoons/
270 grams water, at body
temperature (when you
stick your finger in it,
it does not register as either
warm or cold)

2 cups/**280 grams**
all-purpose flour

1½ cups/**225 grams**
high gluten bread flour

¼ teaspoon active dry yeast

¼ cup/**85 grams** honey

2¼ teaspoons kosher salt

1 cup/**100 grams** pecan halves,
toasted (see page 29)

¾ cup/**90 grams**
dried cranberries

1 cup/**100 grams** fresh
cranberries, roughly chopped

¼ to ½ cup cornmeal,
for the baking sheet

For ten months of the year we make a barely sweet raisin-pecan bread that is an homage to the nutty, hearty raisin-pecan bread from Amy's Bread in New York City. I spent a very short time at Amy's early in my career, learning the very basics of mixing, shaping, proofing, and baking bread. The owner, Amy Scherber, was—and still is—an inspiration to me, not only because of her fabulous bread that is beloved across New York, but also because she is kind, gracious, direct, and as generous a person as you'll ever meet. When I'm in New York I always stop by one of her bakeries to get a few loaves to bring back to Boston. During the winter holidays we change up our standard raisin-pecan for a cranberry-pecan to celebrate the arrival of cranberry season. We knead dried cranberries into the dough and also throw in a generous handful of fresh cranberries. The combination of the sweet chewy dried with the tart juicy fresh makes this a loaf we look forward to all year long.

Note that this takes two days to make, so be sure to plan ahead.

The day before you will be making this bread, make the sponge. Two hours before making the bread, remove the sponge from the fridge.

In a stand mixer fitted with a dough hook attachment or by hand in a large bowl with a wooden spoon, mix the water, all-purpose flour, bread flour, yeast, and sponge for about 2 minutes, until all the ingredients are combined and you have a shaggy, stiff dough. (To prevent the flour from flying out of the mixer bowl, turn the mixer on and off several times until the flour is mixed into the liquid and then keep it on low speed.) Cover the bowl with a piece of plastic wrap and let sit for about 10 minutes. (This is called an autolyse; it allows the water to hydrate the flour, which makes for better mixing down the road.)

Add the honey and salt to the dough and mix on medium-low for 6 to 8 minutes, until the dough is smooth. If it does not come together, let it sit for a few minutes to allow the flour to be absorbed into the dough more, then mix again for a few minutes. The dough should be

somewhat sticky but still smooth, and have the texture of an earlobe (as strange as that sounds). If it's stiffer than this, add a few tablespoons water, or if it's looser than this add a few tablespoons all-purpose flour, and mix until incorporated. Don't add more flour unless it's really soupy. If you're mixing by hand this process will take at least 15 minutes of active kneading. Constantly knead, push, and fold the dough over itself, picking it up from time to time and slapping it onto the counter to incorporate all the ingredients and help develop the dough's structure.

Add the pecans, dried cranberries, and fresh cranberries and mix on low for another 3 to 4 minutes, until the nuts and cranberries are all completely and evenly distributed within the dough. You may need to stop the mixer a few times to pull off any dough that has gathered around the hook or on the sides of the bowl. If you are mixing and kneading by hand, it will take at least 10 minutes to incorporate these ingredients.

Lightly oil a clean large bowl, remove the dough from the mixer bowl, and place it in the oiled bowl. Cover it with an oiled piece of plastic wrap or a damp lint-free towel. Place it in a draft-free warm place (78° to 82°F is ideal; an area near the stove or an oven with only the pilot light on is good) for 2 to 3 hours. The dough will rise a little bit but not a lot, and will feel a little loose and relaxed and somewhat sticky.

Generously flour your hands and work surface and turn the dough out of the bowl. Divide the dough in half with a sharp chef's knife or bench scraper. Shape each half into a rough square. Working with one half at a time, bring the upper right and left corners of the dough to the center of the square and then fold over the top of the dough to meet the corners in the center. Now hold the top part of the dough in both hands, cradling the folded-over part with your fingers, and line up your thumbs in the center of the dough along the seams in the middle. Push at the center of the dough at the seam, nudging away from you with your thumbs to create a taut surface at the outside of the dough. Cup the outer part of the dough in your fingers again and bring your thumbs against the seam again as you nudge the dough away from you. Roll your hands toward you to create more surface tension on the dough as you roll it down to the bottom of the square. Continue nudging and rolling until you have a long loaf that is fat in the middle and tapered at the ends like a football. (At this point you can store the shaped loaves on a baking sheet or flat plate, covered lightly with plastic or a lint-free

Sponge for Cranberry-Pecan Bread

**MAKES ABOUT 1¼ CUPS/
380 GRAMS**

1 cup/**140 grams**
all-purpose flour

⅛ teaspoon active dry yeast

—

Stir together the flour, 1 cup/
240 grams room temperature
water, and the yeast until well
mixed and sloshy. Cover and
leave out at room temperature
for at least 4 hours or up to
8 hours.

Stir the sponge, cover, and
refrigerate overnight. Pull it
out of the fridge 2 hours before
using to bring it back to room
temperature.

towel, in the fridge overnight.
Remove the next day and proceed
as directed.)

Generously sprinkle a baking sheet
with cornmeal to keep the loaves
from sticking to it. Place the shaped
loaves seam side down on the
baking sheet, at least 3 inches
apart. Cover them loosely and
completely with plastic wrap or a
lint-free towel and let them sit at
room temperature for 2 to 3 hours,
until the dough has loosened up
and seems relaxed. It won't pouf up
too much but it will seem much
softer.

Preheat the oven to 400°F and
place racks in the center and
bottom third of the oven. (It's very
important to make sure the oven
comes to temperature before you
place the bread inside! The heat
from the oven ensures that your
loaves will get enough oomph to
rise and grow.) Sprinkle the tops

of the loaves with 2 to 3 tablespoons flour. Slash the loaves on
top with a knife, lame, or razor
blade (see page 27) and place the
baking sheet on the center rack.
Place a rimmed baking sheet or
shallow baking pan filled with about
2 cups water on the rack underneath the bread. (The steam from
the water will create a nice moist
atmosphere, allowing your bread to
grow.) Bake for 30 to 35 minutes,
rotating the baking sheet with the
bread midway through the baking
time, until the bread is dark golden
brown on top and makes a hollow
sound when you thump it on the
bottom.

Let cool for at least 1 hour, directly
on a wire rack.

The bread can be stored in a paper
bag at room temperature for 2 to
3 days. (Plastic seals the air out and
keeps the bread from breathing, so it
can get too soft.)

Fig-Walnut Bread

MAKES 2 LOAVES

Sponge for Fig-Walnut
Bread (page 150), at room
temperature

1¼ cups/**300 grams** water, at
body temperature (when you
stick your finger in it,
it does not register as either
warm or cold)

2 cups/**280 grams**
all-purpose flour

1¾ cups/**260 grams**
high-gluten bread flour

¼ teaspoon active dry yeast

¼ cup/**85 grams** honey

1 tablespoon kosher salt

1½ cups/**180 grams** walnut
halves, toasted (see page 29)

1 cup/**180 grams** dried figs,
stemmed and cut in half

About 2 tablespoons
cornmeal, for the baking sheet

If you looked in my freezer at home you would think I'm preparing for the apocalypse—every shelf is jam-packed with leftover loaves of multigrain bread and ciabatta from the bakery for my weekend brunch feasts. Once a year around the holidays, I clear out the whole freezer to make room for the hearty fig-walnut loaves that we make to celebrate Thanksgiving. A chewy, dense, fragrant loaf, this bread is faintly purplish in color from all the walnuts and filled with tangy dried figs. Toasted and spread with butter, it is the ultimate in simple perfect breakfasts. I try to save at least a dozen loaves so I can enjoy this treat into the new year.

Note that you will need to plan ahead to make this bread, as the sponge needs a full day to develop before you can use it.

The day before you'll be making this bread, make the sponge. Two hours before making the bread, remove the sponge from the fridge.

In the bowl of a stand mixer fitted with a dough hook attachment or by hand in a large bowl with a wooden spoon, mix together the water, all-purpose flour, bread flour, yeast, and sponge on low speed for about 2 minutes, until the mixture comes together and you have a shaggy, stiff dough. (To prevent the flour from flying out of the bowl, turn the mixer on and off several times until the flour is mixed into the liquid, and keep it on low speed.) Cover the bowl with a piece of plastic wrap and let it sit for about 15 minutes. (This is called an autolyse; it allows the water to hydrate the flour, which

makes for better mixing down the road.)

Add the honey and salt and mix for 6 to 8 minutes on medium-low, until the dough is smooth. If it does not come together, let it sit for a few minutes to allow the flour to be absorbed into the dough more, then mix again for a few minutes. The dough should be somewhat sticky but still smooth, and have the texture of an earlobe (as strange as that sounds). If it's stiffer than this add a few tablespoons water, or if it's looser than this add a few tablespoons all-purpose flour, and mix until incorporated. If you're mixing by hand, this process will take at least 15 minutes of active kneading. Constantly knead and push and fold the dough over itself, picking it up

Sponge for Fig-Walnut Bread

MAKES ABOUT 1¼ CUPS/ 380 GRAMS

1 cup/**140 grams** all-purpose flour

⅛ teaspoon active dry yeast

—

Stir together the flour, 1 cup/ 240 grams room temperature water, and the yeast until well mixed and sloshy. Cover and leave out at room temperature for at least 4 hours or up to 8 hours.

Stir the sponge, cover it, and refrigerate overnight. Pull it out of the fridge 2 hours before using to bring it back to room temperature.

from time to time and slapping it onto the counter as you are kneading to incorporate all the ingredients and help develop the dough structure.

Add the walnut halves and figs and mix on low for another 3 to 4 minutes, until the walnuts and figs are all completely and evenly distributed within the dough. You may need to stop the mixer a few times to pull off any dough that's gathered around the hook or on the sides of the bowl. This will take at least 10 minutes if you are mixing and kneading by hand.

Lightly oil a clean large bowl, remove the dough from the mixer bowl, and place it in the oiled bowl. Cover it with an oiled piece of plastic wrap or a damp lint-free towel. Place it in a draft-free warm place (78° to 82°F is ideal; an area near the stove or an oven with only the pilot light on is good) for 2 to 3 hours. The dough will rise up a little bit but not a lot, and it will feel a little loose and relaxed and somewhat sticky.

Generously flour your hands and work surface and turn the dough out of the bowl. Divide the dough in half with a sharp chef's knife or bench scraper. Shape each half into a ball by tucking the edges of the dough underneath and continuing to tuck the edges of the dough underneath until the dough naturally gathers into a ball shape with a taut surface. (At this point you can store the shaped loaves on a baking sheet or flat plate, lightly covered with plastic or a lint-free towel, in the fridge overnight. Remove the next day and proceed as directed.)

Generously sprinkle a baking sheet with cornmeal to keep the loaves from sticking. Place the shaped loaves on the baking sheet at least 3 inches apart. Cover them loosely and completely with plastic wrap and let them sit at room temperature for 2 to 3 hours, until the dough has loosened up and seems relaxed. It won't pouf up too much but it will seem much softer.

Preheat the oven to 400°F and place racks in the center and bottom third of the oven. (It's very important to make sure the oven comes to temperature before you place the bread inside! The heat from the oven ensures that your loaves will get enough oomph to rise and grow.)

Sprinkle the tops of the loaves with 2 to 3 tablespoons flour. Slash the bread on top with a knife, lame, or razor blade (see page 27) and place the baking sheet on the center rack. Place a rimmed baking sheet or shallow baking pan filled with about 2 cups water on the rack underneath the bread. (The steam from the water will create a nice moist atmosphere for the bread to grow.) Bake for 30 to 35 minutes, rotating the baking sheet with the bread midway through the baking time, until the bread is dark golden brown on top and makes a hollow sound when you thump it on the bottom.

Let cool for at least 1 hour, directly on a wire rack.

The bread can be stored in a paper bag at room temperature for 2 to 3 days. (Plastic seals the air out and keeps the bread from breathing, so it can get too soft.)

Honey Whole Wheat Bread

MAKES 2 LOAVES

Soaker (page 152)

Biga (page 152)

½ cup/**75 grams** whole wheat flour

¼ cup/**85 grams** honey

2 tablespoons extra-virgin olive oil

2¼ teaspoons/**7 grams**/ 1 (¼-ounce) packet active dry yeast

2 teaspoons kosher salt

2 tablespoons cornmeal, for the baking sheet

Our production pastry chef, Rachael, is someone you meet and work with and never want to let go. Her dedication to perfection inspires me daily, and her bakers adore her for her tough but compassionate management. She's passionate about pastry and totally obsessed with bread. We wanted to introduce a whole wheat bread option to our sandwich menu so I asked Rachael to come up with a whole grain bread that would be as popular and delicious as our famous focaccia sandwich bread. She hit it out of the park with this gorgeous chewy honey wheat loaf. It's hearty and wheaty with a slightly sweet taste from the honey; it is also so light that the crumb is almost flaky. We made it for our sandwich menu but I love it best in thick slices, warm, and slathered with lots of soft butter. If you are a breadhead like me, it's one of those breads that you might eat all in one sitting, so do like I do and cut off what you want ahead of time and hide the rest.

Plan ahead when making this bread because the biga needs a full day to develop prior to mixing the dough.

Make the soaker and biga the day before you'll be making this bread. Two hours before, remove them from the fridge.

In a large bowl with a wooden spoon, or in a stand mixer fitted with a dough hook attachment, combine the soaker, biga, whole wheat flour, honey, olive oil, yeast, and salt and mix on low speed until fully combined.

If you're using a mixer, knead for around 2 minutes at medium speed. If kneading by hand, flick flour over the work surface, turn out the dough, and knead it until fully elastic, about 5 meditative minutes. To knead by hand, fold the top half of the dough down over itself, give the dough a quarter-turn (90 degrees), and repeat; keep folding the dough on top of itself and turning it a quarter-turn. The dough will break apart into pieces at first but the more you knead it, the more together it will be. After a few minutes it will feel like one mass and have a nice elasticity to it. Cover the dough with plastic wrap or a lint-free towel and let it rest and proof at warm room temperature for 2 to 3 hours, until it has relaxed and grown almost double in size.

Fold the dough, bringing the edges into the center, then turn the dough over and repeat. Cover and let rest for another 30 minutes.

Dust a baking sheet with the cornmeal. Divide the dough in half with a sharp chef's knife or bench scraper and shape each half into a round boule (see page 115). Place the loaves evenly apart on the baking sheet. Cover the loaves with plastic or a lint-free towel and let proof in a warm place in the kitchen for about 1 hour, until the loaves have grown a little bit and are a bit jiggly when you poke them.

Preheat the oven to 400°F and place a rack in the center of the oven. Slash the tops decoratively with a knife, lame, or razor blade (see page 27). Bake for 35 to 40 minutes, rotating the baking sheet midway through the baking time, until the loaves are deep golden brown and sound hollow when you thump them on the bottom.

Remove the loaves from the oven and let cool directly on a wire rack.

The bread is best enjoyed day of. But you can store it in a paper bag at room temperature for up to 3 days. If the bread is 1 day old or more, toast the slices — it's great!

Soaker

MAKES ABOUT 2 CUPS

2¼ cups/**340 grams** whole wheat flour

1 cup/**240 grams** whole milk

1½ teaspoons kosher salt

—

In a medium bowl or container, combine the flour, milk, and salt with a wooden spoon or your hands. It will look like a loose, rough dough. Cover with plastic wrap or a lid and let sit at warm room temperature for 2 hours, then refrigerate overnight. Pull it out of the fridge 2 hours before using to bring it back to room temperature.

Biga

MAKES ABOUT 2¼ CUPS

¼ teaspoon active dry yeast

2⅓ cups/**350 grams** high-gluten bread flour

—

In a medium bowl or container, sprinkle the yeast over 1 cup/240 grams room temperature water. Add the flour and mix with a wooden spoon or your hands until it comes together into a loose dough and all the flour is mixed in. It will be soft and sticky. Cover the biga with plastic wrap or a lid and let sit at warm room temperature for 2 hours, then refrigerate overnight. Pull it out of the fridge 2 hours before using to bring it back to room temperature.

Housemade Nutella Babka

MAKES 2 LOAVES

1 recipe Master Brioche Dough
(page 444)

¼ cup/**40 grams** blanched
hazelnuts

Homemade Nutella
(page 156)

1½ ounces/**40 grams**
bittersweet or semisweet
chocolate, finely chopped
(about ¼ cup)

Hazelnut Syrup (page 157)

As Flour has grown, one of our biggest challenges has been to keep our menu consistent with all our—and your—favorites while also offering enough new items to entice our guests and keep our bakers engaged. We have many exceptional bakers on our team and we wanted a way for them to showcase their skills—hence Pastry of the Month, or POM. Every bakery is encouraged to come up with a POM, and every now and then a POM is so good we decide to offer it as a holiday special. This babka was created by one of our longtime bakers, Matt, who worked for months to make a buttery, chocolatey, tender babka that blew us all away. I had never made babka before and loved learning all the tricks from him. The slicing and twisting and shaping of the babka is really fun, and serves to help the filling bake evenly into the dough so you minimize air pockets and have gorgeous swirls in the final product.

This isn't a difficult recipe but you do need to plan ahead because the brioche dough needs time to rest to be the most flavorful. Toast all the hazelnuts for the different parts of the recipe together to save some time.

Mix the brioche dough and let proof for 6 hours or up to overnight in the fridge as directed.

Preheat the oven to 350°F and place a rack in the center of the oven. Place the nuts on a baking sheet and toast for 6 to 8 minutes, until light golden brown and fragrant; break a few open to check. Remove from the oven (turn off the oven), let the nuts cool, then rough-chop them. Line two 9 x 5-inch loaf pans with

parchment paper or butter them generously, and set them aside. Make the Nutella.

Generously flick flour over the work surface. Divide the brioche dough in half and roll out one half into a rectangle about 20 inches wide from side to side and 12 inches long from top to bottom. Brush off any loose flour from the surface of the dough. Mix the Nutella vigorously with a spoon to soften and loosen it. Using an offset spatula, spread half the Nutella evenly over the dough. Sprinkle half the chopped nuts and half the chocolate evenly over the Nutella. Roll the dough tightly, starting from the top and rolling downward in a spiral like a jelly roll. Repeat with the other half of the brioche dough. Place the dough rolls on a flat plate or baking sheet in the freezer for 10 to 15 minutes. (This will make twisting them together a bit easier to handle, and they'll be less likely to fall apart.)

Remove the dough rolls from the freezer. Cut one of the dough rolls lengthwise straight down the middle completely in half, exposing the layers. Place one cut half across the center of the other cut half, making an X shape. Twist the dough on either side of the center around each other, keeping the exposed cut sides of the dough visible, so that you have a long twisted braid of dough. Fold the dough braid in half like a horseshoe, give it a twist so the Nutella is now hidden inside, and place in a prepared loaf pan, tucking in any overhanging or loose dough. Repeat with the second dough roll. Cover both babkas with plastic wrap or lint-free towels and place in a warm area in the kitchen. Let the babkas proof and grow for 1½ to 2 hours, until they are billowing and soft and full.

Make the hazelnut syrup.

Preheat the oven to 350°F and place a rack in the center of the oven. Remove the plastic wrap or towels and bake the babkas for 35 to 40 minutes, rotating the pans and switching their positions midway through the baking time, until the

babkas are medium golden brown and sound hollow when you thump them on the bottom.

Remove the babkas from the oven and while warm, brush them with the hazelnut syrup. Let cool in the pans on a wire rack.

Babka can be stored in a paper bag at room temperature for 1 day. You can also freeze it, well wrapped in plastic, for up to 2 weeks. Refresh in a 300°F oven for about 10 minutes before serving.

Homemade Nutella

MAKES ABOUT 2 CUPS

½ cup/**75 grams** blanched hazelnuts

1 cup/**240 grams** heavy cream

6 ounces/**170 grams** milk chocolate, finely chopped (about 1 cup)

3 ounces/**85 grams** bittersweet or semisweet chocolate, finely chopped (about ½ cup)

¼ teaspoon kosher salt

—

Preheat the oven to 350°F and place a rack in the center of the oven. Place the hazelnuts on a baking sheet and toast for 8 to 10 minutes, until they are light golden brown and fragrant; break a few open to check. Remove from the oven and let cool.

In a small saucepan, combine the cream and hazelnuts. Bring the mixture to a boil over high heat. Reduce the heat to medium and simmer for 2 to 3 minutes. Place the milk and dark chocolates in a medium metal or heatproof glass bowl. Pour the hot cream and nuts over the chocolate and whisk until the chocolates are melted. Add the salt. Pour the mixture into a blender or food processor and blend until smooth. Transfer to a bowl or storage container and let cool to room temperature. It will thicken and become spreadable.

Nutella can be stored in an airtight container in the fridge for up to 3 weeks. Bring the Nutella to room temperature before using.

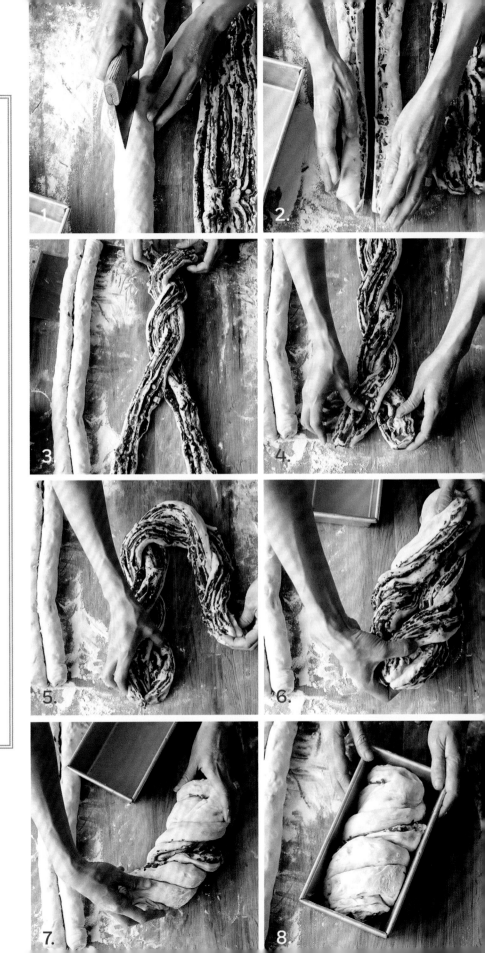

Hazelnut Syrup

MAKES ABOUT ½ CUP

½ cup/**75 grams** blanched hazelnuts

½ cup/**100 grams** sugar

—

Preheat the oven to 350°F and place a rack in the center of the oven. Place the hazelnuts on a baking sheet and toast for 8 to 10 minutes, until light golden brown and fragrant; break a few open to check. Remove from the oven.

In a small saucepan, combine the sugar and hazelnuts with ½ cup/120 grams water. Bring to a boil, then reduce the heat to medium. Simmer for 2 to 3 minutes, until the sugar has dissolved and the hazelnuts have softened. Remove from the heat and let sit for 30 minutes.

Pour the mixture into a blender or food processor and blend until the nuts are completely ground into tiny pieces. Strain through a fine-mesh sieve, discarding the solids.

The syrup can be stored in an airtight container in the fridge for up to 2 months.

Good anytime

Pecan Sandies / 160

Walnut Meltaways / 162

Lemon-Polenta Cookies / 165

Vegan Almond Macaroons / 166

Flour Power Bars / 169

Gluten-Free Double Chocolate–Walnut Brownies / 171

Persian Love Cookies / 174

Gluten-Free Chocolate-Caramel Oreos / 177

Mixed Nut and Honey Whole Grain Biscotti / 180

Anzacs / 182

Ossa dei Morti / 185

Lemon Sugar Cookies with Lemon Glaze / 189

Jessi's Caramel Popcorn Cookies / 191

Thin, Crispy Chocolate Chip Cookies / 194

Double Chocolate Rye Cookies / 196

Mocha Chip Cookies / 199

Raspberry Swirl Meringues / 202

Brown Sugar–Candied Almond Meringues / 205

Keith's Homemade Devil Dogs / 209

Hazelnut-Raspberry Rugelach / 211

Baby Palmiers / 215

Tahini–Black Sesame Spiral Shortbreads / 219

CHAPTER 3

Afternoon
Pick-Me-Up

Pecan Sandies

MAKES 36 COOKIES

1¼ cups/**150 grams**
pecan halves

1¾ cups/**245 grams**
all-purpose flour

1 cup/2 sticks/**225 grams**
unsalted butter, at cool
room temperature

⅔ cup/**80 grams**
confectioners' sugar

2 teaspoons pure
vanilla extract

1½ teaspoons baking powder

1½ teaspoons kosher salt

Simple is best. It's the running theme in my first book, *Flour*. In my career I've seen it all: homespun, molecular gastronomy, architectural sky-high, fancy European. For me it comes down to what's so delicious that I can't stop eating it. It's almost always something super simple like this cookie. It's nutty, delicate, and rich. Everyone who tries them asks for the recipe and it's so easy to make, I know even the most beginner baker will be able to re-create and share these buttery treats with pride.

Preheat the oven to 350°F and place a rack in the center of the oven. Place the pecans on a baking sheet and toast for 8 to 10 minutes, until they start to smell nutty and turn pale golden inside; break a few open to check. Remove from the oven (turn off the oven) and let cool.

Place the pecans in a food processor and pulse 10 to 15 times, until roughly chopped. Remove about ¼ cup/30 grams of the chopped pecans and set them aside. Add ¼ cup/35 grams of the flour to the pecans in the food processor and process until finely ground, about 1 minute. (The flour will help the nuts grind up without becoming a paste.)

Using a handheld electric mixer or a stand mixer fitted with a paddle attachment, beat the butter and confectioners' sugar on medium-high speed until creamy and smooth and light, about 2 minutes. Reduce the mixer speed to low and add the

vanilla, baking powder, and salt. Stop the mixer and use a rubber spatula to scrape the bowl and the paddle. Add the remaining 1½ cups/210 grams flour and the nut-flour mixture and beat on medium for 1 minute. Scrape and beat again until thoroughly combined. Scrape the dough onto a piece of parchment or wax paper and shape into a tight roll about 2 inches in diameter and 10 inches long. Refrigerate until firm, at least 4 hours or up to 5 days. (At this point the cookie dough can be tightly wrapped with plastic wrap and frozen for up to 1 month. Remove from the freezer and let thaw in the refrigerator overnight before using.)

When you're ready to bake the cookies, preheat the oven to 350°F and place a rack in the center of the oven. Line a baking sheet with parchment paper.

Place the reserved ¼ cup/30 grams chopped pecans on a large flat plate or another baking sheet, unwrap the dough, and roll it around in the pecans until totally covered. Use a sharp chef's knife to slice the log into ¼-inch-thick rounds. Place the rounds on the prepared baking sheet cut side down. Bake for about 12 minutes, rotating the baking sheet after about 6 minutes, until the cookies are golden brown.

Remove from the oven and let cool on the baking sheet on a wire rack.

Pecan sandies can be stored in an airtight container at room temperature for up to 3 days.

Walnut Meltaways

MAKES 18 COOKIES

1½ cups/**180 grams** walnut halves, plus 18 walnut halves for decoration

1½ cups/3 sticks/**340 grams** unsalted butter, at cool room temperature

¾ cup/**90 grams** confectioners' sugar, for the dough, plus ½ cup/**60 grams** for garnish

1 tablespoon pure vanilla extract

¾ teaspoon kosher salt

2¾ cups/**385 grams** all-purpose flour

These are similar to Mexican wedding cookies, but with a twist; the walnuts add a slight tannic note that works well with the richness of the cookie. Dusted with a generous amount of confectioners' sugar, these are extraordinarily tender and hard not to eat multiples of. I know this firsthand because when Jonathan, our pastry chef at Flour Harvard, baked a batch of these for a special order, everyone in the kitchen ended up eating so many of them that he had to make another batch. That's a surefire indication of an excellent cookie.

Preheat the oven to 350°F and place a rack in the center of the oven. Place the 1½ cups/180 grams walnuts on a baking sheet and toast for 8 to 10 minutes, until they start to smell nutty and turn pale golden inside; break a few open to check. Remove from the oven and let cool. If you'll be baking the cookies the same day, leave the oven on; otherwise turn it off.

Place the toasted walnuts in a food processor and process until ground into crumbs, about 20 seconds. Using a handheld electric mixer or a stand mixer fitted with a paddle attachment, beat the butter and the ¾ cup/90 grams confectioners' sugar on medium-high speed until creamy and smooth and light, about 2 minutes. Reduce the mixer speed to low and add the ground walnuts, vanilla, and salt. Stop the mixer and use a rubber spatula to scrape the bowl and the paddle. Add the flour

and mix on low for 30 seconds. Scrape and beat again until thoroughly combined. (At this point the dough can be stored in an airtight container in the fridge for up to 1 week or in the freezer for up to 1 month. If frozen, thaw the dough in the fridge before using; when ready to bake, let the dough come back to room temperature, and preheat the oven to 350°F and place a rack in the center of the oven.)

Line a baking sheet with parchment paper. Using a ¼-cup ice cream scoop or a large spoon, scoop the dough into ¼-cup-size balls and place on the prepared baking sheet a few inches apart. Lightly press each with the palm of your hand to flatten slightly. (Try dipping your hand in water to prevent it from sticking to the dough.) Press an untoasted walnut half into the center of each cookie. Bake for 18 to 22 minutes, rotating the baking sheet midway

through the baking time, until the cookies are light golden brown. Remove from the oven and let cool completely on the baking sheet on a wire rack.

Using a sifter or small sieve, dust the cookies with the remaining ½ cup/ 60 grams confectioners' sugar until they are completely white.

Walnut meltaways can be stored in an airtight container at room temperature for up to 3 days. Dust with additional confectioners' sugar to freshen them before serving.

Lemon-Polenta Cookies

MAKES ABOUT 24 COOKIES

1 cup/2 sticks/**225 grams** unsalted butter, at cool room temperature

1 cup/**120 grams** confectioners' sugar

¼ cup/**35 grams** grated lemon zest (about 4 large lemons)

2⅓ cups/**330 grams** all-purpose flour

¼ cup/**45 grams** fine cornmeal

1 teaspoon kosher salt

About ½ cup/**100 grams** granulated sugar

This cookie recipe is a longtime favorite of one of our former pastry chefs, Brian. We had started experimenting with packaging cookies in little bags to offer on our retail shelves. I was adamant that any packaged cookie we made had to be as good on its third or fifth or even seventh day as it was on its first. That's no small feat! Most cookies benefit from being eaten fresh out of the oven. This crunchy, barely sweet, buttery cookie is an exception. It gets more lemony and flavorful after a few days. Packaged in packs of five or six, these were hard to keep on the counter, they sold so quickly. We debuted these cookies a few months after my first baking book came out, and it became one of our most requested recipes. I'm happy to finally be able to share it with you.

In a stand mixer fitted with a paddle attachment, cream the butter for 30 seconds on medium-high speed until light and fluffy. Add the confectioners' sugar and lemon zest and beat for 3 to 4 minutes, until light and creamy. Stir together the flour, cornmeal, and salt until combined and add to the butter mixture. Beat on low for 1 minute, then scrape the bowl and beater and beat again for 30 seconds. The dough will be a bit crumbly.

Line a 9 x 5-inch loaf pan with parchment paper or plastic wrap. Press the dough into the loaf pan, packing it firmly. Chill the dough for at least 2 hours to firm up. (At this point the dough can be removed from the loaf pan, wrapped in plastic, and refrigerated for up to 1 week or double-wrapped and frozen for up to 1 month. If frozen, remove from the freezer the night before you want to bake it and thaw in the refrigerator.)

Preheat the oven to 350°F and place a rack in the center of the oven. Line a baking sheet with parchment paper or butter it. Pour the granulated sugar onto a flat plate. Remove the dough from the fridge, pop it out of the loaf pan, peel off the parchment or plastic, and press all sides of the dough into the sugar until it is totally coated. Slice the dough into ¼-inch-thick slices. Place the slices, cut side down, about 1 inch apart on the prepared baking sheet. Bake for 18 to 22 minutes, rotating the baking sheet midway through the baking time, until the cookies are firm to the touch, golden brown on the edges, pale in the center, and baked all the way through; break one open to check. Remove from the oven and let cool completely on the baking sheet on a wire rack.

The cookies can be stored in an airtight container at room temperature for up to 1 week.

Vegan Almond Macaroons

MAKES ABOUT 15 COOKIES

2½ cups/**250 grams**
sliced skin-on almonds,
for the dough, plus about
½ cup/**50 grams** for garnish

1 cup/**200 grams** sugar

⅓ cup/**80 grams** aquafaba
(liquid from a can of
no-salt-added chickpeas,
or homemade)

¾ teaspoon pure
almond extract

¼ teaspoon kosher salt

One of my favorite recipes from my first book, *Flour*, is a chewy, addictive almond macaroon sandwich cookie. I adore almonds (I always have a handful in my pocket, much to Christopher's chagrin when I forget to take them out when doing laundry), and this recipe came from my former boss and mentor, Chef Jamie. It was a very popular offering at Flour for many years, and I never thought to mess with it until I learned about aquafaba. Aquafaba is the cooking liquid from chickpeas—that thick, viscous water you drain out of the can. For reasons I still don't quite understand, this liquid acts like egg whites in many recipes. There are Facebook groups devoted to aquafaba. It's amazing! We switched out the egg whites for aquafaba in our almond macaroon recipe and it tastes exactly the same . . . and now it is vegan. I didn't think these cookies could get better, but they did.

The batter needs to rest for at least 4 hours (even better, overnight), so plan accordingly when making these chewy treats.

Place the 2½ cups/250 grams almonds, the sugar, aquafaba, almond extract, and salt in a stand mixer fitted with a paddle attachment. Paddle on medium-high speed for 10 minutes. Yes, 10 full minutes! The almonds will slowly break down and eventually the batter should look like thick quicksand. Scrape the batter into an airtight container and refrigerate for at least 4 hours or preferably overnight, to allow it to stiffen up a little bit.

When ready to bake the cookies, preheat the oven to 325°F and place a rack in the center of the oven. Line a baking sheet with parchment paper and spray it very liberally with pan spray—this is a sticky cookie, so don't be shy. Using a small (2-tablespoon) ice cream scoop or large spoon, scoop balls of dough about the size of golf balls onto the prepared baking sheet, spacing them a few inches apart. Press the dough with the palm of your hand to flatten the cookies until they are about ½ inch thick. Sprinkle the cookies liberally with the remaining ½ cup/50 grams almonds and press slightly to adhere. Bake for 26 to 30 minutes, rotating the baking sheet midway through the baking time, until the cookies are totally medium golden brown on top and along the edges and the almonds are lightly toasted. Don't underbake or they will be gummy in the center. Let cool on the baking sheet on a wire rack.

Almond macaroons can be stored in an airtight container at room temperature for up to 1 week.

Flour Power Bars

MAKES 16 BARS

People often say to me, "If I worked at a bakery I would eat sweets all day long!" Lucky for me, that is my life and my work. But it's not quite as glamorous as you might imagine. At our weekly tastings we gather a dozen or more pastries and nibble and study each one in depth. Is this one too tart, maybe that one isn't crispy enough, why is this one baked so lightly? By the time we are done scrutinizing each pastry we have clear marching orders on how to improve. It's necessary work and I love it, but afterward our taste buds are often overwhelmed. Nicole created these gluten-free, sugar-free, vegan snack bars as an antidote to our being overloaded with sugar. They are crunchy, barely sweet, filling, and healthy without tasting so. Everyone loves them—in fact our director of operations, Mike, recently ran the Boston Marathon and ate one of these every five miles to power him through to the end.

1¼ cups/**175 grams** raw whole almonds

½ cup/**70 grams** raw shelled sunflower seeds

2½ cups/**350 grams** raw whole cashews

1½ cups/**150 grams** rolled oats

1 cup/**165 grams** pitted Medjool dates (about 9 large or 16 small)

1 teaspoon kosher salt

¼ teaspoon ground cinnamon

¾ cup/**120 grams** raisins

2 tablespoons chia seeds

½ cup/**170 grams** maple syrup, plus more if needed

Preheat the oven to 325°F and place a rack in the center of the oven. Line a 9 x 5-inch loaf pan with parchment or wax paper. The easiest way to do this is to make a parchment sling 9 inches wide and another one 5 inches wide. Crisscross them in the pan so they come up and over the sides, one on top of the other. Set the pan aside.

Place the almonds on one side of a baking sheet and the sunflower seeds on the other side and toast for 10 to 12 minutes, until lightly golden brown throughout; break a few almonds open to check. Remove from the oven and let cool. When cool enough to handle, place the almonds in a food processor and pulse 2 or 3 times to break them up so they are not all whole but mostly halved. Pour them out into a large bowl and add the sunflower seeds.

Place the cashews, oats, dates, salt, and cinnamon in the food processor and process for 20 to 25 seconds, until they become a fine-ish meal and the nuts are pulverized. Add to the bowl with the almonds and sunflower seeds. Add the raisins and chia seeds and mix with a wooden spoon or rubber spatula until combined. Pour in the maple syrup and mix until thoroughly combined and evenly moistened. Get in there with your hands; mix and squeeze the mixture assertively for about 2 minutes. You'll notice that everything gradually becomes stickier and clumpier. When you can press the mixture between your hands and it holds together well (like packing a wet snowball), it's ready. If the mixture does not come together, drizzle in another tablespoon or two of maple syrup and mix with your hands until it comes together.

Press the mixture firmly and evenly into the prepared loaf pan. Cover with plastic wrap and refrigerate for at least 6 hours or up to overnight.

When you are ready to bake, preheat the oven to 350°F and place a rack in the center of the oven. Line a baking sheet with parchment paper. Remove the power bar from the pan, unwrap it, and use a sharp knife to cut the bar into 16 slices about ½ inch thick. Place on the baking sheet and bake for 15 to 20 minutes, rotating the baking sheet and flipping the bars over once midway through the baking time, until they are evenly golden brown.

Remove from the oven and let cool on the baking sheet on a wire rack.

Power bars can be stored in an airtight container at room temperature for up to 2 weeks.

VARIATION: *Cut the bars, skip baking them at all, keep them in the refrigerator, and eat them raw. One of my bakers and testers, Katie, actually prefers them this way. She drizzles them with a little melted chocolate (about ½ cup/85 grams bittersweet or semisweet vegan chocolate, chopped, melted with 1 tablespoon/15 grams coconut oil) for a delicious vegan candy bar–like treat.*

Double Chocolate-Walnut Brownies

MAKES 16 TO 20 BROWNIES

1 cup/**100 grams** raw walnuts, roughly chopped

8 ounces/**225 grams** unsweetened chocolate, chopped (about 1¼ cups)

½ cup/1 stick/**115 grams** unsalted butter

4 large eggs (about **200 grams**), at room temperature

2 cups/**400 grams** sugar

1 cup/**120 grams** buckwheat flour

3 ounces/**85 grams** semisweet or bittersweet chocolate, chopped into chunks (about ½ cup)

¼ cup/**45 grams** white rice flour

¼ cup/**45 grams** potato starch (not potato flour)

½ teaspoon baking powder

½ teaspoon kosher salt

1 recipe Master Ganache (page 432)

I love posting pictures of our mouthwatering pastries on Instagram. I get so excited when I see a perfect croissant or cookie or brioche that I have to share the pastry love with as many people as possible. Our bittersweet chocolate brownie is a classic: a little chewy and a lot rich and moist and chocolatey. After I posted a picture of a tower of fudgy decadent brownies, one follower begged, "Is there any way you can make these gluten-free?" Using buckwheat and white rice flours and potato starch, I was able to create a gluten-free version of our popular offering. I added a handful of walnuts for extra flavor, but if you are looking for something nut-free feel free to omit them.

Preheat the oven to 325°F and place a rack in the center of the oven. Line a 9 x 13-inch baking pan with parchment paper or butter it generously, and set it aside.

Place the walnuts on an unlined baking sheet and toast for 10 to 12 minutes, until lightly golden brown. Set aside to cool (leave the oven on).

Place the unsweetened chocolate and butter in a heatproof glass or metal bowl and set the bowl over a small pot of simmering water. Whisk until both are melted. Set aside.

Place the eggs in a stand mixer fitted with a whisk attachment and slowly whip in the sugar. Whip for 1 minute total, until frothy and somewhat thick. Remove the bowl from the mixer and use a rubber spatula to fold in the chocolate-butter mixture.

Stir together the buckwheat flour, bittersweet chocolate, rice flour, potato starch, baking powder, salt, and toasted walnuts. Fold the flour mixture into the egg mixture. When thoroughly combined, use a rubber spatula to spread the batter in the prepared pan (the batter will be thick). Bake for 18 to 24 minutes, rotating the baking sheet midway through the baking time, until a knife poked into the center of the brownies comes out with a few wet crumbs on it. Check every few minutes starting at 15 minutes to make sure they don't overbake. If the knife comes out with

liquid batter on it, the brownies need
more time in the oven. If the knife is
dry, you've probably gone too far —
not the end of the world, but you'll
know next time to bake them less so
they are nice and fudgy. Remove the
brownies from the oven and place
the baking pan on a wire rack.

While the brownies are baking, make
the ganache.

Pour the ganache over the brownies
and let cool for a few hours, until the
brownies are cool and the ganache
has thickened. Place them in the
fridge for an hour or so to help with
cutting, if you want super-clean
edges. If you lined the baking pan
with parchment, once the brownies
are chilled you can pop the whole
thing out of the pan onto a cutting
board and cut the brownies into
squares; otherwise, cut the brownies
in the pan.

Brownies can be stored in an airtight
container at room temperature for up
to 3 days.

Persian Love Cookies

MAKES 15 TO 18 COOKIES

2⅔ cups/**270 grams** almond flour

1¾ cups/**210 grams** confectioners' sugar

2 teaspoons kosher salt

1 teaspoon freshly grated nutmeg

1 teaspoon ground cardamom

2 large egg whites (about ¼ cup/**60 grams**), at room temperature

2 teaspoons rose water

½ cup/**175 grams** finely chopped unsalted pistachios

Pomegranate Glaze (opposite)

One of my favorite bakeries is Sofra in Cambridge, Massachusetts. Maura, their incredibly talented pastry chef, is a sugar wizard—I could eat her pastries morning, noon, and night. She deftly combines Middle Eastern flavors and ingredients with perfect technique, and she's one of my pastry idols. This spiced cookie is an homage to all she does to make Boston's life sweeter. It is chewy and nutty and wonderfully fragrant with cardamom, spotted with vivid green pistachios, and drizzled with a pastel-pink glaze. It also happens to be super simple to make, and it is gluten-free. You may think it's not worth it to purchase rose water since there's such a tiny amount in here but trust me, it brings that "I can't quite pinpoint what that flavor is" element that makes these cookies distinctive and irresistible.

Preheat the oven to 350°F and place a rack in the center of the oven. Line a baking sheet with parchment or butter it lightly, and set it aside.

In a large bowl, stir together the almond flour, confectioners' sugar, salt, nutmeg, and cardamom. In a small bowl, whisk together the egg whites and rose water until frothy. Pour the egg whites into the almond flour mixture and mix well, first with a wooden spoon and then with your hands as the dough gets really stiff, until it is well mixed. Pinch off golf ball–size pieces of dough and roll them into balls. Place the pistachios on a flat plate and press each ball firmly in them so it is totally covered; press the nuts in so they stick to the dough. Place the balls on the prepared baking sheet about 2 inches apart and press down until the cookies are flat. Bake for 18 to 22 minutes, rotating the baking sheet midway through the baking time, until the cookies are golden brown on the edges and pale brown in the center.

Remove from the oven and let cool on the baking sheet on a wire rack. While the cookies are cooling, make the pomegranate glaze.

Use a spoon to drizzle the glaze back and forth across each cooled cookie in a zigzag pattern. Let the glaze firm up until it hardens.

The cookies can be stored in an airtight container at room temperature for up to 5 days.

Pomegranate Glaze

MAKES ABOUT ⅓ CUP/ 65 GRAMS

½ cup/**60 grams** confectioners' sugar

1 to 2 tablespoons pure pomegranate juice

—

In a small bowl, whisk together the confectioners' sugar with 1 tablespoon of the pomegranate juice. Slowly whisk in up to an additional 1 tablespoon pomegranate juice to make a thin glaze that drizzles easily.

Pomegranate glaze can be stored in an airtight container at room temperature for up to 1 week; rewhisk before using.

Bake the log for 30 to 40 minutes, rotating the baking sheet midway through the baking time, until the log is browned and firm. Check it by pressing a finger firmly into the middle — it should not give at all. Remove from the oven and let the log cool on the baking sheet for about 30 minutes, until it is cool enough to handle comfortably. Turn the oven down to 175°F.

Transfer the log to a cutting board. Using a serrated knife, slice it on a slight diagonal into ½-inch-thick biscotti. You should get approximately 15 biscotti. (At this point you can transfer the once-baked biscotti to an airtight container and store in the freezer for up to 2 months before finishing them.)

Lay the biscotti flat on the baking sheet and bake until they are completely baked through, about 2 hours. Test the biscotti by poking at the middle of one of the cookies: It should be completely hard. Turn off the oven but leave the biscotti in the oven overnight to dry out and harden further.

The next day the biscotti will have hardened and dried out completely, and are ready to serve.

Biscotti can be stored in an airtight container at room temperature for up to 4 weeks.

Anzacs

1 cup/**140 grams**
all-purpose flour

1½ cups/**150 grams** rolled oats

1¼ cups/**125 grams** desiccated
unsweetened coconut

¾ cup/**120 grams**
golden raisins

⅔ cup firmly packed/
150 grams light brown sugar

½ cup/1 stick/**115 grams**
unsalted butter

2 tablespoons maple syrup

1 teaspoon baking soda

½ teaspoon kosher salt

A few years ago I got an email out of the blue from Yotam Ottolenghi. Yes, THAT Ottolenghi—not that there are so many I would have been unsure. He wanted to do a baker exchange and have some of his pastry chefs come to America and spend time at Flour for inspiration, and we would do the same thing with his bakeries. I thought for all of a nanosecond before sending him a resounding YES. I sent two of my pastry chefs to his bakery kitchens to learn, taste, and share ideas for about two weeks. This was a once-in-a-lifetime opportunity, so I tagged along for part of the journey. It remains one of the most thought-provoking and creative trips I have ever taken.

At one point, in their commissary the bakers were packing up all sorts of delightful treats. White chocolate–raspberry bark, dark chocolate honeycomb, and some unassuming little cookies they called Anzacs. I took a few samples of each and shoved them in my bag for later. Later ended up being about a week later when I got back to Boston and found them in my luggage. The bark and honeycomb were crushed to bits and the cookies were smashed in little pieces. But I tried them anyway, and the cookies blew me away. So much so that I brought the cookie bits to my meeting the next day with my baking team and we all inhaled them. Even a week later, in shreds, these cookies were phenomenal. It turns out that is true to their name. Anzac is an acronym for the Australian and New Zealand Army Corps (ANZAC) established in World War I, and these biscuits (or cookies) were sent to soldiers because they traveled well and didn't spoil easily. A week in my bag and they were still chewy, airy, nutty, crunchy, sweet—all the things you want in a perfect cookie.

Preheat the oven to 350°F and place a rack in the center of the oven. Line a baking sheet with parchment paper or butter it lightly, and set it aside.

In a large bowl, stir together the flour, 1 cup/100 grams of the oats, 1 cup/100 grams of the coconut, the golden raisins, and brown sugar until thoroughly mixed. Place the butter, maple syrup, and ¼ cup/60 grams water in a small saucepan and bring to a boil. Remove from the heat and whisk in the baking soda and salt until it bubbles. Immediately add the liquid to the oat mixture and stir until the dough comes together.

In a small bowl, stir together the remaining ½ cup/50 grams oats and ¼ cup/25 grams coconut. Using a tablespoon measure, one at a time scoop out rounded balls of cookie dough and roll them around in the oat-coconut mixture. Place on the prepared baking sheet about 3 inches apart. Bake for 18 to 20 minutes, rotating the baking sheet midway through the baking time, until the cookies are golden brown all over. Remove them from the oven and let cool on the baking sheet on a wire rack.

Anzacs can be stored in an airtight container for up to 2 weeks (or in your luggage for up to a week!).

Ossa dei Morti

MAKES ABOUT 2 DOZEN COOKIES

1½ cups/**210 grams**
whole almonds

2 large eggs (about **100 grams**),
at room temperature

1 large egg white (about
30 grams), at room
temperature

1¾ cups/**350 grams** sugar

½ teaspoon pure
almond extract

1 cup/**140 grams**
all-purpose flour

½ teaspoon baking powder

¼ teaspoon kosher salt

Probably the place Christopher and I travel to most is New York City. It's an easy 3½-hour train ride and our list of "just opened/must go" restaurants perpetually beckons. Sullivan Street Bakery is a must each visit. I'm obsessed with their slabs of cracker-thin, simply dressed flatbreads, the slightly sour chestnut-colored Pugliese bread, and their airy, crunchy "ossi di morti" cookies that come in a beautiful little package perfect for gifting (or eating on the train ride home). Translated, the name means "bones of the dead" and they truly look pale and bony and not super attractive. But what they lack in appearance they make up for in taste. Christopher especially loves them, so I wanted to replicate them for him. Nicole, our executive pastry chef, must have tested a dozen recipes until she perfected this one. It's super crispy and light like a meringue but more satisfying, and it goes great with a coffee.

We'd had these on our counters at Flour for a few years when we hired an Italian baker, Mirko. After a few months on our team, Mirko shyly took me aside to let me know we were misspelling this cookie's name—it should be *ossa dei* morti. Mirko, thank you!

Preheat the oven to 325°F and place a rack in the center of the oven. Place the almonds on a baking sheet and toast for 10 to 12 minutes, until they are light gold and start to smell deliciously nutty; break a few open to check. Let cool, then roughly chop into large pieces either by hand or by pulsing in a food processor. Set aside.

Line a baking sheet with parchment paper or butter it lightly, and set it aside.

In a stand mixer fitted with a whisk attachment, whip together the whole eggs, egg white, sugar, and almond extract on medium-high speed for 6 to 8 minutes, until the mixture is thick and leaves a ribbon when you lift a spoonful of the mixture and drop it back into itself. Combine the flour, baking powder, salt, and chopped almonds in a small bowl. Fold the flour mixture into the egg-sugar mixture until completely combined. The batter will be stiff and thick; you may need to switch to mixing it with your hands. Immediately fill a pastry bag fitted with a large round tip at least ½ inch across, or a plastic pastry bag with the end snipped to make a ½-inch opening, with the batter. Pipe out slender 3-inch-long "bones" onto the prepared baking sheet about 3 inches apart. These spread wide so try to keep your piping skinny. Continue piping until all of the batter is used. The batter stiffens with time and becomes harder and harder to pipe, so pipe quickly. (If you prefer, instead of piping out the "bones," you can let the batter sit at room temperature to stiffen. Within an hour it will be firm enough that you can hand-roll it into a long skinny snake and cut it into 3-inch-long cookies.)

Bake for 12 to 15 minutes, rotating the baking sheet midway through the baking time, until the cookies are light golden brown and completely baked through. Remove from the oven and let cool completely on the baking sheet on a wire rack.

Ossa can be stored in an airtight container at room temperature for up to 2 weeks.

Chocolate Chip Cookies

MAKES 18 TO 20 COOKIES

1 cup/2 sticks/**225 grams**
unsalted butter, at room
temperature

1 cup/**200 grams**
superfine sugar

½ cup firmly packed/
110 grams light brown sugar

1 large egg (about **50 grams**),
at room temperature

2 teaspoons pure
vanilla extract

2 cups/**280 grams**
all-purpose flour

1¼ teaspoons kosher salt

1 teaspoon baking soda

10 ounces/**230 grams**
semisweet or bittersweet
chocolate chips (1½ cups)

Not to brag, but Flour makes THE BEST chocolate chip cookies in the world. Hands down. One of our longest-tenured managers, Nick, has been with us over a dozen years and he has eaten at least one a day every day he's worked here. I might have him beat—I've been at it a few years longer and I'm just as addicted. A few years back a guest asked me if I'd ever tried Tate's chocolate chip cookies and was I able to replicate the recipe? He brought me a bag and begged me to figure out how to make them. Harrumph. I was not about to spend time on a cookie that sat on a supermarket shelf for weeks. But if you've had one, you know—as I found out—that these are super-crunchy cookies with a slightly salty edge and rich flavor. Challenge accepted! I took our recipe and added a touch more salt, took out an egg, added some water to allow the dough to melt more easily, increased the sugar (which turns to caramel in the oven), and baked them extra long until they became nice and crispy.

Be sure to use really great chocolate and plan ahead for the dough to rest overnight, and you'll be rewarded with the ultimate thin, crispy chocolate cookie.

—

In a stand mixer fitted with a paddle attachment, by hand with a wooden spoon, or with a handheld electric mixer, beat the butter, superfine sugar, and brown sugar on medium speed until the mixture is light and fluffy, about 5 minutes (10 minutes if mixing by hand). Stop the mixer and use a rubber spatula to scrape the sides and bottom of the bowl and the paddle a few times; the sugars and butter love to collect here and stay unmixed. Beat in the egg,

3 tablespoons plus 1 teaspoon (50 grams) water, and the vanilla on medium until thoroughly combined, 2 to 3 minutes. Again scrape the bowl and the paddle to make sure the egg is thoroughly incorporated.

In a medium bowl, mix together the flour, salt, and baking soda. Add the chocolate chips to the flour mixture and toss to combine. Turn the mixer to low, or continue to use a wooden spoon if mixing by hand, and slowly blend the flour–chocolate mixture into the butter-sugar mixture. Mix until the flour and chocolate are totally incorporated.

For best results, scrape the dough into an airtight container and let it rest in the refrigerator for at least 3 to 4 hours or up to overnight before baking. (The unbaked dough can be stored in the refrigerator for up to 1 week.)

When ready to bake, preheat the oven to 350°F and position a rack in the center of the oven. Line a baking sheet with parchment paper.

Drop the dough in ¼-cup balls onto the prepared baking sheet, spacing them about 2 inches apart. Press the dough down slightly with the palm of your hand. Bake for 20 to 24 minutes, rotating the baking sheet midway through the baking time, until the cookies are deep golden brown all the way through.

Remove the cookies from the oven and let them cool on the baking sheet on a wire rack for 5 to 10 minutes, then transfer them to the rack and let cool completely.

The cookies can be stored in an airtight container at room temperature for up to 3 days.

Double Chocolate Rye Cookies

MAKES 22 TO 24 COOKIES

¾ cup/**90 grams** walnut halves

9 ounces/**255 grams** bittersweet chocolate

6 ounces/**170 grams** unsweetened chocolate

½ cup/1 stick/**115 grams** unsalted butter

½ teaspoon pure vanilla extract

1½ cups/**300 grams** sugar

4 large eggs (about **200 grams**), at room temperature

½ cup/**60 grams** rye flour

½ teaspoon baking powder

¼ teaspoon kosher salt

Our double chocolate cookie is, to me, the perfect cookie. It's extremely chocolatey and rich, full of both dark chocolate chunks and bits of unsweetened chocolate. The cookie part itself is chewy and soft, and when you get one of the slightly caramelized edge pieces it's really amazing. At Flour, we launched a whole grain campaign to introduce more whole grains into our baking and this was the first pastry we changed. Granted, these could never be considered health food. However, if you are going to bake, why not use a whole grain flour to make it incrementally better for you . . . and better tasting. Rye flour is a bit nutty and offers more flavor than all-purpose flour; adding it to this cookie dough has the subtle effect of making the cookie slightly less sweet and showcasing the chocolate flavor even more.

—

Preheat the oven to 350°F and position a rack in the center of the oven. Place the walnuts on a baking sheet and toast for 8 to 10 minutes, until they start to smell fragrant and are lightly golden brown when you break one in half. Remove them from the oven and let cool. Roughly chop them and set aside.

Chop 5 ounces/140 grams of the bittersweet chocolate and 4 ounces/ 115 grams of the unsweetened chocolate into large chunks and place them with the butter in a metal or heatproof glass bowl. Set the bowl over a pot of simmering water and heat, stirring occasionally, until completely smooth. Remove from the heat, whisk in the vanilla, and let cool

for about 20 minutes so it's not piping hot.

In a stand mixer fitted with a whisk attachment, whisk together the sugar and eggs for about 5 minutes on medium-high speed, until light and thick and pale yellow. With the mixer on low, slowly add the chocolate-butter mixture and whisk for about 15 seconds. It will not be completely mixed at this point but that's okay, because you will finish combining all the ingredients by hand.

Chop the remaining 4 ounces/ 115 grams bittersweet chocolate into 1-inch chunks and shave the remaining 2 ounces/55 grams unsweetened chocolate into fine

shavings. In a medium bowl, stir together the rye flour, the chopped bittersweet chocolate, shaved unsweetened chocolate, baking powder, salt, and toasted walnuts. Remove the bowl from the mixer, add the rye flour mixture, and fold it in by hand until the dough is completely homogeneous.

For best results, scrape the dough into an airtight container and let it rest in the refrigerator for at least 3 to 4 hours or up to overnight before baking. (The unbaked dough can be stored in the refrigerator for up to 1 week.)

Preheat the oven to 350°F and position a rack in the center of the oven. Line a baking sheet with parchment paper.

Drop the dough in ¼-cup scoops onto the prepared baking sheet, spacing them about 2 inches apart. Bake for 10 to 12 minutes, rotating the baking sheet midway through the baking time, until the cookies are just starting to crack on the edges and the centers are soft but not liquidy when you press them.

Remove the cookies from the oven and let them cool on the baking sheet on a wire rack for 5 to 10 minutes, then transfer them to the rack and let cool completely.

The cookies can be stored in an airtight container at room temperature for up to 3 days.

Mocha Chip Cookies

MAKES 20 TO 22 COOKIES

1 cup/2 sticks/**225 grams**
unsalted butter, at cool room
temperature

1 cup firmly packed/
220 grams light brown sugar

½ cup/**100 grams**
superfine sugar

2 large eggs (about **100 grams**),
at room temperature

1 teaspoon pure vanilla extract

2¼ cups/**270 grams** rye flour

¼ cup/**25 grams** finely ground
espresso or coffee

1 teaspoon baking soda

½ teaspoon kosher salt

12 ounces/**335 grams**
bittersweet or semisweet
chocolate chips (2 cups)

At my first baking job at Bentonwood Bakery, every morning we baked off humongous cookies of all flavors: standard chocolate chip, oatmeal, and peanut butter, along with less traditional flavors like a chocolatey, chewy, coffee-filled mocha chip. Rick, the pastry chef and owner, packed these cookies with freshly ground coffee for a bracing jolt of caffeine and intense flavor. I've been playing around with rye flour lately; I love the nutty, mellow flavor it adds, and tried it in these cookies for a fabulous upgrade. When we made these for the photo shoot for this book, Kristin, our photographer, deemed them her favorite of everything we had baked thus far. Typically at the end of every day of shooting, all the extra pastries got shared with neighbors, friends, or staff. It made me so happy to see that she wrapped up a large stack of these to take home for herself and her husband.

In a stand mixer fitted with a paddle attachment, by hand with a wooden spoon, or using a handheld electric mixer, beat the butter, brown sugar, and superfine sugar on medium speed until light and fluffy, about 5 minutes (10 minutes if mixing by hand). Stop the mixer and use a rubber spatula to scrape the sides and bottom of the bowl and the paddle a few times; the sugars and butter love to collect here and stay unmixed. Beat in the eggs and vanilla on medium until thoroughly combined, 1 to 2 minutes. Again scrape the bowl and the paddle to make sure the eggs are thoroughly incorporated.

In a medium bowl, mix together the rye flour, espresso, baking soda, salt, and chocolate chips. Turn the mixer to low, or continue to use a wooden spoon if mixing by hand, and slowly blend the flour mixture into the butter-sugar mixture. Mix until the flour and chocolate are totally incorporated.

Scrape the dough into an airtight container and let it rest in the refrigerator overnight before baking. (The unbaked dough can be stored in the refrigerator for up to 1 week.)

When you're ready to bake, preheat the oven to 350°F and place a rack in the center of the oven. Line a baking sheet with parchment paper.

Drop the dough on the prepared baking sheet in ¼-cup balls, spacing them about 2 inches apart. Press the dough down slightly with the palm of your hand. Bake for 15 to 18 minutes, rotating the baking sheet midway through the baking time, until the cookies are golden brown on the edges and slightly soft in the center. Don't let them get brown through and through — you want these slightly underbaked so they are soft and chewy in the center.

Remove the cookies from the oven and let them cool on the baking sheet on a wire rack for 5 to 10 minutes, then transfer them to the rack and let cool completely.

The cookies can be stored in an airtight container at room temperature for up to 3 days.

Raspberry Swirl Meringues

MAKES 8 MERINGUES

Raspberry Coulis
(page 204)

1 cup/**120 grams**
confectioners' sugar

½ teaspoon kosher salt

8 large egg whites (about
1 cup/**240 grams**), at room
temperature

1 cup/**200 grams**
superfine sugar

About 3 ounces/**85 grams**
bittersweet chocolate, finely
shaved (½ cup; optional)

I had never thought to put fruit into a meringue cookie until I visited Ottolenghi in London and was blown away by their gorgeous raspberry meringues. At this iconic bakery piles of meringues sprayed with raspberry sauce are the focal point of their pastry counter. Back in Boston we tried to replicate these beauties and came upon a different way of incorporating the raspberry flavor. Instead of spraying the sauce (called a coulis) we swirled it in with . . . chopsticks. Chopsticks are the ideal tool for making deep divots in the meringue and then swirling the coulis in a spiral throughout the meringue. This makes a stunning cookie that is light and fruity and truly unique. We sometimes add shaved bittersweet chocolate to the meringue for a decadent variation.

—

Make the raspberry coulis and set aside.

Preheat the oven to 175°F and place a rack in the center of the oven. Line a baking sheet with parchment paper and spray it liberally with pan spray. Set it aside.

Sift the confectioners' sugar and salt into a small bowl together and set aside.

In a stand mixer fitted with a whisk attachment, beat the egg whites on medium speed until the wires of the whisk leave a slight trail in the whites, 3 to 4 minutes.

With the mixer on medium, add the superfine sugar in three increments, whipping for about 1 minute between additions. Increase the mixer speed to medium-high and beat for about 1 minute. The meringue should be glossy and stiff and look a bit like soft Cool Whip or shaving cream. Remove the bowl from the mixer and fold in the confectioners' sugar and the chocolate, if you are using it. The meringue will soften up a bit with the sugar folded in.

Use a ½-cup ice cream scoop, large soup ladle, or ½-cup measuring cup to spoon out baseball-size mounds of meringue onto the prepared baking sheet. You should get about 8 meringue mounds. Use a small teaspoon to make a divot in the center of each mound and fill with ½ to 1 teaspoon of the coulis.

This next part is tricky. You are going to use a pair of chopsticks held together or a slender spoon handle to swirl the coulis around into the meringue. Start by pointing the chopsticks at a 45-degree angle, not straight up and down, into the well of coulis. Scoop just underneath the coulis, lift the chopsticks through the meringue, and pull up and swirl one-and-a-half swirls through the meringue in a circular motion, starting with a small circle and moving outward. Pull the chopsticks out of the meringue and repeat, starting from the center and swirling outward but this time in the opposite direction. Don't press the meringue down too much while you're doing this, or you'll flatten it out and won't get a nice billowy cloud. It's tempting to keep swirling the coulis, but then you'll end up with a faded pink meringue and not a distinct white-and-fuchsia swirl. Also try to avoid letting the coulis run down the sides and onto the parchment, or it will settle underneath the meringue while baking and oxidize into an off-putting purple-green color. Repeat with the remaining 7 meringues.

Bake for about 4 hours, until the meringues are firm to the touch. Turn off the oven, crack the oven door open, and let the meringues dry out for at least 8 hours or up to overnight before serving.

The meringues can be stored in an airtight container at room temperature for up to 5 days.

Raspberry Coulis

MAKES ¼ CUP

¾ cup/**95 grams** fresh or frozen raspberries

1½ tablespoons sugar

1 teaspoon fresh lemon juice

Combine the raspberries, sugar, and lemon juice in a food processor and process on low speed until it becomes liquid. Strain the coulis through a fine-mesh sieve and discard the seeds. Refrigerate the coulis for at least 1 hour to chill.

Coulis can be stored in an airtight container in the fridge for up to 1 week.

Brown Sugar–
Candied Almond Meringues

MAKES 12 TO 15 MERINGUES

Candied Almonds
(page 207)

8 large egg whites (about
1 cup/**240 grams**),
at room temperature

1 cup/**200 grams**
superfine sugar

½ cup firmly packed/
110 grams light brown sugar

½ teaspoon kosher salt

Flour's almond meringue clouds were among my favorite afternoon snacks for years. It's funny how you can be totally obsessed with a pastry day in and day out and then one day you try it and it no longer does the trick. After inhaling bits and pieces of almond meringue from my backpack pretty much daily, I realized I wanted something more from this cookie: more almond and more I-can't-stop-eating-this-ness. "What if we made an almond praline and folded that into the meringue?" Nicole wondered during one of our regular morning brainstorming sessions. Brilliant! Meringues are a very sweet confection already, and cooking the almonds with caramelized sugar adds a bitter note that nicely offsets the sweetness. Brown sugar as well as white echo the caramely molassesy notes in the meringue and helps keep the inside of these slightly chewy and taffy-like.

Make the candied almonds and let them cool. Chop them very roughly by hand or in a food processor — I like the almonds to be in halves and thirds, no smaller. Set aside.

Preheat the oven to 200°F and place a rack in the center of the oven. Line a baking sheet with parchment paper or butter it lightly; set aside.

In a medium metal or heatproof glass bowl, whisk together the egg whites, superfine sugar, and brown sugar. Place the bowl over a pot of simmering water so that the bottom of the bowl is above the water. (This is called a bain-marie; it is a nice gentle way to heat up ingredients

that might overcook, such as egg whites.) Cook, whisking the mixture constantly, until it is hot hot hot to the touch, 8 to 10 minutes. When you put your finger into the mixture it should feel too hot to keep your finger in place. Whisk in the salt. Transfer the mixture to a stand mixer fitted with a whisk attachment. Whip on high speed for about 3 minutes, until the whites turn to stiff glossy meringue and hold a very firm peak. Set aside about ¼ cup of the candied almonds for garnish and fold the rest into the meringue. Using a large spoon or ¼-cup ice cream scoop, scoop out large rounded mounds of

Candied Almonds

MAKES ABOUT 2½ CUPS

1½ cups/**210 grams** whole raw almonds

½ cup/**100 grams** sugar

¼ teaspoon ground cinnamon

¼ teaspoon kosher salt

—

Preheat the oven to 350°F and place a rack in the center of the oven. Line a baking sheet with parchment paper and set it aside.

Place the almonds, sugar, cinnamon, salt, and ¼ cup/60 grams water in a large saucepan. Cook over medium heat, stirring constantly with a wooden spoon, until the sugar crystallizes onto the almonds and turns a sandy white, 8 to 10 minutes depending on the heat of your stove. It may seem like there's no way it will become sandy, but be patient and keep stirring, and soon you'll be rewarded with coated nuts. Remove from the heat and pour the nuts out onto the prepared baking sheet.

Bake for 8 to 10 minutes, until the almonds are slightly toasted inside; break a few open to check — they should be pale golden brown. Cool completely on the baking sheet.

Candied almonds can be stored in an airtight container at room temperature for up to 2 weeks.

meringue and place them on the prepared sheet. Use the back of a spoon to make decorative peaks and valleys in the mounds. Sprinkle evenly with the remaining candied almonds. Bake for 2 hours 30 minutes, rotating the baking sheet a few times during the baking time.

Remove from the oven and cool completely on the baking sheet on a wire rack before serving.

Meringues can be stored in an airtight container at room temperature for up to 1 week.

Keith's Homemade
Devil Dogs

MAKES 15 TO 18 PASTRIES

Creamy Vanilla Frosting
(page 210)

2 cups/**280 grams**
all-purpose flour

½ cup/**60 grams** Dutch-
processed cocoa powder

1 teaspoon baking powder

½ teaspoon baking soda

½ teaspoon kosher salt

½ cup/1 stick/**115 grams**
unsalted butter, melted
and cooled

2 ounces/**55 grams** bittersweet
chocolate, melted and cooled
(a scant ¼ cup chopped
chocolate or chips)

1 cup/**200 grams** sugar

1 large egg yolk (about
20 grams; save the white for
the Creamy Vanilla Frosting),
at room temperature

2 teaspoons pure
vanilla extract

½ cup/**120 grams** whole milk,
at room temperature

½ cup/**120 grams** crème
fraîche, at room temperature

One of my very first cookbook testers, Keith, had no experience baking professionally but was an eager home baker. By the time I finished writing my first book, *Flour*, I was proud that Keith had learned how to be a better baker from testing almost every recipe. He got so good, in fact, that we hired him to be a baker at Flour. He worked his way up to become an assistant pastry chef before he left to pursue other baking opportunities. While at Flour, Keith developed this recipe for homemade Devil Dogs; they were a favorite of his growing up and he knew I loved trying quality versions of anything from the junk food aisle. I still have never tried the original Drake's version but I don't see any reason to. These are soft and rich and chocolatey and I can't imagine anything in a box coming anywhere close.

⸻

Make the frosting and set it aside.

Preheat the oven to 350°F and place racks in the center and bottom third of the oven. Line two baking sheets with parchment paper and set them aside.

In a medium bowl, stir together the flour, cocoa powder, baking powder, baking soda, and salt. In a small bowl, whisk together the melted butter and chocolate. Add the sugar and whisk until well combined. Add the egg yolk and vanilla and whisk until combined. Add the milk and crème fraîche and whisk until well combined.

Make a well in the flour mixture and pour the chocolate-butter mixture into the middle. Use a rubber spatula to fold all the ingredients together. The consistency will be thick but stirrable.

Fill a pastry bag fitted with a 1-inch tip with the batter. Pipe the batter into 1-inch-wide, 3-inch-long, somewhat flat ovals (around ½ inch thick), 2 to 3 inches apart on the prepared baking sheets; the batter will spread a lot. (If you pipe the batter too thickly, it will spread too much and bake off in a blob.)

Place one baking sheet on the center rack and the other below it. Bake for about 10 minutes, rotating the baking sheets and switching their positions midway through the baking time, until the tops of the cakes are no longer sticky and don't leave a residue on your finger but the cakes are still soft to the touch.

Remove from the oven and let the cakes cool completely on the baking sheets on wire racks.

Peel the little cakes from the parchment. Fill a small pastry bag fitted with a small round tip with the frosting. Pipe frosting on the flat side of half the cakes, then sandwich them together with the unfrosted cakes, flat side down. Eat as many as you can before someone steals them, but if you have any left, Devil Dogs can be stored in an airtight container at room temperature for up to 1 day.

Creamy Vanilla Frosting

MAKES ABOUT 1¼ CUPS

¼ cup/**50 grams** superfine sugar

1 large egg white (about **30 grams**), at room temperature

¾ cup/1½ sticks/**170 grams** unsalted butter, cut into chunks, at room temperature

1 cup/**120 grams** confectioners' sugar

2 tablespoons whole milk

1 teaspoon pure vanilla extract

½ teaspoon kosher salt

In a small metal or heatproof glass bowl, whisk together the superfine sugar and egg white to make a thick slurry. Place the bowl over a small pot of simmering water and whisk occasionally until the slurry is hot to the touch. It will thin out a bit as the sugar melts. Scrape the sugar–egg white slurry into a stand mixer fitted with a whisk attachment. Whip on medium-high speed for 6 to 8 minutes, until the mixture cools.

Add the butter and whip on medium until the butter is thoroughly incorporated, about 2 minutes.

Add the confectioners' sugar, milk, vanilla, and salt and whip on medium until the frosting is smooth and satiny. It may look broken (i.e., curdled, like the butter is separating from the frosting) at first but keep whipping until it comes together.

The frosting can be stored in an airtight container at room temperature for up to 3 days or in the refrigerator for up to 2 weeks. Before using, place the frosting in a stand mixer fitted with a paddle attachment and mix until the frosting smooths out again. If it breaks, warm up the frosting by placing the bowl in a larger bowl of hot water, whisking occasionally until the frosting softens, and beat again.

Hazelnut-Raspberry Rugelach

MAKES 32 RUGELACH

1 cup/2 sticks/**225 grams**
unsalted butter, at room
temperature

1 cup/8 ounces/**225 grams**
cream cheese, at room
temperature

2 cups/**280 grams**
all-purpose flour

½ teaspoon kosher salt

Hazelnut Butter
(page 213)

⅔ cup/**200 grams**
raspberry jam

2 tablespoons
confectioners' sugar

I've never worked directly with Nancy Silverton but I feel like she's been a mentor my entire pastry career. I've read her books cover to cover and baked my way through most of them; the first pastry chef I ever worked for, Rick Katz, received much of his training working for her, so the lessons I gleaned from her books were reiterated when Rick was teaching me how to bake. At one point early on I even cold-called her to inquire about moving to L.A. to work for her. She could not have been kinder in letting me know that she didn't have a position at the time but to keep on pursuing my passion. I learned how to make rugelach—a flaky tender cookie—from her book *Pastries from the La Brea Bakery*. Her recipe served as a jumping-off point for us at Flour and we now offer different flavors like orange-chocolate and walnut-cinnamon during the Rosh Hashanah holidays. My favorite version is this homemade hazelnut butter and jam rugel that reminds me of eating a peanut butter and jelly sandwich in flaky, buttery cookie form.

In a stand mixer fitted with a paddle attachment, mix the butter and cream cheese together on medium speed until well mixed, about 1 minute. Add the flour and salt and mix on low until the flour is completely mixed in. Remove the dough from the mixer and wrap it lightly in plastic wrap, or place it a clean bowl and cover it with plastic wrap. Refrigerate for 1 hour.

Generously flick flour over the work surface. Remove the dough from the fridge, unwrap it, place it on the work surface, and roll the dough into a rectangle about 24 inches wide from side to side and 18 inches long from top to bottom. (The dough is a dream to work with, and you should have no trouble rolling it into a nice thin rectangle.) Divide the dough into thirds by eye and fold the left third of the dough in toward the center, then fold the right third of the dough on top of that, similar to folding a business letter. You will now have a rectangle that is about 8 inches wide and 18 inches long. Rotate the dough rectangle counterclockwise 90 degrees (a quarter-turn) so it's now

Hazelnut Butter

MAKES ABOUT 1½ CUPS

1½ cups/**190 grams** raw
skin-on hazelnuts

⅓ cup/**115 grams** honey

2 tablespoons/**30 grams**
unsalted butter

⅛ teaspoon kosher salt

—

Preheat the oven to 350°F
and place a rack in the middle
of the oven. Place the hazelnuts
on a baking sheet and toast for
8 to 10 minutes, until the nuts
are lightly toasted and golden
brown; break a few open to
check. Remove from the oven
and let cool until just cool
enough to handle. Rub the
nuts in a rough towel to loosen
and remove any loose skins;
discard the skins. Place the
nuts, honey, butter, and salt in
a food processor or blender
and blend on medium-high
speed until the nuts are
pulverized and resemble coarse
peanut butter, about 2 minutes.
Use immediately, before the oil
separates from the mixture.

18 inches wide from side to side and
8 inches long from top to bottom.
(This is called giving the dough a
trifold and turn. You are going to do
this twice more for a total of three trifolds and turns.)

Here we go with the second trifold
and turn: Roll this out to a rectangle
approximately 22 inches wide and
12 inches long. Again divide the
dough in thirds by eye, fold the right
third in toward the center, the left
third on top of that, and then rotate
the dough counterclockwise 90
degrees.

Roll the dough to approximately
18 inches wide and 12 inches long,
then give the dough a trifold and
turn so the dough packet is about
9 x 12 inches. At this point the dough
is done!

Cut the dough in half and wrap each
half well in plastic. Place the dough
in the fridge to rest for at least 1 hour
or up to 3 days. (You can also store
the dough in the freezer for up to
2 weeks; transfer it to the fridge to
thaw the day before you plan to
use it.)

Preheat the oven to 350°F and
place a rack in the center of the oven.
Make the hazelnut butter and set it
aside. Line a baking sheet with
parchment paper.

To shape the rugelach: Generously
flick flour over the work surface, then
roll out one dough piece into a circle
about 14 inches across. Trim the
dough if needed to make it a circle.
Spread half the hazelnut butter
evenly over the whole circle, then
spread half the jam on top of that.

(If the jam is too stiff to spread, stir
it vigorously to loosen it up or
microwave it to warm it slightly so
it's spreadable.) Using a sharp knife
or a pizza cutter, cut the dough into
16 wedges by slicing the dough in
half and then in quarters, then
slicing each quarter in half and then
in half again. Starting from the
widest part of one wedge, roll it down
toward the point. Place the shaped
rugel on the prepared baking sheet.
Repeat with the rest of the dough
wedges. Repeat with the second half
of dough, the remaining hazelnut
butter, and the remaining raspberry
jam. (At this point the shaped
rugelach may be frozen on the
baking sheet. Once frozen, transfer
them to an airtight container and
store in the freezer for up to 2 weeks.
Bake directly from the freezer,
adding up to 5 minutes to the baking
time, as needed.)

Bake for 35 to 40 minutes, rotating
the baking sheet midway through
the baking time, until the rugelach
are medium golden brown throughout. The hazelnut butter might leak
out a bit but that's okay — you can
cut off any excess when the rugelach
cool.

Remove from the oven and let cool
on the baking sheet on a wire rack.
Dust with the confectioners' sugar
before serving.

Rugelach can be stored in an
airtight container at room temperature for up to 2 days.

Baby Palmiers

½ recipe/12 ounces/**340 grams**
Master Puff Pastry Dough
(page 442) or store-bought
all-butter puff pastry

½ cup/**100 grams** sugar

¼ teaspoon kosher salt

"Does the world really need another palmier recipe?" Christopher asked me when I brought a few dozen to a dinner party after a long day of recipe testing. I watched as Emily, one of our friends' daughters, sandwiched them with ice cream, while their other daughter Lucy scooped them into whipped cream, drizzled them with chocolate sauce, and passed them around. Toddler twins Dean and Iola were double-fisting these sweet, crunchy caramelized cookies and Christopher—yes, the one who worried that the world was overrun with palmier recipes—was popping them like potato chips. First one, then two, then we stopped counting. These are classics and everyone should make them at least once, both for the sheer joy of making puff pastry from start to finish and to fall into a sugar coma after eating them without stopping. We add a pinch of salt to the sugar when layering these and we rest them overnight in the freezer, which allows the sugar to melt. Upon baking they caramelize into glass-like shatter. Wait until they are fully cooled to enjoy.

Generously flick flour over the work surface, unwrap the puff pastry, and roll it out to a rectangle about 9 x 14 inches. Working fairly quickly so the butter in the dough doesn't start to melt, trim the rectangle, rotate it so that it is 14 inches wide from side to side and 9 inches long from top to bottom, and brush off any loose flour. Sprinkle about two-thirds of the sugar and the salt evenly across the rectangle and gently press it into the dough by rolling the rolling pin lightly across the dough.

Fold the top part of the dough down to the middle of the rectangle. Fold the bottom part of the dough up to meet the top part. Sprinkle the rest of the sugar on the bottom flap of exposed dough. Carefully fold the top half down on top of the sugared bottom half. Press down gently so that the sugar stays mostly inside.

Using a sharp chef's knife, slice the dough into ½-inch-thick slices. Place the palmiers cut side down on a baking sheet or flat plate and freeze for at least 8 hours. (At this point the palmiers can be transferred to a plastic freezer bag and frozen for up to 1 month. The time in the freezer will melt the sugar so you get really caramelized crunchy palmiers.)

Preheat the oven to 350°F and place a rack in the center of the oven. Line a clean baking sheet with parchment paper. Place the palmiers cut side up about 2 inches apart on the baking sheet. Bake for 30 to 40 minutes, rotating the baking sheet midway through the baking time, until the palmiers are golden brown through and through and the sugar is caramelized. Remove from the oven and let cool completely on the baking sheet on a wire rack.

Palmiers can be stored in an airtight container at room temperature for up to 3 days.

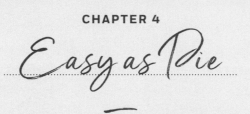

CHAPTER 4

Easy as Pie

Fresh Fruit Tart

MAKES ONE 8-INCH TART, TO SERVE 6 TO 8

1 recipe Master Pâte Sucrée
(page 437)

½ recipe/1 cup/**340 grams**
Master Pastry Cream
(page 434)

½ cup/**120 grams** heavy cream

4 or 5 fresh medium
strawberries

1 ripe kiwi, or 4 or 5 large
green seedless grapes

1 ripe Champagne mango

1 cup/**110 grams** fresh
blackberries

1 cup/**125 grams** fresh
raspberries

1 cup/**125 grams** fresh
blueberries

I learned a million and one things while working at Payard Patisserie in New York City. It was a classic French kitchen filled with classically trained French pastry chefs. I picked up kitchen French full of slang and swears, I learned how to *chablonner un biscuit joconde* (which means to cover a thin cake with chocolate), I became a pro at rolling the heads of dozens of brioches à tête at four in the morning. I also learned tricks on how to extend the life of fresh fruit for several days when making a fruit tart. Every morning I would build stunning tarts with vivid berries and fresh currants and sliced apricots and then I would paint the fruit meticulously with a clear gelatin coating called nappage. The nappage kept the fruit looking fresh for a few days, which meant the tart could sit for several days and still be presentable. When I put fresh fruit tarts on the menu at Flour, I took a different approach. I wanted just the fruit—no nappage. This meant the tarts would only last a day. The fruit had to be perfectly ripe and fresh and able to stand on its own. It's a fleeting treat for sure but your reward is a delicate, crispy, sweet shell filled with fresh vanilla cream and piled high with the juiciest, ripest fruit, ready to eat out of hand.

Make the pâte sucrée. Make the pastry cream and set it aside.

Remove the pâte sucrée from the refrigerator, unwrap it, and knead it slightly to make it malleable if it feels stiff. Using a rolling pin, press the dough to flatten it into a disk about ½ inch thick. Generously flick flour over the work surface and the dough. Make sure the surface you are rolling on is well floured so that the dough does not stick to it; likewise, make sure the disk itself is floured well enough to keep the rolling pin from sticking to it. Carefully roll out the disk into a circle about 10 inches in diameter. Roll from the center of the disk outward and gently rotate the disk 90 degrees (a quarter-turn) after each roll to ensure that the disk gets stretched out evenly into a nice circle. Use a bench scraper to help move the dough by scraping underneath the dough and moving it around. Don't worry if the dough breaks a bit, especially toward the edges. You can easily patch these tears up once you've lined the tart pan.

Once the dough circle is about 10 inches in diameter, dock it by poking it all over with a fork or a pastry docker (see page 24). Roll it gently around the rolling pin, then unfurl it over an 8-inch tart pan. Press the dough into the tart pan, taking care to press into the corners. Trim the edge of the shell even with the top of the tart pan. Use any scraps or odd pieces to patch up any tears or missing bits. Make sure the entire tart pan is completely covered with dough, and press one last time all the way around to ensure that any holes have been patched up.

Refrigerate the tart shell for at least 30 minutes to let the dough rest; the gluten needs a little time to relax so it doesn't shrink in the oven. (At this point you can wrap the tart shell well in plastic wrap and refrigerate for up to 3 days or freeze it for up to 2 weeks.)

Preheat the oven to 350°F and place a rack in the center of the oven. Place the tart shell on a baking sheet and bake for 25 to 30 minutes, rotating the baking sheet midway through the baking time, until it is golden brown all around. Remove from the oven and let cool completely on a wire rack. (At this point the tart shell can be stored, well wrapped, at room temperature for up to 1 week.)

In a medium bowl, whip the heavy cream until it holds a peak and is thick and soft. Fold the pastry cream into the whipped cream until thoroughly combined.

Gently pop the tart shell out of the pan. Place the tart shell on a serving plate. (Hint: The tart shell has a tendency to slide around a bit, so anchor it to the plate by putting a small spoonful of the pastry cream mixture directly on the plate before placing the tart shell on it.) Fill the tart shell with the pastry cream mixture and spread it evenly with a spatula.

Stem and quarter the strawberries and place them on top of the cream with one cut side down, spaced randomly but evenly. Peel the kiwi and slice it in half lengthwise. Slice each half into ½-inch-thick half-moons. (If using green grapes instead of kiwis, slice the grapes in half.) Place the kiwi slices in the cream against the cut side of the strawberries. Peel the mango and cut it into thin slices about 1 x 1 inch. Place the mango in the cream next to the kiwi. Slice the blackberries in half if they are large and place them in the cream in random places. Fill the empty spots on the tart with raspberries, blueberries, and any extra mango. The goal is to cover the whole tart with fruit and not have any cream visible. The tart must be eaten the same day it is assembled or it will get soggy. If not serving the tart immediately, store it in the refrigerator; serve within 6 hours.

Spring Ricotta Pie
with Fresh Berries

MAKES ONE 9-INCH PIE

1 recipe Master Pâte Sucrée (page 437)

1 pound/**455 grams** whole milk ricotta cheese

½ cup/**120 grams** crème fraîche

½ cup/**100 grams** sugar

¼ cup/**60 grams** heavy cream

1 large egg (about **50 grams**), at room temperature

3 large egg yolks (about **60 grams**), at room temperature

1 tablespoon grated lemon zest (about 1 large lemon)

2 teaspoons pure vanilla extract

¼ teaspoon kosher salt

1 pint/**250 grams** fresh blueberries, raspberries, or blackberries, or an assortment

Not the same as cheesecake, ricotta pie is a traditional Italian dessert often served at parties and holiday gatherings. I had never heard of it when Nicole suggested it as a special dessert on our Easter menu. Jess Larsen, the pastry chef who opened our Back Bay location, grew up making these for her family dinners and she brought one for us to try. It was intriguingly grainy and sweet, and we ate the whole thing during a manager meeting. I wanted ours to be a little lighter and brighter, and even milkier and less sugary. Adding crème fraîche helps achieve all these things, and some fresh lemon zest sharpens up all the creamy flavors. Covered in berries, it is a lovely way to welcome the spring season.

Make the pâte sucrée.

Remove the pâte sucrée from the refrigerator, unwrap it, and let it soften for about 15 minutes at room temperature. You have about 15 minutes when the dough reaches the perfect rolling temperature: not so cold that it breaks when you roll it, but not so warm that it sticks to everything. Using a rolling pin, bang and flatten the dough into a disk about ½ inch thick. If the dough is too cold, keep pressing it with the rolling pin to flatten and soften it. If it's too warm, place it back in the fridge so it firms up a bit, or roll it out between two large sheets of parchment paper. Flick flour over the work surface and the dough and carefully roll out the disk into a circle about 11 inches in diameter. Make sure the surface you are rolling on is well floured so that the dough does not stick to it; likewise, make sure the disk itself is floured well enough to keep the rolling pin from sticking to it. Roll from the center of the disk outward and gently rotate the disk 90 degrees (a quarter-turn) after each roll to ensure that the disk gets stretched out evenly into a nice circle. Don't worry if the dough breaks a bit, especially toward the edges. You can easily patch these tears up once you've lined the pie plate.

Once the dough circle is about 11 inches in diameter, dock it by poking it all over with a fork or a pastry docker (see page 24). Roll it gently around the rolling pin, then unfurl it over a 9-inch ceramic, glass, or aluminum pie plate. Press the dough well over the bottom and up the sides of the pie plate. Trim the edge of the dough even with the edge of the pie plate. Use any scraps or odd pieces to patch up any tears or missing bits. Make sure the entire pie plate is completely covered with dough and press one last time all the way around to ensure that any holes have been patched up.

Refrigerate the pie shell for at least 30 minutes to let the dough rest. (At this point you can wrap the pie shell well in plastic wrap and refrigerate for up to 1 day or freeze it for up to 2 weeks. If frozen, thaw the shell overnight in the fridge before proceeding.)

Preheat the oven to 350°F and place a rack in the center of the oven. Bake the pie shell for 30 minutes, until the bottom is golden brown. Remove it from the oven. (At this point the pie shell can be stored, well wrapped in plastic, at room temperature for up to 5 days.)

Place the ricotta, crème fraîche, sugar, heavy cream, whole egg, egg yolks, lemon zest, vanilla, and salt in a large bowl and whisk together until completely smooth. Carefully pour the mixture into the pie shell. (The shell does not have to be cool; you can pour the filling in as soon as the shell comes out of the oven.) Bake the pie for 35 to 45 minutes, rotating it midway through the baking time,

until the filling is set and just starting to brown on top.

Remove from the oven and let cool on a wire rack. Refrigerate for at least 1 hour before serving. Top the pie with the berries just before serving.

Leftover pie can be stored in the fridge, well wrapped, for up to 3 days.

Plum-Frangipane Tart

MAKES ONE 10-INCH TART, TO SERVE 10 TO 12

1 recipe Master Pâte Sucrée (page 437)

1 recipe Master Frangipane (page 433), at room temperature

1½ pounds/**680 grams** ripe red plums (about 7 small or 5 medium)

¼ cup/**60 grams** apricot preserves

One of the easiest ways to celebrate summer fruits is with this frangipane tart. I love it with sweet-tart plums but you can make it with peaches, nectarines, cherries, and/or apricots. In cold weather, poach pears or quince for a winter variation. Fruit is nestled deep into a thick layer of almond cream that is baked into a crispy tart shell. When it comes out of the oven you glaze it with apricot preserves to add shine and a little sweetness. As with most fruit desserts, so much rides on the ripeness of your fruit. So wait until you have fruit that begs to be eaten out of hand and use it instead for this fantastic dessert.

Make the pâte sucrée. Make the frangipane and set aside.

Remove the pâte sucrée from the refrigerator, unwrap it, and let it soften for about 15 minutes at room temperature. You have about 15 minutes when the dough reaches the perfect rolling temperature: not so cold that it breaks when you roll it, but not so warm that it sticks to everything. Using a rolling pin, bang and flatten the dough into a disk about ½ inch thick. If the dough is too cold, keep pressing it with the rolling pin to flatten and soften. If it's too warm, place it back in the fridge so it firms up a bit or roll it out between two large sheets of parchment paper. Flick flour over the work surface and the dough and carefully roll out the disk into a circle 12 inches in diameter. Make sure the surface you are rolling on is well floured so

the dough does not stick to it; likewise, make sure the disk itself is floured well enough to keep the rolling pin from sticking to it. Roll from the center of the disk outward and gently rotate the disk 90 degrees (a quarter-turn) after each roll to ensure that the disk gets stretched out evenly into a nice circle. Don't worry if the dough breaks a bit, especially toward the edges. You can easily patch these tears up once you've lined the tart pan.

Once the dough circle is 12 inches in diameter, dock it by poking it all over with a fork or a pastry docker (see page 24). Roll it gently around the rolling pin, then unfurl it over a 10-inch tart pan set on a baking sheet. Press the dough into the tart pan, taking care to press it into the corners. Trim the edge of the dough

even with the top of the tart pan. Use any scraps or odd pieces to patch up any tears or missing bits. Make sure the entire tart pan is completely covered with dough, and press one last time all the way around to ensure that any holes have been patched up.

Refrigerate the tart shell for at least 30 minutes to let the dough rest. (At this point you can wrap the tart shell well in plastic wrap and refrigerate for up to 1 day or freeze it for up to 2 weeks. If frozen, thaw in the fridge overnight before proceeding.)

Preheat the oven to 350°F and place a rack in the center of the oven. Bake the tart shell on the baking sheet for 30 minutes, rotating it midway through the baking time, until the bottom is golden brown. Remove it from the oven and let cool completely on the baking sheet on a wire rack. Keep the oven on. (At this point, the tart shell can be stored, well wrapped in plastic, at room temperature for up to 5 days.)

Using a wooden spoon, stir the frangipane well to loosen it up so it is spreadable. Scrape it into the tart shell and use an offset spatula to spread it evenly. Quarter the plums, discarding the pits; if the plums are large, cut them in sixths. Place the plums cut side up/skin side down around the edge of the tart shell in a circle, all touching. Press the plums down gently into the frangipane.

Repeat with the rest of the plums, making smaller concentric circles and filling the center of the tart, covering as much of the frangipane as possible.

Bake for 1 hour 10 minutes to 1 hour 20 minutes, rotating the tart midway through the baking time, until the frangipane is golden brown and the plums are soft and jammy. Remove the tart from the oven.

In a small saucepan, combine the apricot preserves with 1 tablespoon water and heat over medium heat until the preserves are liquid. Using a pastry brush, brush the preserves over the whole tart while warm, focusing on glazing the plums. Let cool to room temperature before serving.

The tart can be stored at room temperature, well covered, for up to 2 days.

Almond Joy Tart

MAKES ONE 8-INCH TART, TO SERVE 8 TO 10 PEOPLE

2 cups/**280 grams** whole raw almonds

½ cup/**60 grams** plus 1 tablespoon Dutch-processed cocoa powder

¾ cup/**140 grams** coconut oil, melted and cooled

9 tablespoons/**190 grams** maple syrup

½ teaspoon kosher salt

⅓ cup/**80 grams** full-fat coconut milk

1 teaspoon pure vanilla extract

¼ cup/**15 grams** unsweetened flaked coconut, for garnish

Every month or two, the pastry chefs at each Flour location offer a special dessert on their pastry counters. It might be something they've made in another job or something they are playing around with at home or an idea from one of their bakers. It's an opportunity for them to flex their pastry muscles and for our guests to enjoy new treats regularly. I am inspired by what the chefs come up with and I look forward to trying the new specials every month. This Almond Joy Tart is the creation of our Flour Fort Point pastry chef, Jessi, who started as a pastry cook and slowly worked her way up to running one of our busiest locations. I asked her how she came up with this crunchy, coconutty, decadent tart: "I was brainstorming for a January special and keeping in mind that a lot of people make New Year's resolutions to eat healthier, cut out gluten, and/or go vegan. I like the challenge of making something amazing that fits within those limits." This tart is worth making all year round.

Preheat the oven to 350°F and place a rack in the center of the oven. Place the almonds on a baking sheet and toast for 8 to 10 minutes, until they are light golden brown inside; break a few open to check. Remove from the oven and turn the oven off.

To make the crust: Place 1½ cups/ 210 grams of the almonds, 1 tablespoon of the cocoa powder, 6 tablespoons/70 grams of the coconut oil, 3 tablespoons/60 grams of the maple syrup, and ¼ teaspoon of the kosher salt in a food processor and pulse until the nuts are finely chopped. The consistency should be

stiff but easy to mold, like cookie dough. If the mixture is too loose to work with, refrigerate it for up to 20 minutes, until it stiffens up. Press the crust into the sides of an 8-inch tart pan with a removable bottom. First build up the edges so that they are about ¼ inch thick all the way around, then press the remainder of the crust into the bottom of the ring. Refrigerate for 15 to 20 minutes, until the crust is set.

To make the filling: In a small saucepan, combine the remaining 6 tablespoons/70 grams coconut oil, the coconut milk, and remaining

6 tablespoons/130 grams maple syrup and heat over low heat. When the coconut oil is melted, add the remaining ½ cup/60 grams cocoa powder and the vanilla and whisk until smooth.

Spread a thin layer of the filling over the bottom of the crust, just enough so the almonds have something to adhere to. Arrange the remaining ½ cup/70 grams whole almonds in an even layer so that they cover most of the filling. Sprinkle evenly with the remaining ¼ teaspoon salt.

Refrigerate for about 10 minutes to set the almonds in place.

Pour the remaining filling into the crust over the almonds. (If the filling is not liquid, reheat gently until it is pourable.) Gently nudge the filling into place so that it completely covers the almonds and the top is smooth. Refrigerate for about 30 minutes to set the filling.

When ready to serve, remove the tart from the fridge and let sit at room temperature for about 10 minutes to let the coconut oil soften up, then run a small paring knife around the edge to release it. Place one hand under the base of the tart and push it up and out of the outer ring. Transfer the tart to a flat serving plate.

Garnish with the flaked coconut, slice, and serve.

The tart can be stored, well wrapped, in the refrigerator for up to 3 days; serve chilled.

Lime Cream Pie

with Brown Sugar Graham Crust

MAKES ONE 9-INCH PIE

Brown Sugar Graham Cracker
Pie Shell (page 238)

1⅔ cups/**535 grams**
sweetened condensed milk
(from two 14-ounce cans)

¾ cup plus 2 tablespoons/
210 grams fresh lime juice
(about 7 limes)

4 large egg yolks (about
80 grams), at room
temperature

2 teaspoons grated lime zest
(about 2 limes)

¼ teaspoon kosher salt

1½ cups/**360 grams**
heavy cream

3 tablespoons/**22 grams**
confectioners' sugar

1 teaspoon cornstarch

If you bake to make those you love happy, as I do, then sometimes you end up making things you're not familiar with but
your beloved pines for. Key lime pie had reached iconic status in
the Chang-Myers household as The Pastry We Never Have. I had
never made or eaten key lime pie, so I was having a hard time
understanding what Christopher was so in love with. We spent a
long weekend in Florida a few years back, and at a local restaurant I finally got my first taste of this classic pie. It was good but
I can't say I was blown away. Key limes are tarter than regular
limes, and the purported floral flavor they impart was less
impactful than I expected. Back home I wanted to see what we
could create based on the same flavors but using regular limes.
We made a simple lime pie with fresh regular limes and topped
it with soft limey whipped cream. Sweetened condensed milk
gives the lime custard a velvety smooth texture and nicely
rounds out the sharpness of the lime. The graham cracker crust
puts it over the top. Now at home this pie has become The Pastry
We Don't Have Often Enough.

Make the pie shell and set it aside.

Preheat the oven to 350°F and
place a rack in the center of the oven.

In a large bowl, combine the
condensed milk, lime juice, egg
yolks, 1 teaspoon of the lime zest, and
the salt. Whisk until smooth, then
pour into the pie shell. Bake for 30 to
40 minutes, rotating the pie midway
through the baking time, until the pie
is set but still a little wobbly when
you shake it.

Remove from the oven and let cool
completely on a wire rack. (At this
point the pie can be stored in an
airtight container in the fridge for up
to 2 days.)

In a large bowl with a whisk, or in a
stand mixer fitted with a whisk
attachment, combine the cream,
confectioners' sugar, cornstarch,
and remaining 1 teaspoon lime zest
and whip until the cream is firm but
not too stiff — you want it to be
billowing and fluffy but whipped

enough to hold its shape when you pipe it. Fill a pastry bag fitted with a large star tip with the whipped cream and pipe rows of S-shapes, shingling each row next to the previous one, across the top of the pie. Alternatively, spread the whipped cream on top of the pie and smooth it out with an offset spatula. Serve immediately.

The pie can be stored in an airtight container in the fridge for up to 1 day.

Brown Sugar Graham Cracker Pie Shell

MAKES ONE 9-INCH PIE SHELL

16 squares/**130 grams** graham crackers

3 tablespoons firmly packed/**40 grams** light brown sugar

¼ teaspoon kosher salt

3 tablespoons/**45 grams** unsalted butter, melted

Preheat the oven to 350°F and place a rack in the center of the oven.

In a food processor, grind the graham crackers, brown sugar, and salt into fine crumbs. Pour the crumbs into a large bowl and add the butter. Stir with a wooden spoon or mix using your hands until the crust comes together. Press the crust evenly over the bottom and up the sides of a 9-inch ceramic, glass, or aluminum pie plate. Bake for 15 to 18 minutes, rotating the pan midway through the baking time, until the shell is golden brown and baked through. Remove from the oven and let cool on a wire rack.

The shell can be stored, well wrapped, at room temperature for up to 1 week.

Double Lemon Cream Tart

MAKES ONE 10-INCH TART, TO SERVE 10

1 recipe Master Pâte Sucrée (page 437)

1½ recipes/about 3½ cups/ **1,125 grams** Master Lemon Curd (page 435)

½ cup/1 stick/**115 grams** unsalted butter, cut into 8 pieces, at room temperature

2 large egg whites (about ¼ cup/**60 grams**), at room temperature

½ cup/**100 grams** sugar

⅛ teaspoon pure vanilla extract

1 teaspoon grated lemon zest, for garnish

Our lemon curd is bracingly tart. We used to make lemon bars from this curd at Flour, and I instructed the staff to make sure guests knew how lemony they were so they would be prepared. My mom, who happens to dislike lemon, took it one step further. For the first three months or so after we opened, she worked the pastry counter; when a guest ordered a lemon bar, she would advise them against it. "They are very lemony! Very sour! Get something else!" I couldn't understand why the bars were not selling until I overheard Mom directing yet another customer to a pop tart or brownie instead. Mooooooom! I loved those bars (still do), but here is a variation that even my lemon-averse mom enjoys. In this tart you make two layers of lemon: the first is the original lemon bar lemon curd (pucker up!) and the second is the curd made richer and creamier and super luscious with a deca-dent amount of butter. The butter is emulsified into the lemon curd to create a lemon pudding–like layer that tempers the straight curd. Topping the tart with meringue stars turns this dessert into a gussied-up lemon meringue pie.

Make the pâte sucrée. Remove it from the refrigerator about 15 minutes before using to soften slightly, and unwrap it. Using a rolling pin, press the dough to flatten it into a disk about ½ inch thick. Generously flick flour over the work surface and dough, and carefully roll out the disk into a circle about 12 inches in diameter. Make sure the surface you are rolling on is well floured so the dough does not stick to it; likewise, make sure the disk is floured well enough to keep the rolling pin from sticking to it. Roll from the center of the disk outward and gently rotate the disk 90 degrees (a quarter-turn) after each roll to ensure the disk gets stretched out evenly into a nice circle. Use a bench scraper to help you move the dough by scraping underneath the dough and moving it around. Don't worry if the dough breaks a bit, especially toward the edges. You can easily patch these tears up once you've lined the tart pan.

Once the dough circle is about 12 inches in diameter, dock it with a pastry docker (see page 24) or by poking it all over with a fork. Roll it gently around the rolling pin, then unfurl it over a 10-inch tart pan. Press the dough into the tart pan, taking care to press it into the corners. Trim the edge of the dough even with the top of the tart pan. Use any scraps or odd pieces to patch up any tears or missing bits. Make sure the entire tart pan is completely covered with dough, and press one last time all the way around to ensure that any holes have been patched up.

Refrigerate the tart shell for at least 30 minutes to let the dough rest (the gluten needs a little time to relax so it doesn't shrink in the oven). (At this point you can wrap the tart shell well in plastic wrap and refrigerate for up to 3 days or freeze it for up to 2 weeks. If frozen, thaw in the fridge overnight before proceeding.)

Preheat the oven to 350°F and place a rack in the center of the oven. Place the tart pan on a baking sheet and bake the tart shell for 25 to 30 minutes, rotating the baking sheet midway through the baking time, until the shell is golden brown all around. Remove it from the oven and let cool on the baking sheet on a wire rack. Keep the oven on. (At this point, the tart shell can be stored, well wrapped, at room temperature for up to 1 week.)

Make the lemon curd. Scrape about 1½ cups/485 grams of the lemon curd into the baked tart shell and spread it evenly to cover the bottom of the shell. (The curd can be used hot.) Bake until the curd is set, about 15 minutes, rotating the baking sheet midway through the baking time. When you jiggle the baking sheet, the curd should no longer be wobbly, and there will be small bubbles along its edge. Remove the tart from the oven and let cool to room temperature.

If the curd was made ahead and is cold, gently warm up the remaining 2 cups/640 grams curd to room temperature in a small saucepan. Use a handheld electric mixer, immersion blender, or stand mixer fitted with a whisk attachment to mix in the butter, about 1 tablespoon at a time, waiting until each bit is totally mixed in before adding the next. The curd will get creamy and lighter in color.

When the tart is cooled to room temperature, spread the creamy, buttery curd on top in an even layer. Refrigerate for at least 6 hours to firm up the fillings.

Right before serving, whisk together the egg whites, sugar, and vanilla in a medium metal or heatproof glass bowl to make a thin slurry. Place the bowl over a small pot of simmering water and whisk for a few minutes, until the mixture is very hot to the touch. Scrape the whites into a stand mixer fitted with a whisk attachment and whip on high speed until the whites turn into a shiny, glossy meringue that holds stiff peaks and the mixture is cool, about 5 minutes. Fill a pastry bag fitted with a small star tip with the meringue and pipe small and large stars randomly across the surface of the tart. Use a blowtorch to brown the tops of the stars, or place the tart under the broiler for a minute or two until the meringue stars start to brown. Garnish with the lemon zest. Place one hand under the base of the tart and push it up and out of the outer ring. Transfer the tart to a flat serving plate. Slice into thin wedges and serve.

The tart can be stored in the fridge, well wrapped, for up to 2 days.

Cherry Crumb Pie

MAKES ONE 9-INCH PIE

1 recipe Master Single-Crust Pâte Brisée (page 438)

Butter Crumbs (page 244)

3 pounds/**1,360 grams** fresh sweet cherries, stemmed and pitted (about 6 cups/**750 grams** pitted)

½ cup/**100 grams** sugar

¼ cup/**30 grams** cornstarch

½ teaspoon pure vanilla extract

¼ teaspoon kosher salt

When I see cherries in the grocery store, I know it is really summer. In Boston, prior to cherry season, summer days can sometimes still get breezy and downright chilly. But the arrival of cherries means the hot sun is finally shining all day long, and that's when I jump to making as many things with cherries as I can—as well as eating as many as I can. For this crumb pie you make a buttery crumb mixture that you partially bake in advance so that it doesn't get too soggy. Some of the crumbs bake into the cherry juice and get all soft and jammy and some brown into more of a crunchy streusel top. The season is short; I make up for it by making this pie as often as I can.

Make the pâte brisée. Remove it from the fridge about 15 minutes before using it to soften slightly.

Generously flick flour over the work surface and roll out the pâte brisée into a circle about 11 inches wide. Dock it with a pastry docker (see page 24) or by poking it all over with a fork. Invert a 9-inch ceramic, glass, or aluminum pie plate on top of the circle and trim the dough neatly and evenly so it is about an inch larger than the pie plate all around. Turn the pie plate right side up and press the dough circle into it, across the bottom and up the sides, allowing the edge of the dough to fall over the edge of the pie plate. Use any scraps or odd pieces to patch up any tears or missing bits. Make sure the entire pie plate is completely covered with

dough and press one last time all the way around to ensure that any holes have been patched up. Pleat the dough with your thumb and forefinger for a pretty edge, or trim the dough neatly so it overhangs the pie plate about ½ inch all the way around. Refrigerate the pie shell for at least 30 minutes. (At this point you can wrap the pie shell well in plastic wrap and refrigerate for up to 1 day or freeze it for up to 2 weeks. If frozen, thaw in the fridge overnight before proceeding.)

Preheat the oven to 350°F and place a rack in the center of the oven.

Remove the pie shell from the fridge, place it on a baking sheet, and line it with parchment paper. Pour pie weights, uncooked beans, or uncooked rice directly onto the parchment; fill the pie shell all the way to the top. Blind bake the pie shell (see page 21) for 35 to 45 minutes, rotating the baking sheet midway through the baking time, until light brown all the way through. (You will have to lift up the parchment and pie weights to peek at the shell.) Remove from the oven and let cool on a wire rack. When the pie weights have cooled down, remove them carefully from the pie shell and discard the parchment.

While the pie shell is baking, make the butter crumbs. Set aside.

In a large bowl, combine the cherries, sugar, cornstarch, vanilla, and salt. Toss well to combine. Pour the cherries into the pie shell and gently press the cherries down to fill the shell. Sprinkle evenly with the butter crumbs. Place the pie on a baking sheet to catch any drips and bake for 1 hour to 1 hour 10 minutes, rotating the baking sheet midway through the baking time, until the butter crumbs are golden brown and the cherries are starting to bubble. Remove from the oven and let cool completely on a wire rack before serving.

Cherry pie can be stored at room temperature, well wrapped, for up to 2 days.

Butter Crumbs

MAKES ABOUT 1¾ CUPS/260 GRAMS

4 tablespoons/½ stick/**60 grams** unsalted butter

1 cup/**120 grams** cake flour, sifted after measuring

3 tablespoons firmly packed/**40 grams** light brown sugar

3 tablespoons/**40 grams** superfine sugar

¼ teaspoon ground cinnamon

¼ teaspoon ground ginger

¼ teaspoon kosher salt

—

Preheat the oven to 350°F and place a rack in the center of the oven. Line a baking sheet with parchment paper and set it aside.

Melt the butter in a small saucepan or in the microwave. Place the cake flour, brown sugar, superfine sugar, cinnamon, ginger, and salt in a medium bowl and drizzle the melted butter on top. Stir with a rubber spatula or wooden spoon until the butter is mostly mixed into the flour mixture. Continue mixing with your hands until all the ingredients come together into crumbs and are clumpy. Break apart any large clumps. Spread the crumbs on the prepared baking sheet and bake for about 15 minutes, just until they start to bake through a bit. Remove from the oven and let cool.

Butter crumbs can be stored in an airtight container in the fridge for up to 1 month.

Bittersweet Chocolate-Orange
Truffle Tart with Salted Caramel

MAKES ONE 8-INCH TART, TO SERVE 8 TO 10

1 recipe Master Pâte Sucrée (page 437)

Salted Caramel Sauce for Truffle Tart (page 246)

Candied Orange Slices (page 248)

¾ cup/**180 grams** heavy cream

½ cup/**120 grams** whole milk

1 tablespoon grated orange zest (about 1 large orange)

8 ounces/**225 grams** excellent-quality bittersweet chocolate, finely chopped

2 large egg yolks (about **40 grams**), at room temperature

2 tablespoons/**30 grams** unsalted butter, at room temperature

¼ teaspoon kosher salt

They say you can't judge a book by its cover but try to square that with the adage "You eat with your eyes." One of the tarts I love to eat most is a decadent chocolate truffle tart. It is velvety smooth and very classic. Dusted with cocoa powder, it's simple and elegant. For special occasions I love to dress up this tart a few ways—first by adding a thin, rich layer of salted caramel and then by topping it off with shimmering slices of glossy candied orange. It looks way more complicated and involved than it really is, especially when you realize that every component can be made in advance. This is the dessert to make when you want to impress your in-laws or your favorite person.

Make the pâte sucrée. Make the caramel sauce and candied orange slices, and set aside.

Remove the pâte sucrée from the refrigerator, unwrap it, and let it soften for about 15 minutes at room temperature. You have about 15 minutes when the dough reaches the perfect rolling temperature: not so cold that it breaks when you roll it, but not so warm that it sticks to everything. Using a rolling pin, bang and flatten the dough into a disk about ½ inch thick. If the dough is too cold, keep pressing it with the rolling pin to flatten and soften. If it's too warm, place it back in the fridge so it firms up a bit, or roll it out between two large sheets of parchment paper. Lightly flick flour over the work surface and the dough and carefully roll out the disk into a circle 10 inches in diameter. Make sure the surface you are rolling on is well floured so that the dough does not stick to it; likewise, make sure the disk itself is floured well enough to keep the rolling pin from sticking to it. Roll from the center of the disk outward and gently rotate the disk 90 degrees (a quarter-turn) after each roll to ensure that the disk gets stretched out evenly into a nice circle. Don't worry if the dough breaks a bit, especially toward the edges. You can easily patch these tears up once you've lined the tart pan.

Once the dough circle is 10 inches in diameter, use a fork to poke a few holes in the dough. (Don't poke too many holes, or the shell will not hold the caramel in place.) Roll it gently around the rolling pin, then unfurl it over an 8-inch tart pan set on on a baking sheet. Press the dough well over the bottom and up the sides of the tart pan. Trim the edge of the dough even with the edge of the tart pan. Use any scraps or odd pieces to patch up any tears or missing bits. Make sure the entire tart pan is completely covered with dough; press one last time all the way around to ensure that any holes have been patched up.

Refrigerate the tart shell for at least 30 minutes to let the dough rest. (At this point you can wrap the tart shell well in plastic wrap and refrigerate for up to 1 day or freeze it for up to 2 weeks. If frozen, thaw the shell overnight in the fridge before proceeding.)

Preheat the oven to 350°F and place a rack in the center of the oven. Bake the tart shell on the baking sheet for 30 minutes, rotating the baking sheet midway through the baking time, until the bottom is golden brown. Remove the tart shell from the oven and let cool on a wire rack. (At this point, the tart shell can be stored, well wrapped, at room temperature for up to 5 days.)

In a small saucepan, combine the cream, milk, and orange zest and heat over medium-high heat until just before it comes to a boil, when small bubbles have started to form around the edge of the pan. Place the chopped chocolate in a medium metal or heatproof glass bowl. Pour the hot cream mixture through a fine-mesh sieve over the chocolate and let stand for about 1 minute, then whisk gently until the chocolate is completely melted and the mixture is thoroughly combined. Slowly whisk in the egg yolks one by one. Add the butter and salt and whisk until the butter is completely mixed in. Let the chocolate filling sit at room temperature for about 1 hour until it thickens up and is no longer completely liquid. (The chocolate filling can be stored in an airtight container in the fridge for up to 3 days. Warm it so it is spreadable before using.)

Place the tart shell on a baking sheet and pour the salted caramel into the shell. Let the caramel fully cool until it doesn't move around when you tilt the baking sheet. Pour the cooled chocolate filling into the shell over the caramel. It should come to the top of the shell.

Salted Caramel Sauce for Truffle Tart

MAKES A SCANT 1 CUP

1 cup/**200 grams** sugar

½ cup/**120 grams** heavy cream

1 teaspoon kosher salt

Place the sugar in a small saucepan and slowly pour in about ⅓ cup/ 80 grams water. Stir gently to moisten the sugar. Brush the sides of the pan with a pastry brush dipped in water if there are any sugar crystals clinging to the pan. Place the saucepan over high heat and bring the syrup to a boil. Don't stir the mixture once it's on the heat and don't jostle the pan (you want to avoid crystallization of the syrup, which can happen if the pan is disturbed while the syrup is coming to a boil).

Let the syrup boil rapidly without moving the pan until it starts to caramelize, 1 to 2 minutes. The sugar syrup will boil furiously at first, then slowly thicken as the water boils off. Some of the syrup around the edge will start to color to a golden yellow like a butterscotch candy — at this point swirl the pan to even out the coloring and caramelization. As soon as the caramel is a deep golden brown like dark maple syrup (it may even start to smoke a bit), immediately reduce the heat to low and slowly and carefully add the cream. (Be careful — the steam that rises when the cream hits the caramel is extremely hot.) Let the caramel and cream sputter for a few seconds, until the sputtering settles down, then turn the heat back up to medium and whisk until it all comes together, about 10 seconds. Add the salt and stir to combine.

Caramel sauce can be stored in an airtight container in the fridge for up to 2 weeks. Rewarm until it is pourable before using.

Lay the circles on the prepared baking sheet (they won't all fit at once so lay out as many as you can). Whisk the egg for the egg wash in a small bowl with a fork. Use a pastry brush to brush the egg wash over the perimeter of one circle. Place 2 heaping tablespoons of the blueberry filling in the middle of the circle. Carefully fold the circle over the filling to make a half-moon, keeping the filling inside, and press firmly around the edge of the circle to seal. Repeat to fill the remaining circles. (At this point you can freeze the hand pies on the baking sheet until solid, transfer them to an airtight container, and store in the freezer for up to 2 weeks. When you're ready to bake the pies, remove them from the freezer and bake as instructed, adding up to 5 minutes to the baking time.)

Brush the tops of the hand pies with the remaining egg wash and sprinkle them evenly with the sanding sugar. Bake for 35 to 45 minutes, rotating the baking sheet midway through the baking time, until the pies are evenly golden brown. Remove from the oven and let cool.

Hand pies should be enjoyed the same day they are baked, but they can be stored in an airtight container at room temperature overnight. If you're serving them the next day, refresh them in a 300°F oven for about 8 minutes.

Fresh Peach Crostatas

**MAKES 6 CROSTATAS, EACH ENOUGH FOR ONE VERY HUNGRY PERSON
OR FOR TWO MODERATELY HUNGRY PEOPLE TO SHARE**

1 recipe Master Double-Crust
Pâte Brisée (page 439)

About ½ recipe/1 cup/
210 grams Master Frangipane
(page 433)

2¼ pounds/**1,020 grams** ripe
fresh peaches (about
7 medium), pitted and sliced
thinly (about 5 cups)

⅓ cup/**70 grams**
superfine sugar

5 tablespoons/**40 grams**
cornstarch

½ teaspoon pure
vanilla extract

¼ teaspoon kosher salt

1 large egg (about **50 grams**),
for egg wash

2 teaspoons sanding sugar

I learned how to make the best free-form open-faced crostatas from my very first pastry chef and mentor, Rick Katz. During the holidays we roasted cases and cases of pears with lots of butter and ginger and sugar and baked large pear crostatas that were more popular than pumpkin and pecan and apple pies. I took that lesson with me and we now make hundreds of pear crostatas at Flour every Thanksgiving and Christmas. But don't make these just in the winter months. What makes these crostatas so incredible is the flaky, buttery pie dough. Once you master this dough, you can—and should—make any fruit into a crostata, like I do here with fragrant, juicy peaches. Line the crostatas with almond cream and pile them high with as much ripe fruit as you can fit.

Did you know that inside the peach pit is a little kernel that tastes almost exactly like an almond? This commonality makes peaches (and all other stone fruits) a natural pairing with almonds. The flavors go remarkably well together, making these fresh peach crostatas my favorite.

Make the pâte brisée. Make the frangipane and set aside. Line a baking sheet with parchment paper and set it aside. Remove the pâte brisée from the fridge about 15 minutes before using it to soften slightly.

Divide the pâte brisée into 6 equal pieces and press them with your hands into small, flat disks about 4 inches in diameter. Generously flick flour over the work surface and roll each disk into a circle about 8 inches in diameter. Be sure to flour the pâte brisée as well as the work surface as you are rolling so the dough doesn't stick to the rolling pin or the work surface. Start from the center of the disk and roll outward, then rotate the disk 90 degrees (a quarter-turn) and repeat. Keep doing this until the circle is around 8 inches across and fairly thin.

In a large bowl, combine the peaches, superfine sugar, cornstarch, vanilla, and salt and toss with your hands to combine them all together.

Use the back of a spoon or a small offset spatula to spread about 1½ tablespoons of the frangipane in the middle of each of the dough circles, leaving a 2-inch border.

Pile the peaches in the center of the dough circles on top of the frangipane, distributing the fruit evenly and layering and shingling the slices nicely. Working your way around each circle, fold the exposed dough in toward the center, folding it over the peaches, until you have 5 or 6 pleats and just the center is exposed, with a bit of peach peeking through. Carefully transfer the assembled crostatas to the prepared baking sheet. Refrigerate for at least 1 hour before baking. (At this point, the crostatas can be covered well with plastic wrap and refrigerated for up to 1 day.)

Preheat the oven to 350°F and place a rack in the center of the oven. Whisk the egg for the egg wash in a small bowl with a fork. Use a pastry brush to brush the egg wash all over the crostatas, then sprinkle evenly with the sanding sugar. Bake for 1 hour 10 minutes to 1 hour 20 minutes, rotating the baking sheet midway through the baking time, until the pleats in the crostatas are golden brown. Make sure the folds are all completely browned so that you don't have any chewy under-baked bits of dough in the crostatas.

Remove the crostatas from the oven and let cool on a wire rack for about 2 hours. Serve warm or at room temperature.

The crostatas can be stored at room temperature in an airtight container for up to 2 days.

S'mores Pie

MAKES ONE 9-INCH PIE

Milk Chocolate Graham
Cracker Pie Shell
(page 262)

2 cups/**480 grams**
heavy cream

4 ounces/**115 grams** milk
chocolate, finely chopped
(about ¾ cup)

1 ounce/**30 grams** bittersweet
or semisweet chocolate, finely
chopped (scant 3 tablespoons)

1 tablespoon brewed coffee

4 large egg yolks (about **80
grams**), at room temperature

2 tablespoons/**30 grams** sugar

½ teaspoon kosher salt

¼ teaspoon pure
vanilla extract

Marshmallow Meringue
(page 262)

In my first book, *Flour*, I share the recipe for a lemon meringue pie that I tested on one of my closest friends, Jenn, and her family. Her son Matthew was around five at the time and he loved the pie so much he asked if I could stay in their spare bedroom forever so I could make him this pie. Fast-forward a decade and Matthew is now a strapping teenager taller than his mom and me. When I told him about my new book he immediately made the suggestion of a s'mores pie. I loved this idea! I tweaked my favorite milk chocolate pot de crème recipe from my Rialto days and baked it in a graham cracker crust. Billowing piles of Swiss meringue are piled on top and torched with a blowtorch to give the characteristic burnt marshmallow flavor. I presented this to Matthew as a parting gift before he left for boarding school, and he proclaimed it his new favorite pie.

Make the pie shell and set it aside.

Preheat the oven to 350°F and place a rack in the center of the oven.

In a medium saucepan, heat the cream over medium-high heat until just before it comes to a boil, when small bubbles have started to form around the edge of the pan. Place the milk and dark chocolates together in a small metal or heat-proof glass bowl and set the bowl over a pot of simmering water, stirring occasionally until the chocolate is melted and the mixture is well combined. Remove the bowl from over the water. Pour the hot cream over the melted chocolate, add the coffee, and whisk until thoroughly combined.

Place the egg yolks in a medium bowl and slowly whisk in the sugar. Using a small ladle, ladle a little of the hot cream mixture into the egg yolk mixture; whisk it in to temper the eggs (see page 29). Continue adding the hot cream mixture to the egg yolk mixture until it is all combined.

Pour the pudding back into the saucepan and place it on the stove over medium-low heat. Cook slowly, stirring continuously with a wooden spoon or rubber spatula for 5 to 6 minutes, until the pudding thickens and when you swipe a finger across the back of the spoon, the pudding holds the line. (First the mixture will be liquid and loose, then as you continue to stir, the mixture at the

Milk Chocolate Graham Cracker Pie Shell

MAKES ONE 9-INCH PIE SHELL

16 squares/**130 grams** graham crackers

2 tablespoons/**25 grams** sugar

⅛ teaspoon kosher salt

3 tablespoons/**45 grams**
unsalted butter, melted

2 tablespoons finely chopped milk chocolate
(about 1½ ounces/**40 grams**)

Preheat the oven to 350°F and place a rack in the center of the oven.

In a food processor, grind the graham crackers, sugar, and salt into fine crumbs. Pour the crumbs into a large bowl and add the melted butter. Stir with a wooden spoon until the mixture comes together. Press the crumb mixture evenly over the bottom and up the sides of a 9-inch ceramic, glass, or aluminum pie plate. Bake for 12 to 15 minutes, rotating the pie plate midway through the baking time, until the shell is golden brown and baked through. Remove from the oven and immediately sprinkle the milk chocolate evenly over the shell; let the residual heat of the shell melt the chocolate. Using a pastry brush, spread the melted chocolate evenly over the shell. This gives the shell some protection from the filling and helps keep it crispy.

The shell can be made up to 1 week in advance and stored, well wrapped, at room temperature.

Marshmallow Meringue

MAKES 6 TO 8 CUPS

4 large egg whites (about ½ cup/**120 grams**),
at room temperature

⅔ cup/**135 grams** sugar

1 teaspoon pure vanilla extract

Pinch of kosher salt

In a medium metal or heatproof glass bowl, whisk together the egg whites, sugar, vanilla, and salt. Place the bowl over a pot of simmering water and whisk until the mixture is hot to the touch, about 4 minutes. (You will know when it is ready when you stick your finger in it and automatically say OUCH.) Pour the mixture into a stand mixer fitted with a whisk attachment and whip on high speed for 6 to 8 minutes, until the meringue is glossy, shiny, and cool to the touch. Use immediately.

the pie shell and bake for about 20 minutes, until the edges of the pudding start to set.

Remove the pie from the oven and let cool on a wire rack for about 15 minutes. Refrigerate the pie for at least 4 hours before topping. (At this point, the untopped pie can be stored in an airtight container in the refrigerator for up to 2 days.)

Make the marshmallow meringue. Pile it high on top of the pie and use the back of a spoon to make decorative spikes in the meringue. Using a blowtorch, caramelize the entire top of the pie until it is golden brown. If you do not have a torch, place the pie on a baking sheet under the broiler; rotate the sheet every few minutes until the meringue is toasted, 4 to 6 minutes total. Refrigerate the pie for at least 2 hours to firm up the meringue. Serve chilled. For the cleanest cutting, heat a long, thin knife under hot running water and dry with a towel, then slice the pie; reheat and dry the knife between slices.

Leftover pie can be stored in the fridge, well covered, for up to 1 day. The meringue will start to weep after that, so it's best eaten the same day it is made.

bottom of the pan will start to get a little thicker. Be sure to scrape the bottom of the pan with the spoon and stir continuously. The pudding will start to let off a little steam as it gets thicker. As soon as you see wisps of steam coming from the pan you know the pudding is getting close to done.) Immediately strain the pudding through a fine-mesh sieve into a clean heatproof bowl. Stir in the salt and vanilla. Pour the pudding directly into

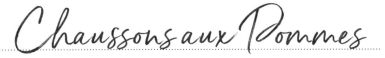

Chaussons aux Pommes

MAKES 6 CHAUSSONS

Growing up, I used to eat Pepperidge Farm apple turnovers on special Sundays when my mom felt indulgent. I learned to pop them in the toaster oven at a very early age and I loved watching the puff pastry slowly swell and turn golden brown. I rarely waited for them to cool before eating them and inevitably burned the roof of my mouth. But it was always worth it. These chaussons are the grown-up version of those turnovers. They are named after their oval shape (*chausson* is the French word for "slipper") and filled with a slightly chunky apple butter scented with vanilla. Careful scoring on the top gives them an impressive presentation. Be sure to bake them fully so you don't end up with chewy dough; the puff pastry should shatter and send flakes flying in a million directions when you bite into these.

Vanilla Apple Butter
(page 272)

⅔ recipe/1 pound/**455 grams** Master Puff Pastry Dough (page 442) or Master Quick Puff Pastry Dough (page 440), or 1 pound/**455 grams** store-bought all-butter puff pastry

1 large egg (about **50 grams**), for egg wash

1 firm tart apple (such as Granny Smith), peeled, cored, and sliced into ⅛-inch-thick slices (you'll need 18 to 24 slices)

1 large egg yolk (about **20 grams**), for egg wash

Make the apple butter and set it aside. Make the puff pastry.

Preheat the oven to 350°F and place a rack in the center of the oven. Line a baking sheet with parchment paper and set it aside.

Generously flick flour over the work surface and roll the puff pastry into a rectangle roughly 18 inches wide and 12 inches long. Use a 6-inch round cake pan or can as a template to cut six 6-inch circles from the puff pastry. Wrap the scraps and save them for another use. Give each circle a back-and-forth roll with the rolling pin to turn it into an 8-inch-long oval.

Whisk the whole egg for the egg wash in a small bowl with a fork. Use a pastry brush to brush the egg wash along the edge of each oval. Scoop about ¼ cup apple butter on one half of each oval, then shingle 3 or 4 slices of apple to cover the apple butter. Fold the oval in half and press down firmly along the edge to seal in the apples. Gently press down on the apples and apple butter to fill the chaussons fully. Arrange the chaussons on the prepared baking sheet. Refrigerate for about 15 minutes to rest and relax the puff pastry.

Add the egg yolk to the remaining egg wash and whisk it in with a fork. Use the pastry brush to carefully brush egg wash over each chausson. With a small sharp paring knife, trace a sun ray pattern on each chausson, starting at one corner of the chausson on the folded edge and tracing outward toward the edge in a curved pattern. Don't cut all the way through.

Bake for 40 to 50 minutes, rotating the baking sheet midway through the baking time, until the chaussons are golden brown on top and along the sides. Remove the chaussons from the oven and let cool on a wire rack.

Chaussons can be stored at room temperature, well wrapped in plastic wrap or in an airtight container, for up to 3 days. Refresh in a 300°F oven for 6 to 8 minutes before serving.

Vanilla Apple Butter

MAKES ABOUT 1½ CUPS

4 large tart apples (such as Granny Smith; about 2 pounds/**900 grams**), peeled, cored, and roughly chopped (about 4 cups)

⅔ cup/**135 grams** sugar

3 tablespoons/**45 grams** unsalted butter

Seeds scraped from ½ vanilla bean (see page 28)

Pinch of kosher salt

—

Place the apples, sugar, butter, vanilla seeds, and salt in a medium saucepan. Cook over low heat, stirring occasionally, until the apples break down and the mixture thickens and turns golden brown, 30 to 40 minutes. The apples will let out a lot of water at first and bubble a lot, then will slowly start to caramelize and get a bit darker. There may still be some large pieces of apple, which is fine. Remove from the heat and let cool.

Apple butter can be stored in an airtight container in the refrigerator for up to 4 days, or frozen for up to 2 weeks. Thaw before using.

Old-Fashioned
Double-Crust Apple Pie

MAKES ONE 9-INCH PIE, TO SERVE 8 PEOPLE

1 recipe Master Double-Crust Pâte Brisée (page 439)

4 or 5 medium Granny Smith apples, peeled, cored, and sliced ¼ to ½ inch thick (4 cups)

4 or 5 medium McIntosh or Rome apples, peeled, cored, and sliced ¼ to ½ inch thick (4 cups)

¾ cup firmly packed/**170 grams** light brown sugar

¼ cup/**35 grams** all-purpose flour

¼ teaspoon kosher salt

⅛ teaspoon ground cinnamon

⅛ teaspoon freshly grated nutmeg

1 tablespoon/**15 grams** unsalted butter, at room temperature

1 large egg (about **50 grams**), for egg wash

2 tablespoons sanding or pearl sugar

I've made lattice pies, crumb pies, bottom-crust-only pies—but my favorite is an old-fashioned double-crust pie. The double crust is easy to pull off, it allows for a higher (and thus to me, better) crust-to-fruit ratio, and it also shows off my super-flaky, tender pie crust. Macerating the apples softens them, which means you can pack more apples into your pie. The more fruit, the better! Nicole taught me the trick of dotting the apples with butter before covering them with the top crust, for a richer filling.

—

Make the pâte brisée. Remove it from the fridge about 15 minutes before using it to soften slightly.

Roll out three-quarters of the pâte brisée into a circle about ⅛ inch thick and 12 inches across. (Wrap the remaining dough in plastic and refrigerate to use for the top crust.) Dock it with a pastry docker (see page 24) or by poking it all over with a fork. Line a 9-inch ceramic, glass, or aluminum pie plate with the dough circle, leaving a ¼-inch-wide lip around the edge to allow for shrinkage in the oven. Refrigerate the pie shell for at least 30 minutes. (At this point you can wrap the pie shell well in plastic wrap and refrigerate for up to 1 day or freeze it for up to 2 weeks. If frozen, the pie shell can be baked straight from frozen.)

Preheat the oven to 325°F and place a rack in the center of the oven.

Combine the apples, brown sugar, flour, salt, cinnamon, and nutmeg in a medium bowl. Let macerate at room temperature for about 30 minutes. This softens the apples so you can pack more of them into the pie.

Remove the pie shell from the fridge and line it with parchment paper. Pour pie weights, dried beans, or uncooked rice directly onto the parchment; fill the pie shell all the way to the top. Blind bake the pie shell (see page 21) for about 30 minutes, rotating the pie pan midway through the baking time, until the shell is light brown all over. Remove from the oven and let cool on a wire rack. When the pie weights have cooled down enough, remove them carefully from the pie shell and discard the parchment.

Pile the apples and any juices into the pie shell, lightly pressing down to compact them. Dot the butter evenly

over the apples. Roll out the remaining dough into a circle about 9½ inches in diameter and use a fluted pastry wheel to give the dough a pretty edge. Drape it carefully over the apples. Press gently to adhere the dough to the edges of the pie crust. Score the top with five 2-inch slits to make a star shape.

Whisk the egg for the egg wash in a small bowl with a fork. Use a pastry brush to brush the egg wash on the top crust. Sprinkle with the sanding sugar. Place the pie on a baking sheet to catch any drips and bake for 1 hour 10 minutes to 1 hour 20 minutes, rotating the baking sheet midway through the baking time, until the top is evenly golden brown. Remove from the oven and let cool on a wire rack. Serve warm or at room temperature.

The pie can be stored in an airtight container at room temperature for up to 2 days.

Autumn Pear Tarte Tatin

MAKES ONE 9-INCH TART, TO SERVE 8 TO 10

About ¼ recipe/5½ ounces/
150 grams Master Puff Pastry
Dough (page 442) or Master
Quick Puff Pastry Dough (page
440), or 5½ ounces/**150 grams**
store-bought all-butter puff
pastry

1½ cups/**300 grams** sugar

6 tablespoons/¾ stick/
85 grams unsalted butter

2 teaspoons pure
vanilla extract

¼ teaspoon kosher salt

8 to 10 medium Bosc pears
(3 to 4 pounds/**1,360 to
1,820 grams**), peeled,
halved, and cored

1 cup/**240 grams** crème
fraîche, for serving

The oft-told story of the traditional tarte tatin is that in the 1800s in France, the Tatin sisters ran an inn together. One day one of the sisters forgot to put in the bottom crust when making her apple tart. She threw the crust on top and put the whole thing in the oven and crossed her fingers. When the tart came out of the oven she inverted it, and the butter and sugar had combined with the juice of the apples to create a rich caramel that sauced the whole tart. It's a classic recipe for many reasons: It's stunning; the buttery caramel slowly cooks down the apples into concentrated apple essence; the puff pastry bakes up flaky and crispy. Apples are traditional but you can make almost any fruit into a tatin. Here I use Bosc pears to show off their gorgeous bell shape. The original recipe instructs you to cook sugar and butter and fruit together in a cast-iron skillet on the stove to a deep caramel and then add the puff pastry and transfer the whole thing into the oven to finish. Lacking a cast-iron skillet, I make mine in a cake pan with a butter-sugar caramel that I've cooked ahead of time. It simplifies the process a bit and also allows me to regulate the color of the caramel coating.

Make the puff pastry. Line a baking sheet with parchment paper and set it aside.

Generously flick flour over the work surface and roll out the puff pastry to a 9-inch circle. Place the puff circle on the parchment-lined baking sheet and refrigerate for at least 30 minutes while you prepare the caramel and pears.

Generously butter a 9-inch cake pan or spray it with pan spray and set

aside. Don't use a springform pan; if you do, line it well with aluminum foil before buttering or spraying it. Preheat the oven to 400°F and place a rack in the center of the oven.

Place the sugar in a small saucepan and slowly pour in about ¾ cup/ 180 grams water. Stir gently to moisten the sugar. Brush the sides of the pan with a pastry brush dipped in water if there are any sugar crystals clinging to the side of the pan. Place the saucepan over high heat and bring the syrup to a boil. Don't stir the mixture once it's on the heat and don't jostle the pan — you want to avoid crystallization of the syrup, which can happen if the pan is disturbed while the syrup is coming to a boil.

Let the syrup boil rapidly without moving the pan until it starts to caramelize, 1 to 2 minutes. The sugar syrup will boil furiously at first, then slowly thicken as the water boils off. Some of the syrup around the edge will start to color to a golden yellow like a butterscotch candy — at this point swirl the pan to even out the coloring and caramelization. Turn the heat down to medium and keep swirling the saucepan gently until the caramel is a deep golden-brown amber, 5 to 6 minutes. Once the sugar has started to caramelize, watch it carefully. It may smoke a little bit, which is just fine. As soon as the caramel has reached a deep dark amber, immediately add the butter; watch out, as it will sputter and spatter. Whisk the butter into the caramel until the butter is completely incorporated. The caramel will seize up at first and get foamy; eventually the hardened caramel will melt and combine with the butter. Whisk in the vanilla and salt, and immediately pour the caramel into the prepared pan. Swirl the pan until the bottom is evenly coated with caramel.

Immediately place the pear halves in the cake pan, on their sides with their stems pointing toward the center. Then fill the center of the cake pan with pear halves, cut side up. Pack the pears in as tightly as you can;

they cook down and shrink a bit so don't be afraid to really pack them in there. Remove the puff pastry circle from the fridge and drape it on top of the pears; tuck the edges of the pastry into the pan. Bake for 1 hour to 1 hour 10 minutes, rotating the cake pan midway through the baking time, until the puff pastry is golden brown through and through.

Remove from the oven and let cool on a wire rack for at least 2 hours until it reaches room temperature. (This allows the caramel to thicken and the pears to cool so they'll hold their shape when you remove the tart from the pan.)

When the tart is no longer hot, tilt the cake pan a little; if there is a lot of juice, carefully drain it off by holding down the baked dough with one hand and gently tilting the pan so the juice can run out. Discard the juice. When most of the juice has been removed, place a large serving platter on top of the cake pan and quickly invert everything so the puff pastry circle is on the plate and the fruit is on top of it. Carefully lift off the cake pan. Rearrange the fruit if necessary, as sometimes it gets jostled loose and falls off the pastry. Serve with generous dollops of crème fraîche on the side.

Leftover tarte tatin can be stored in an airtight container at room temperature for up to 2 days. Refresh in a 300°F oven for 8 to 10 minutes before serving.

VARIATION: *To make the traditional apple tarte tatin, substitute 8 to 10 medium Granny Smith or other firm apple for the pears.*

Have your cake and eat it, too

Vanilla Bean Cupcakes
with Creamy Ginger Frosting / 281

Hummingbird Cupcakes / 283

Super Bowl Cupcakes / 287

Lemon Meringue Cupcakes / 289

Vegan Hostess Cupcakes / 293

Olive Oil Cake with Fresh Grapes / 297

Syrian Nutmeg Cake / 298

Japanese Cotton Cheesecake / 300

Plum Upside-Down Cake / 303

Ginger-Peach Crumb Cake / 306

Simple Lemon Spiral / 309

Eggnog Cheesecake with Gingerbread People / 312

Orange-Almond Pudding Cake
with Chocolate Ganache / 317

Funfetti Angel Food Cake / 319

Lamingtons / 323

Stone Fruit and Berry Financier Cake
with Toasted Meringue / 325

Strawberries and Cream Chiffon Cake / 329

Sarah's Adult Spice Cake / 333

Malted Chocolate Cake / 337

Ashley's Birthday Cake / 343

Passion Fruit Crêpe Cake / 349

CHAPTER 5

Let Them Eat Cake

Vanilla Bean Cupcakes
with Creamy Ginger Frosting

MAKES 12 JUMBO OR 16 REGULAR CUPCAKES

2 cups/**240 grams** cake flour, sifted after measuring

1⅓ cups/**270 grams** sugar

1 teaspoon baking powder

½ teaspoon baking soda

½ teaspoon kosher salt

½ cup/1 stick/**115 grams** unsalted butter, at cool room temperature

Seeds scraped from 1 vanilla bean (see page 28)

½ cup/**110 grams** vegetable oil (such as canola)

2 large eggs (about **100 grams**), at room temperature

2 large egg yolks (about **40 grams**), at room temperature

⅔ cup/**160 grams** fat-free buttermilk, at room temperature

Creamy Ginger Frosting (page 282)

One of the most gratifying parts of writing a cookbook is when a reader bakes something from your recipe successfully. After all, isn't that the whole point—to share your recipes so that others can replicate the things you love for the people they love? I hadn't really thought about how the bakers on my team might also fall into this camp. Sarah, one of our top pastry chefs at Flour, excitedly told me about how often she uses the Flour cookbook at home. She knows each of the recipes by heart inside and out from making them in grand scale at the bakery. But at home when she only wants to bake one cake, not forty, she turns to my book. She's got a creative streak and she mixes and matches the recipes to create her own. This cupcake recipe is a happy result. She took our vanilla cake recipe, turned it into a cupcake, and frosted it with a ginger-spiked version of our red velvet cupcake frosting. It's a tremendous combination.

—

Preheat the oven to 350°F and place a rack in the center of the oven. Line a 12-cup jumbo muffin tin or 16 cups of two 12-cup regular muffin tins with muffin papers, or butter and flour the cups. Set aside.

In a stand mixer fitted with a paddle attachment, mix the cake flour, sugar, baking powder, baking soda, and salt on low speed for about 30 seconds, until well combined. Add the butter in 5 or 6 increments and paddle on low for 3 to 4 minutes, until the butter is well incorporated into the flour mixture. The mixture will look like coarse meal, or if the butter is a little softer than room

temperature it may come together as a soft dough.

Place the vanilla seeds in a small bowl and add the oil, whole eggs, and egg yolks. Whisk until combined and the seeds are dispersed in the mixture. With the mixer on low, slowly pour the vanilla mixture into the flour-butter mixture. Turn the mixer up to medium and beat the batter for about 90 seconds. The batter will go from looking thick and clumpy and yellowish to light and fluffy and whitish. Stop the mixer once or twice and scrape down the sides and bottom of the bowl and the paddle to make sure all the ingredients are incorporated. Turn the mixer down to low and add the buttermilk. Beat on medium for about 30 seconds more. Again, scrape the bowl and paddle once or twice. Scoop the batter into the prepared muffin tin cups, filling them about three-quarters full.

Bake for 25 to 30 minutes, rotating the muffin tin(s) midway through the baking time, until the cupcakes are golden brown and bounce back when you press them in the middle, and a cake tester inserted into the middle of a cupcake comes out clean. Remove from the oven and let cool in the tin(s) on a wire rack.

While the cupcakes are baking, make the creamy ginger frosting.

Frost the cooled cupcakes and serve.

The cupcakes can be stored in an airtight container in the fridge for up to 2 days. Remove from the fridge a few hours before serving so the cupcakes and frosting are at room temperature when you serve them.

Creamy Ginger Frosting

MAKES ABOUT 2½ CUPS

1 cup/**240 grams** whole milk

¼ cup/**35 grams** all-purpose flour

1 cup/**200 grams** sugar

1 cup/2 sticks/**225 grams** unsalted butter, cut into cubes, at room temperature

1 tablespoon grated fresh ginger (about a 1-inch knob)

1¼ teaspoons ground ginger

1 teaspoon pure vanilla extract

¼ teaspoon kosher salt

In a medium saucepan over medium heat, whisk the milk and flour until the mixture starts to thicken and become pasty, 3 to 4 minutes. Once it becomes visibly thicker, count to 30 while continuously whisking. Remove from the heat and scrape it into a stand mixer fitted with a paddle attachment, or into a medium bowl and use a handheld electric mixer. Let it sit uncovered for about 1 hour at room temperature, paddling it every 10 minutes or so to help it cool off.

When it is room temperature, paddle the mixture on low speed and slowly add the sugar until it is incorporated. Add the butter piece by piece with the mixer on low until it is all added. Mix in the grated ginger, ground ginger, vanilla, and salt. Turn the speed up to medium and beat for 6 to 8 minutes. The frosting will look curdled and clumpy at first, then gradually it will start to look creamy. When the frosting is entirely smooth it is ready to use.

The frosting can be stored in an airtight container in the refrigerator for up to 1 week. Before using, transfer to a stand mixer fitted with a paddle attachment and beat to bring it back to a silky consistency; this will take a long time. It's best to remove it from the refrigerator about 8 hours in advance so that when you beat it again, it doesn't separate.

Hummingbird Cupcakes

¾ cup/**75 grams** pecan halves

1⅓ cups/**185 grams**
all-purpose flour

1 teaspoon baking powder

½ teaspoon baking soda

½ teaspoon kosher salt

¼ teaspoon ground cinnamon

1 cup plus 2 tablespoons/
225 grams sugar

2 large eggs (about **100 grams**),
at room temperature

½ cup/**110 grams** vegetable oil
(such as canola)

2 very ripe medium bananas,
mashed (about **200 grams**)

1 cup/**225 grams** crushed
pineapple, drained

2 tablespoons crème fraîche

1 teaspoon pure vanilla extract

Magic Sally Frosting
(page 284)

Hummingbird cake is the brilliant melding of soft banana cake and sweet crushed pineapple, slathered in tangy cream cheese frosting. It hails from Jamaica—the original recipe was included as part of a marketing effort in the late 1960s to encourage Americans to visit this beautiful, welcoming island. That recipe then appeared in *Southern Living* magazine—and it has become the most requested recipe in the magazine's history. It has been fittingly described as "the cake that doesn't last." You usually see these as a tall layered cake, but I prefer our recipe in cupcake form so you can get a higher (and better) frosting-to-cake ratio.

Preheat the oven to 350°F and place a rack in the center of the oven. Place the pecans on a baking sheet and toast for 8 to 10 minutes, until they are lightly toasted inside; break a few open to check. Remove from the oven and let cool. Leave the oven on. Chop the pecans into small pieces and set aside.

Line a 12-cup jumbo muffin tin or 18 cups of two 12-cup regular muffin tins with muffin papers, or butter and flour the cups. Set aside.

In a medium bowl, stir together the flour, baking powder, baking soda, salt, and cinnamon. In a stand mixer fitted with a whisk attachment, whip the sugar and eggs on medium-high speed until the mixture falls back onto itself in languid ribbons when you lift the whisk out of the bowl and wave it back and forth. Turn the mixer to low and slowly drizzle in the oil. Turn off the mixer and remove the bowl. Fold in the bananas, pineapple, crème fraîche, and vanilla.

Fold in the flour mixture and pecans until all the ingredients are well combined. Divide the batter evenly among the prepared muffin tin cups. Bake for 25 to 30 minutes, rotating the muffin tin(s) midway through the baking time, until the cupcakes are golden brown and bounce back when you press them in the middle, and a cake tester inserted into the middle of a cupcake comes out clean. Remove from the oven and let cool completely in the tin(s) on a wire rack.

While the cupcakes are baking, make the frosting.

Fill a pastry bag fitted with a star tip with the frosting (see page 24) and frost the cooled cupcakes. Serve.

The cupcakes can be stored in an airtight container in the fridge for up to 2 days. Remove a few hours before serving so the cupcakes and frosting are at room temperature when you serve them.

Magic Sally Frosting

MAKES ABOUT 3 CUPS

¾ cup plus 2 tablespoons/
7 ounces/**200 grams** cream
cheese, cut into small pieces

½ cup/**50 grams**
superfine sugar

1 large egg white
(about **30 grams**),
at room temperature

14 tablespoons/1¾ sticks/
200 grams unsalted butter,
cut into small pieces, at cool
room temperature

1 cup/**120 grams**
confectioners' sugar

½ teaspoon pure
vanilla extract

¼ teaspoon kosher salt

"Magic buttercream" is what we at Flour call Swiss meringue buttercream, because it's so easy to make and use, it is like magic. Early on in her Flour career, Nicole took a trip to Paris. A song in a French department store with a chorus that sounded like "Sally . . . Sally Sally cream cheese!" caught her ear; when she returned, she renamed our cream cheese frosting "Sally" and it stuck. (To this day we have not figured out exactly what the song really said.) Mix the two together to make a silky, creamy, fluffy frosting that goes great on pretty much everything.

—

Microwave the cream cheese for 30 seconds on medium power, or leave it out in a warm place for at least 4 hours to soften.

In a small metal or heatproof glass bowl, whisk together the superfine sugar and egg white to make a thick slurry. Place the bowl over a small pot of simmering water (make sure the pot is big enough that the bowl sits above the water and not directly touching it, or you may end up with scrambled egg whites) and whisk occasionally until the mixture is hot to the touch, 2 to 3 minutes. (When you stick your finger in the mixture it should be so hot you immediately remove your finger.) It will thin out a bit as the sugar melts.

Pour the sugar–egg white mixture into a stand mixer fitted with a whisk attachment. Whip on medium-high speed for 4 to 6 minutes, until the mixture cools. Add the butter and

whip on medium until the butter is thoroughly incorporated. Add the cream cheese and beat on medium, scraping the sides of the bowl and the paddle a few times, until thoroughly combined. Add the confectioners' sugar, vanilla, and salt and whip on medium until the frosting is smooth and satiny.

The frosting can be stored in an airtight container in the refrigerator for up to 2 weeks. Before using, place the frosting in a stand mixer fitted with a paddle attachment and mix until the frosting smooths out again. It will look broken and curdled for a while until it warms up, but don't panic — just keep beating it and be patient.

Super Bowl Cupcakes

MAKES 8 JUMBO OR 12 REGULAR CUPCAKES

½ cup/**60 grams** Dutch-processed cocoa powder

1½ ounces/**40 grams** semisweet chocolate chunks, roughly chopped, or chocolate chips (about ¼ cup)

1 cup/**240 grams** boiling water

2 cups/**240 grams** cake flour, sifted after measuring

1⅓ cups/**265 grams** sugar

1 teaspoon baking powder

½ teaspoon baking soda

½ teaspoon kosher salt

1 cup/2 sticks/**225 grams** unsalted butter, at room temperature

¼ cup/**60 grams** crème fraîche

2 large eggs (about **100 grams**), at room temperature

2 large egg yolks (about **40 grams**), at room temperature

Peanut Butter Frosting (page 288)

1 cup/**50 grams** pretzel twists

2 cups/**45 grams** Ruffles-style potato chips, crushed slightly

2 ounces/**60 grams** milk chocolate, roughly chopped into small ¼-inch pieces (⅓ cup)

I am hardly a sports fan, but you can't live in New England and not get caught up in the rabid fanaticism that surrounds the Patriots (or the Red Sox or the Celtics or the Bruins). Boston is a sports town and I've grown to love helping our innumerable fans celebrate all the big championship games. When I first suggested a chocolate cupcake covered in peanuts and pretzels and potato chips, Nicole looked at me sideways. I didn't grow up with typical American junk food and she knows I don't have a taste for it. But Christopher is in his element in the chips aisle at the supermarket and when he proposed this for our annual Super Bowl menu I knew it would be a winner. They are salty and sweet and nutty and chocolatey and you'll win every food Super Bowl with these.

Combine the cocoa powder and semisweet chocolate in a small heatproof bowl. Pour the boiling water over them and whisk until the mixture is completely combined and smooth. Set aside and let cool (about 2 hours at room temperature or 30 minutes in the refrigerator, whisking every 10 minutes if refrigerated).

Preheat the oven to 350°F and place a rack in the center of the oven. Line a 12-cup regular muffin tin or 8 cups of a 12-cup jumbo muffin tin with muffin papers, or butter and flour the cups. Set aside.

In a stand mixer fitted with a paddle attachment, combine the cake flour, sugar, baking powder, baking soda, and salt on low speed for about 10

seconds, until thoroughly mixed. With the mixer on low, add the butter in small pieces and mix until the butter is completely incorporated, 30 to 40 seconds, and the mixture resembles dough. In a separate bowl, whisk together the crème fraîche, whole eggs, and egg yolks. With the mixer on low, pour the crème fraîche mixture into the flour mixture. Turn the mixer up to medium-high and beat for about 1 minute, until the batter is fluffy and light. Stop the mixer a few times and scrape down the sides and bottom of the bowl and the paddle. Turn the mixer to low and slowly pour in the chocolate mixture. Mix for about 10 seconds to combine. Scrape the sides and bottom of the bowl and the paddle, then mix on medium for about 30 seconds, until the chocolate is thoroughly incorporated.

Fill the prepared muffin tin cups about three-quarters full with the batter. Bake for 25 to 35 minutes, rotating the muffin tin midway through the baking time, until the centers of the cupcakes spring back when you poke them and a cake tester inserted into the middle of a cupcake comes out clean.

Remove from the oven and let cool briefly in the tin on a wire rack. Remove from the tin when cool enough to handle, remove the muffin papers if you used them, and let the cupcakes cool completely.

While the cupcakes are cooling, make the frosting.

Spread the cupcakes with generous heaping spoonfuls of the frosting. Garnish the cupcakes with the pretzels, potato chips, and milk chocolate pieces. Serve immediately or store in an airtight container at room temperature for up to 2 days. GO PATS!

Peanut Butter Frosting

MAKES ABOUT 4 CUPS, ENOUGH TO FROST 12 REGULAR CUPCAKES AND HAVE EXTRA TO SNACK ON WHILE FROSTING

⅔ cup/**135 grams** superfine sugar

2 large egg whites (about ¼ cup/**60 grams**), at room temperature

1 cup/2 sticks/**225 grams** unsalted butter, cut into small pieces, at room temperature

1 cup/**120 grams** confectioners' sugar

2 tablespoons whole milk

1 teaspoon pure vanilla extract

¼ teaspoon kosher salt

1 cup/**260 grams** crunchy peanut butter

In a small metal or heatproof glass bowl, whisk together the superfine sugar and egg whites to make a thick slurry. Place the bowl over a small pot of simmering water (make sure the pot is small enough that the bowl sits above the water and not directly touching it, or you may end up with scrambled egg whites) and cook, whisking occasionally, until the mixture is hot to the touch. (When you stick your finger in the mixture it should be so hot you immediately remove your finger.) It will thin out a bit as the sugar melts.

Pour the sugar–egg white mixture into a stand mixer fitted with a whisk attachment. Whip on medium-high speed for 4 to 6 minutes, until the mixture cools. Add the butter and whip on medium until the butter is thoroughly incorporated, 3 to 4 minutes. Add the confectioners' sugar, milk, vanilla, and salt. Whip on medium until the mixture is smooth and satiny. Add the peanut butter and whip until fluffy and well combined.

The frosting can be stored in an airtight container at room temperature for up to 3 days or in the refrigerator for up to 2 weeks. Before using, place the frosting in a stand mixer fitted with a paddle attachment and mix until it smooths out again.

Lemon Meringue Cupcakes

MAKES 8 JUMBO OR 12 REGULAR CUPCAKES

About ½ recipe/1 cup/
280 grams Master Lemon
Curd (page 435)

2 cups/**240 grams** cake flour,
sifted after measuring

1⅓ cups/**270 grams** sugar

1 teaspoon baking powder

½ teaspoon kosher salt

¼ teaspoon baking soda

½ cup/1 stick/**115 grams**
unsalted butter, at room
temperature

2 tablespoons grated lemon
zest (about 2 large lemons)

½ cup/**110 grams** vegetable oil
(such as canola)

2 large eggs (about **100 grams**),
at room temperature

2 large egg yolks (about
40 grams), at room
temperature

1 teaspoon pure vanilla extract

⅔ cup/**180 grams**
fat-free buttermilk, at room
temperature

Fluffy Marshmallow Frosting
(page 290)

We sell a lot of cupcakes at Flour. A LOT. So many that we even have special boxes with special holders to hold the cupcakes for everyone who buys one. We always have chocolate with vanilla frosting and every month we feature a special seasonal flavor. These lemon curd–filled meringue-topped cupcakes are probably our most popular monthly special. And no wonder—lemony cake gets amped up with a shot of lemon curd in the middle and then toasted vanilla marshmallow meringue covers the top in dramatic fashion. It's like eating lemon meringue pie in cupcake form—what's not to love?

Make the lemon curd and set it aside in the fridge.

Preheat the oven to 350°F and place a rack in the center of the oven. Line a 12-cup regular muffin tin or 8 cups of a 12-cup jumbo muffin tin with muffin papers, or butter and flour the cups generously. Set aside.

In a stand mixer fitted with a paddle attachment, combine the cake flour, sugar, baking powder, salt, and baking soda on low speed for about 10 seconds, until mixed. With the mixer on low, add the butter and lemon zest and continue to mix until the butter is just barely incorporated, 20 to 25 seconds, and the mixture resembles dough. Turn off the mixer. In a separate bowl, whisk together the oil, whole eggs, egg yolks, and vanilla. Pour the oil mixture into the flour mixture. Gradually turn the mixer up to medium-high and beat for 2 minutes, until the batter is fluffy and light. Stop the mixer a few times and scrape down the sides and bottom of the bowl and the paddle. Turn the mixer to low and slowly pour in the buttermilk. Mix for about 10 seconds to combine. Scrape the sides and bottom of the bowl and the paddle, then mix on medium for about 30 seconds, until the buttermilk is thoroughly mixed in.

Divide the batter evenly among the prepared muffin tin cups. You want to fill the cups all the way to the top so you get a little cupcake top. Bake for 25 to 30 minutes, rotating the muffin tin midway through the baking time. The cupcakes should spring back when you poke the tops in the center and a cake tester inserted into the middle of a cupcake should come out clean.

Continues...

Remove the cupcakes from the oven and let cool completely in the tin on a wire rack. Remove the cupcakes from the muffin tin.

While the cupcakes are cooling, make the fluffy marshmallow frosting.

Use a melon baller or a small 1-inch circle cutter to scoop out the center of each cupcake, going about two-thirds of the way down to the bottom of the cupcake. (Eat these scraps as your reward for making these delicious cupcakes.) Fill a pastry bag fitted with a small round tip with the lemon curd and pipe it into the cupcakes all the way to the top, or use a small teaspoon to fill the centers with the curd. Top each cupcake with a heaping scoop of meringue frosting and use the back of a spoon to spread it over the top. Firmly tap on the frosting with the back of the spoon and lift it to create spikes and swirls. Use a blowtorch to carefully torch the tops of the cupcakes to create a browned meringue top. If you do not have a torch, place the frosted cupcakes under the broiler on a baking sheet and rotate the sheet every few minutes until the sides and top are toasted, 8 to 12 minutes total. Serve immediately, or store in an airtight container at room temperature for no more than 6 hours.

Fluffy Marshmallow Frosting

MAKES ABOUT 4 CUPS

1¼ cups/**250 grams** sugar

6 large egg whites (about ¾ cup/**180 grams**), at room temperature

¾ teaspoon pure vanilla extract

½ teaspoon kosher salt

In a small metal or heatproof glass bowl, whisk together the sugar and egg whites to make a thick slurry. Place the bowl over a small pot of simmering water (make sure the pot is small enough that the bowl sits above the water and not directly touching it, or you may end up with scrambled egg whites) and cook, whisking occasionally, until the mixture is very hot to the touch, 6 to 8 minutes. (When you stick your finger in the mixture it should be so hot you immediately remove your finger.) It will thin out a bit as the sugar melts.

Scrape the sugar–egg white mixture into a stand mixer fitted with a whisk attachment and whip on medium-high speed for 6 to 8 minutes, until the frosting cools, is fluffy and glossy, and looks like shaving cream. Add the vanilla and salt and whip until mixed in. Use immediately.

Vegan Hostess Cupcakes

MAKES 12 REGULAR CUPCAKES

1½ cups/**210 grams** all-purpose flour

½ cup/**100 grams** superfine sugar

⅓ cup/**40 grams** Dutch-processed cocoa powder

2 tablespoons firmly packed light brown sugar

1 teaspoon baking soda

¼ teaspoon kosher salt

¼ cup/**55 grams** vegetable oil (such as canola)

1 teaspoon pure vanilla extract

Soy Ganache (page 295)

Vegan Marshmallow (page 294)

1 ounce/**30 grams** vegan white chocolate, melted

A handful of celebrities are known just by one name. In the television and movie world there's Oprah, of course, and Brad and Angelina. It's even more common in the music world where most everyone knows Madonna and Prince and Beyoncé and Questlove. Questlove, it turns out, is also a food fanatic. So much so that he hosts annual Food Salons at which he invites chefs to cook and a hundred or so of his friends to partake in a food celebration. A few years ago I was asked to participate in a Food Salon along with three other chefs—Bryce Shuman, Amanda Cohen, and Kwame Onwuachi. We were giddy at the prospect of cooking at the Salon and we brainstormed putting together a meal made of "Childhood Favorites" made with a healthy and/or vegetable focus. As the team pastry chef I had a blast coming up with a dessert tasting menu: white sweet potato–filled Oreos, rice crispy–pea treats with crunchy peas, adzuki bean–filled Pop Tarts, eggplant-tomato Newtons, and these vegan Hostess cupcakes. I filled our vegan chocolate cupcakes with an eggless meringue made with aquafaba (the cooking liquid from chickpeas) and glazed the tops with a shiny chocolate ganache made with soy milk. They were so unbelievably delicious no one believed they could be vegan. I'm excited for you to try this recipe—it is as fun to make as it is to eat.

Preheat the oven to 350°F and place a rack in the center of the oven. Line a 12-cup regular muffin tin with muffin papers, or oil and flour the cups. Set aside.

In a medium bowl, mix together the flour, superfine sugar, cocoa powder, brown sugar, baking soda, and salt. In a separate bowl, whisk together 1 cup/240 grams cold water, the oil, and the vanilla. Pour the oil mixture into the flour mixture and mix them together with a wooden spoon until the batter is smooth and homogeneous. Pour

Vegan Marshmallow

MAKES ABOUT 1 CUP

This makes more marshmallow than you need for the cupcakes, but it's hard to whip up a smaller amount. If your mixer's whisk isn't engaging with the aquafaba because there isn't enough in the bowl, consider doubling the recipe.

¼ cup/**90 grams** aquafaba
(liquid from a can of no-salt-added chickpeas, or homemade)

¼ cup/**50 grams** sugar

¼ teaspoon pure vanilla extract

—

Place the aquafaba in a stand mixer fitted with a whisk attachment. Whip on medium-high speed for about 2 minutes, until the aquafaba gets foamy and thick. Slowly add the sugar and vanilla and whip on medium-high for 8 to 10 minutes, until the marshmallow is thick and fluffy. It will take a long time to thicken but once it does, it will magically become exactly like meringue. Use immediately.

the batter evenly into the prepared muffin tin cups, filling the cups about three-quarters full.

Bake for 18 to 24 minutes, rotating the muffin tin midway through the baking time, until the cupcakes spring back when you touch them lightly in the middle and a cake tester inserted into the middle of a cupcake comes out clean. Let cool in the muffin tin on a wire rack for about 30 minutes, then remove the cupcakes from the tin and let them cool completely directly on the rack.

While the cupcakes are baking, make the soy ganache and vegan marshmallow. Pour the ganache into a small bowl and let it cool to room temperature so that it is cool to the touch but still somewhat liquid. If the ganache firms up too much, rewarm it slightly in the microwave or a bain-marie; don't warm it so much that it gets runny.

When the cupcakes are completely cool, use a small teaspoon or a spoon handle to scoop out a divot in the center of each cupcake, about 1½ inches deep and 1 inch wide. Set aside the pieces of cake you take out. Fill each hole with a spoonful of the marshmallow and top with a piece of the saved cake. Use an offset spatula or knife to spread the cupcake tops with the ganache, covering them fully. Make a cornet out of parchment paper (see page 25) and fill it with the melted white chocolate. Draw a decorative swirl across each of the cupcakes. Serve immediately or within a few hours of filling.

These cupcakes should be eaten the same day they are made.

Soy Ganache

MAKES ABOUT 1 CUP

4 ounces/**115 grams** vegan
semisweet chocolate

½ cup/**120 grams**
plain soy milk

—

Chop the chocolate and place
in a medium metal or heatproof glass bowl. In a small
saucepan, heat the soy milk
until just before it comes to a
boil, when small bubbles
collect along the sides of the
pan. Pour the soy milk over the
chocolate and let stand for
about 30 seconds. Slowly
whisk the chocolate and soy
milk together until the
chocolate is completely melted
and the ganache is smooth.

The ganache can be stored in
an airtight container in the
refrigerator for up to 3 days.
If refrigerated, melt it in a
bain-marie (see page 31) or in
the microwave before using.

Olive Oil Cake

with Fresh Grapes

MAKES ONE 9-INCH CAKE, TO SERVE 8 TO 10

¾ cup/**180 grams** plain whole milk Greek yogurt

¾ cup/**165 grams** olive oil

¾ cup/**150 grams** superfine sugar

2 large eggs (about **100 grams**), at room temperature

2 large egg yolks (about **40 grams**), at room temperature

1 tablespoon grated lemon zest (about 1 large lemon)

2 tablespoons fresh lemon juice (about ½ large lemon)

¼ teaspoon pure almond extract

1¼ cups/**175 grams** all-purpose flour

¾ cup/**75 grams** almond flour

2 teaspoons baking powder

¼ teaspoon kosher salt

1 cup seedless green grapes (about 5 ounces/**150 grams**)

2 tablespoons confectioners' sugar, for garnish

The idea of putting olive oil in a cake baffled me. I had always associated olive oil with roasting vegetables and making classic vinaigrettes, never ever with baking. Nicole, our executive pastry chef, made this for us as a muffin-of-the-month flavor. The muffin was so fruity and rich! I was hooked. In addition to the basic muffin, we've made this into a gluten-free version and a vegan version. But I like it best baked as a whole cake, glammed up with juicy, sweet grapes on top.

Preheat the oven to 325°F and place a rack in the center of the oven. Line the bottom of a 9-inch cake pan with a parchment paper circle (see page 23) and set it aside.

In a medium bowl, whisk together the yogurt, olive oil, superfine sugar, whole eggs, egg yolks, lemon zest, lemon juice, and almond extract. In a large bowl, whisk together the all-purpose flour, almond flour, baking powder, and salt. Pour the yogurt mixture into the flour mixture and fold them together until fully combined. Scrape the batter into the prepared cake pan. Slice the grapes in half and arrange them cut side up in concentric circles on top of the batter.

Bake for 1 hour 10 minutes to 1 hour 20 minutes, rotating the cake pan midway through the baking time, until the cake springs back when you press it in the middle and a cake tester inserted into the middle of the cake comes out clean. Remove from the oven and let cool completely in the pan on a wire rack. When cool, carefully invert the cake onto a flat plate and lift off the pan; peel off the parchment. Place a serving plate on top of the cake and turn it right side up so the grapes are on top.

Using a fine-mesh sieve, dust the cake evenly with the confectioners' sugar to finish.

Leftover cake can be stored in an airtight container at room temperature for up to 2 days.

Syrian Nutmeg Cake

MAKES ONE 9-INCH CAKE, TO SERVE 10

1¾ cups firmly packed/
385 grams light brown sugar

1 cup/**150 grams** whole
wheat flour

1 cup/**140 grams**
all-purpose flour

½ cup/1 stick/**115 grams**
unsalted butter, melted
and cooled

1 cup/**240 grams** Greek yogurt

1 cup/**120 grams** walnuts,
roughly chopped

1 large egg (about **50 grams**),
at room temperature

1 teaspoon baking powder

1 teaspoon lightly packed
freshly grated nutmeg

½ teaspoon baking soda

¼ teaspoon kosher salt

½ cup/**120 grams** heavy cream

½ cup/**120 grams**
crème fraîche

2 tablespoons
confectioners' sugar

¼ teaspoon pure
vanilla extract

This is not a fancy, glamorous cake, but it is a sleeper hit in the flavor department. It comes from one of our pastry chefs, Rachael, who remembers her mother making it for her when she was growing up. The spicy nutmeg and tannic walnuts make perfect partners; I add whole wheat flour to the cake to make it a bit heartier. The crème fraîche topping is creamy and tangy and dresses the cake up enough that you could serve it at a dinner party.

Preheat the oven to 350°F and place a rack in the center of the oven. Line the bottom of a 9-inch cake pan with a parchment paper circle (see page 23) and set it aside.

In a stand mixer fitted with a paddle attachment, combine the brown sugar, whole wheat flour, all-purpose flour, and melted butter. Mix on low speed until the butter is totally incorporated and the mixture is sandy and crumby.

Remove about 1 cup/160 grams of the crumb mixture and press it over the bottom of the prepared pan. Press firmly to make an even layer over the bottom of the pan.

Add the yogurt, walnuts, egg, baking powder, nutmeg, baking soda, and salt to the remaining crumbs. Mix on medium or by hand until the mixture is homogeneous, about 30 seconds using a mixer, about 1 minute by hand. Scrape the batter on top of the crumbs in the pan and spread it out evenly.

Bake for 1 hour to 1 hour 10 minutes, rotating the cake pan midway through the baking time, until the cake springs back when you press it in the middle and a cake tester inserted into the middle of the cake comes out clean. Remove from the oven and let cool completely in the pan on a wire rack.

Carefully invert the cake onto a flat plate and lift off the pan; peel off the parchment. Place a serving plate on top of the cake and turn it right side up so the softer cake part is on top. Set aside.

In a stand mixer fitted with a whisk attachment, using a handheld electric mixer, or in a bowl using a whisk, whip the heavy cream, crème fraîche, confectioners' sugar, and vanilla together until fluffy and light. Spread the whipped cream evenly on top of the cake. Use the back of a spoon or a knife to make a circular pattern on the cream. Serve immediately.

Leftover cake can be stored in an airtight container in the fridge for up to 3 days. Be sure to remove the cake from the fridge a few hours before serving so it can come to room temperature.

Japanese Cotton Cheesecake

MAKES ONE 8-INCH CHEESECAKE, TO SERVE 8

5 large eggs (about **250 grams**), at room temperature

1 cup/8 ounces/**225 grams** cream cheese

½ cup/**120 grams** crème fraîche

3 tablespoons/**45 grams** unsalted butter, at room temperature

1 teaspoon grated lemon zest

1 teaspoon pure vanilla extract

½ cup plus 1 tablespoon/ **115 grams** superfine sugar

½ cup/**60 grams** cake flour, sifted after measuring

¼ teaspoon kosher salt

1 tablespoon confectioners' sugar, for garnish

This Asian cheesecake bears little resemblance to its dense, rich New York cousin—or to any other cheesecake I've ever had, for that matter. I had my first taste of this featherlight cheesecake while visiting relatives in Taiwan. I loved it so much I started experimenting as soon as I got back from traveling. My dear friend Alina, who grew up in Japan, became my official taste tester as I tried various formulas. She deemed this one the best: It is whisper light and fluffy, melts in your mouth, is gently sweet but not very, and has a little tang from the cream cheese and the crème fraîche. You can see how it gets its name from its incredibly soft, delicate, wispy texture.

Preheat the oven to 400°F and place a rack in the center of the oven. Line the bottom of an 8 x 3-inch round cake pan with a parchment paper circle (see page 23) or generously butter ONLY the bottom of the pan. Set it aside.

Separate the eggs and place the whites in a stand mixer fitted with a whisk attachment. Place the yolks in a small bowl. Set both aside.

Place the cream cheese in a metal or heatproof glass bowl and place over a pot of simmering water. Stir occasionally until the cream cheese softens and melts and becomes totally smooth. Whisk in the crème fraîche and butter until well combined. Remove from the heat and whisk in the lemon zest and vanilla. Whisk in the egg yolks and 3 tablespoons/40 grams of the

superfine sugar. Sprinkle the cake flour and salt evenly over the top. Use the whisk to gently fold in the flour.

Whip the egg whites on medium speed until you start to see the wires of the whisk leave a trail in the whites. Slowly add the remaining superfine sugar, 1 tablespoon at a time, whipping all the while, until all the sugar is mixed in. Continue whipping for another 30 seconds or so, until the whites hold a soft peak and look a bit like soft seafoam. Stop the mixer and take a few spoonfuls of the whites. Gently fold them into the cream cheese mixture. Once that mixture has been lightened up with some of the whites, go ahead and add the rest of the whites and fold gently and quickly to combine thoroughly. Carefully pour the batter

into the prepared cake pan. Place the pan in a larger roasting pan or another baking dish that is at least as tall as the cake pan. Place both pans in the oven and fill the larger pan with water so that it comes about one-quarter of the way up the side of the cake pan. (This will protect the cheesecake from baking in direct heat, giving it a nicer texture.) The cake is really light so if you pour in too much water it will float. Bake the cheesecake for 35 to 40 minutes, until the top of the cake is golden brown and it doesn't give when you press it gently in the middle.

Turn off the oven and crack the oven door so that it cools off. Leave the cheesecake in the cooling-off oven for 2 hours so that it cools slowly, which keeps the top from cracking.

Remove the cheesecake pan from the pan of water and let it cool completely on a wire rack, at least another 2 hours. It will deflate by a half inch or so. Run a knife around the edges of the cheesecake. Very quickly invert the cheesecake onto a flat plate, lift off the pan, carefully peel off the parchment, then invert it right side up on a serving plate. Refrigerate for at least 2 hours.

Dust the cheesecake with confectioners' sugar before serving.

The cheesecake can be stored in an airtight container in the fridge for up to 4 days.

Plum Upside-Down Cake

MAKES ONE 9-INCH CAKE

¾ cup/**150 grams** sugar,
for the caramel

3 tablespoons/**45 grams**
unsalted butter, at room
temperature, for the caramel

⅔ cup/**135 grams** sugar,
for the cake

4 firm, ripe medium black or
red plums, pitted and sliced
about ¼ inch thick
(about 2 cups)

1½ cups/**210 grams**
all-purpose flour

⅔ cup/**135 grams** sugar,
for the cake

1 teaspoon baking powder

½ teaspoon baking soda

½ teaspoon kosher salt

¾ cup/1½ sticks/**170 grams**
unsalted butter, at room
temperature, for the cake

2 large eggs (about **100 grams**),
at room temperature

½ cup/**120 grams** crème
fraîche, at room temperature

2 tablespoons whole milk,
at room temperature

2 teaspoons pure
vanilla extract

This is my favorite kind of cake: It isn't overly sweet since the plums have a bit of tartness, the caramel is a little bitter, and the cake itself is tender and buttery. It's also visually impressive, with the plums bleeding into the cake and the caramel dripping down the sides. Serve this on its own for breakfast or a snack, or with ice cream or whipped cream for a terrific summer dessert.

—

Preheat the oven to 350°F and place a rack in the center of the oven. Line the bottom of a 9-inch cake pan with a parchment paper circle (see page 23) and spray the pan liberally with pan spray or butter the bottom and sides generously. Set aside.

Place the sugar for the caramel in a small saucepan and slowly pour in about ⅓ cup/80 grams water. Stir gently to moisten the sugar. Brush the sides of the pan with a pastry brush dipped in water if there are any sugar crystals clinging to the pan. Place the saucepan on high heat and bring to a boil. Don't stir the mixture and don't jostle the pan — you want to avoid crystallization of the syrup, which can happen if the pan is disturbed while the syrup is coming to a boil. After 3 to 4 minutes the syrup will come to a furious boil; several minutes later, as more water evaporates, it will boil a bit more languidly, and finally it will start to color and look golden yellow like a butterscotch candy. Once the sugar has started to

caramelize, watch it carefully and have the 3 tablespoons/45 grams of butter ready to go. At this point it's safe to swirl the pan around to even out the caramelization. Don't walk away from the stove, as the caramel cooks quickly when it gets to this stage. Turn the heat down to medium and keep gently swirling the saucepan until the caramel is a dark amber, the color of Samuel Adams lager. As soon as the caramel has reached dark amber, immediately add the butter; watch out, as it will sputter and spatter and get foamy. Whisk the butter into the caramel until completely melted and incorporated.

Carefully pour the caramel into the prepared pan. Swirl the pan until it is evenly coated with caramel. Tightly shingle the plums in concentric circles in the pan, covering all the caramel. The caramel will harden, but don't worry — it will melt again as it bakes. Shingle a second layer of plums if you have extra fruit. Set aside.

In a stand mixer fitted with a paddle attachment, combine the flour, the sugar for the cake, the baking powder, baking soda, and salt on low speed for about 10 seconds, until mixed. With the mixer on low, add the butter for the cake and continue to mix until the butter is completely incorporated, 30 to 40 seconds, and the mixture looks like crumbs. With the mixer on low, add the eggs. Turn the mixer up to medium-high and beat for about 1 minute, until the batter is fluffy and light. Stop the mixer a few times and scrape down the sides and bottom of the bowl and the paddle. In a separate bowl, whisk together the crème fraîche, milk, and vanilla. Turn the mixer to low and slowly pour in the crème fraîche mixture. Mix for about 10 seconds to combine. Scrape the sides and bottom of the bowl and the paddle, then mix on medium-high for about 30 seconds, until the crème fraîche mixture is thoroughly incorporated.

Scrape the batter on top of the plums and spread it evenly. Bake for 50 to 60 minutes, rotating the cake pan midway through the baking time, until the cake is medium golden brown and springs back when you press it in the middle with your finger, and a cake tester inserted into the middle of the cake comes out clean.

Remove the cake from the oven, transfer it to a wire rack, and let cool for at least 2 hours to allow the caramel to thicken and the plums to settle.

Run a knife around the edge of the cake. Place a serving plate on top of the pan, hold tight, and carefully and quickly invert the cake onto the plate. Caramel may run off the plate, so be careful! Lift off the pan and peel off the parchment. Arrange any plums that may have become dislodged. Serve warm or at room temperature.

The cake can be stored in an airtight container at room temperature for up to 3 days.

Ginger-Peach
Crumb Cake

MAKES ONE 10-INCH CAKE, TO SERVE 12 TO 15

Crumb Topping
(opposite)

10 tablespoons/1¼ sticks/
140 grams unsalted butter,
melted and cooled

1¼ cups/**250 grams** sugar

2 large eggs (about **100 grams**),
at room temperature

1 cup/**240 grams** crème
fraîche, at room temperature

1 cup/**240 grams** whole milk,
at room temperature

1 teaspoon pure vanilla extract

3¼ cups/**455 grams**
all-purpose flour

¼ cup/**40 grams** finely
chopped crystallized ginger

1 tablespoon baking powder

1 teaspoon ground ginger

½ teaspoon baking soda

½ teaspoon kosher salt

1 pound/**455 grams** ripe
peaches (about 3 medium),
pitted and roughly
chopped (2 cups)

Crunchy and nutty, redolent with ginger, soft and sweet from the ripe peaches, this cake is a showstopper. Not because it is particularly fancy-looking, but because of how incredibly rich and delicious it is. It is full of juicy fruit that keeps it moist, and it gets better as it sits and all the flavors continue to mingle and deepen. Make this cake early in the week and keep it on the counter to snack on, for breakfast, and for after dinner all week long.

—

Make the crumb topping and set aside.

Preheat the oven to 350°F and place a rack in the center of the oven. Line the bottom of a 10-inch cake pan with a parchment paper circle (see page 23) and spray the pan liberally with pan spray or butter the sides and bottom generously. Set aside.

In a medium bowl, whisk together the melted butter and sugar. Whisk in the eggs until thoroughly combined. Slowly whisk in the crème fraîche until smooth. Whisk in the milk and vanilla. Set aside.

In a large bowl, stir together the flour, crystallized ginger, baking powder, ground ginger, baking soda, and salt until well mixed. Make a well in the center of the flour mixture and pour in the crème fraîche mixture. Using a rubber spatula, gently fold the dry ingredients into the wet ingredients until about halfway combined. Add the peaches and continue to fold until combined and

there are no more dry patches of flour. Scoop the batter into the prepared cake pan. Sprinkle it generously and evenly with the crumb topping.

Bake for 1 hour 15 minutes to 1 hour 30 minutes, rotating the cake pan midway through the baking time, until the cake is golden brown on top and the center springs back when you press it, and a cake tester inserted into the middle of the cake comes out clean. Remove from the oven and let cool on a wire rack.

To remove the cake from the pan, run a knife around the edge of the cake. Place a flat plate on top of the cake. Invert the pan and plate and pop the cake out; lift off the pan and peel off the parchment. Place a flat serving plate on the cake and invert the cake right side up again. Slice the cake into wedges and serve.

The cake can be stored in an airtight container at room temperature for up to 4 days.

Crumb Topping

MAKES 1¼ CUPS/205 GRAMS

½ cup/**50 grams** chopped pecans

½ cup/**100 grams** superfine sugar

2 tablespoons firmly packed
light brown sugar

2 tablespoons/**30 grams**
unsalted butter, at cool room temperature

⅛ teaspoon ground cinnamon

⅛ teaspoon ground ginger

⅛ teaspoon kosher salt

Pinch of ground cloves

Preheat the oven to 350°F and place a rack in the center of the oven. Place the pecans on a baking sheet and toast until light golden brown, about 8 minutes. Remove from the oven and place in a medium bowl. Let cool for about 15 minutes, until they are no longer hot to the touch.

Add the superfine sugar, brown sugar, butter, cinnamon, ginger, salt, and cloves to the bowl with the pecans. Using your fingers, mix in the butter until you have a crumbly topping.

Crumb topping can be stored in an airtight container in the fridge for up to 1 week.

Simple Lemon Spiral

SERVES 10 TO 12 PEOPLE

1 recipe Master Lemon Curd (page 435)

Lemon Syrup (page 310)

4 large eggs (about **200 grams**), separated, at room temperature

1 cup/**200 grams** sugar

2 tablespoons fresh lemon juice (about ½ large lemon)

3 large egg whites (about ⅓ cup/**90 grams**), at room temperature

¾ cup/**90 grams** all-purpose flour

⅛ teaspoon kosher salt

1 cup/**240 grams** heavy cream

I was a budding pastry cook when my pastry chef and mentor, Rick, painstakingly taught me how to taste. Not how to eat, not how to bake, not how to enjoy, but how to TASTE. Everything we made, he would show me how a little more salt or a little less time in the oven would affect the overall effect in our mouths. I learned to take one bite of something first to clear my palate and then to take a second bite to truly taste whatever I was eating. To this day when I'm tasting a mousse or fried rice or anything at all, I take two bites: one to clear and one to judge. This lemon spiral has so few ingredients (eggs, sugar, lemon, flour, cream, butter, vanilla, salt) that every one has to be in perfect proportion to make a final product that sings. So the sponge cake is airy, not too sweet, begging for moisture and flavor. The syrup is like a sucking on a lemon SweeTart, and there's plenty of it to soak into the dry cake. The curd is bracingly sharp and tempered with a big dollop of whipped cream. Yes, the spiral is simple. But when done perfectly it will stop you in your tracks. It stopped Jody and Christopher back in 1995 when I was interviewing for the pastry chef position at their restaurant, Rialto. I presented this lemon spiral to them along with an unassuming crème caramel. Together, these desserts showed what I'd learned from Rick: taste and taste and taste again until it is perfect.

—

Make the lemon curd and lemon syrup and set them aside.

Preheat the oven to 350°F and place a rack in the center of the oven. Line a 13 x 18-inch rimmed baking sheet with parchment paper and spray the parchment liberally with pan spray. Set aside.

Make the sponge cake: In a stand mixer fitted with a whisk attachment, or in a large bowl using a handheld electric mixer, beat together the egg yolks, ¼ cup/50 grams of the sugar, and the lemon juice on high speed for 6 to 8 minutes (10 to 12 minutes with a handheld mixer), until thick and voluminous. Stop the mixer once

MAKES ABOUT 1¼ CUPS

½ cup/**120 grams** fresh lemon
juice (about 4 large lemons)

½ cup/**100 grams** sugar

—

In a small saucepan, combine
the lemon juice and sugar with
½ cup/120 grams water and
bring to a boil, stirring to
dissolve the sugar. Remove
from the heat and let cool.

Lemon syrup can be stored in
an airtight container in the
fridge for up to 2 weeks.

or twice during whipping and scrape
the sides of the bowl and the whisk to
make sure you get all the sugar and
yolk to mix evenly. Transfer to a large
bowl and set aside.

Clean the mixer bowl and the whisk
attachment (or the handheld mixer
beater) thoroughly — they must be
spotlessly clean — and refit the mixer
with the whisk or beater. Place all
7 egg whites in the bowl and beat on
medium for 1 to 2 minutes, until you
can see the wires of the whisk
leaving a slight trail in the whites and
they hold soft peaks. (The whites will
start to froth and turn into bubbles
and eventually the yellowy viscous
part will disappear.) To test for the
soft peak stage, stop the mixer and
lift the whip out of the whites; the
whites should peak and then droop.

With the mixer on medium speed,
add the remaining ¾ cup/150 grams
sugar very slowly, taking about 1 full
minute to add it all. Whip on medium
for another 2 to 3 minutes, until the
whites are glossy and shiny and hold
a stiff peak when you slowly lift the
whip straight up and out of the egg
whites.

Using a rubber spatula, gently fold
about one-third of the whipped
whites into the egg yolk mixture to
lighten it. Then gently fold in the
remaining egg whites. Sift the flour
and salt over the top, then fold them
in gently until the flour disappears
completely. Spread the batter evenly
in the prepared pan; use an offset
spatula to smooth the batter so it is
even. Concentrate on spreading the
batter toward the corners and the
edges of the baking sheet — the
center will be easier to fill once the
edges are filled with batter. Don't
worry about the top being perfectly
smooth.

Bake, rotating the baking sheet
after 7 to 9 minutes to ensure even
baking, until the top of the cake is
firm and dry when you touch it on top
and is very pale golden brown, 15 to
18 minutes total.

Remove the cake from the oven and
let it cool in the pan on a wire rack for
10 minutes.

Run a paring knife around the edge
of the cake to release it from the
sides of the baking sheet. Invert the
cake directly onto the back of a clean

baking sheet. Peel off the parchment and replace it with a piece of clean parchment. Invert the cake again onto a wire rack so the bottom of the cake is back on the bottom and the top of the cake is back on top. Let cool on the parchment on a wire rack for 10 to 15 minutes, until cool to the touch.

Use a pastry brush to brush the cake evenly with the lemon syrup. Soak and soak and soak until all the syrup is used up. (This cake is called a sponge cake for a reason: It IS a sponge. It needs to soak up all of the syrup so that it isn't dry.) Set the cake aside.

Whip the cream by hand in a medium bowl with a whisk, in a bowl with a handheld electric mixer, or in a stand mixer fitted with a whisk attachment on medium speed until it holds stiff peaks. Carefully fold in 1 cup/310 grams of the lemon curd until fully combined. Set aside the remaining curd in the fridge for finishing the spiral. Spread the lemon cream evenly across the cake, leaving a 1-inch border on all four edges of the cake. Carefully roll the cake, starting at the narrow end and rolling the cake up jelly-roll style, narrow end to narrow end, confidently nudging the cake along. Use the parchment to help you push it in shape until you have a cake roll enclosed in the parchment. The final cake spiral will be about 12 inches wide. Place the parchment-wrapped spiral back on the baking sheet and push it to the edge of the sheet. Place a few cans or other heavy objects that can go in the freezer against the spiral to help keep its round shape. Put in the freezer for at least 4 hours or up to overnight, until frozen.

To finish the spiral, at least 3 hours before serving, remove the cake from the freezer and place it on a cutting board. Dip a chef's knife in very hot water to heat, then dry off the knife and trim about ½ inch off each end of the spiral. Using an offset spatula, carefully frost the entire log with the remaining lemon curd. Carefully transfer the spiral onto a long serving platter. Let the cake thaw at room temperature for about 3 hours or in the fridge for about 8 hours. Slice with a hot thin knife and use a pie server to move slices to serving plates. Serve immediately.

Leftover cake can be stored in an airtight container in the fridge for up to 4 days.

Eggnog Cheesecake
with Gingerbread People

MAKES ONE 9-INCH CHEESECAKE, TO SERVE 8 TO 12

A great eggnog balances spicy nutmeg and cinnamon with mellow vanilla, and all are brought into focus by deep, rich bourbon or rum. It's creamy and strong and tastes like a party. I turn this traditional flavor into a holiday cheesecake and make it even more festive with mini gingerbread people to decorate each serving. The dough for the gingerbread people also acts as the crust, but if you want to simplify the recipe, use the graham cracker crust from the S'mores Pie (page 261; omit the chocolate) and skip the gingerbread people decoration. Top instead with a generous shower of freshly grated nutmeg.

Gingerbread Crust and People
(page 314)

3 cups/1½ pounds/**680 grams**
cream cheese

1½ cups/**300 grams** vanilla
sugar (see page 26)

¾ teaspoon freshly
grated nutmeg

½ teaspoon ground cinnamon

4 large eggs (about
200 grams), at room
temperature

⅓ cup/**80 grams** crème fraîche

5 tablespoons/**75 grams**
bourbon or dark rum

2 teaspoons pure
vanilla extract

½ teaspoon kosher salt

Make the gingerbread crust and people as directed. Set them aside.

Pull the cream cheese out at least 2 hours before making the cheesecake or place it in the microwave for 20 to 30 seconds at medium power to soften to room temperature.

Preheat the oven to 325°F and place a rack in the center of the oven.

In a stand mixer fitted with a paddle attachment, beat the cream cheese until it is totally soft and creamy. Scrape the bowl well and keep beating to ensure there are no lumps. Add the vanilla sugar, nutmeg, and cinnamon. Scrape well and keep beating. Add the eggs one at a time, mixing until incorporated. Scrape again and keep beating. Add the crème fraîche, bourbon, vanilla,

and salt. You guessed it — scrape and keep on beating. Strain the cheesecake batter through a fine-mesh strainer (to catch any lumps) into the crust. Wrap the whole bottom and sides of the springform pan in aluminum foil to prevent leaking.

Place the springform pan in a larger roasting pan and place the whole thing in the oven. Pour water into the roasting pan so it comes halfway up the sides of the springform pan. Bake for 1 hour 10 minutes to 1 hour 20 minutes, until the filling is set but still a tiny bit wobbly. You may need to cover the cheesecake lightly with foil if it starts to brown.

Turn off the oven but leave the cheesecake in the oven to cool — this will help prevent cracking. Remove from the oven after about 1 hour.

Place the cheesecake in the fridge until you're ready to serve. Top the cake with gingerbread people for garnish.

The cheesecake can be stored in an airtight container in the fridge for up to 3 days. Store the people separately at room temperature in an airtight container, adding them back to the cheesecake before serving.

Continues...

Gingerbread Crust and People

**MAKES ENOUGH FOR ONE 9-INCH CHEESECAKE
AND 10 TO 15 GINGERBREAD PEOPLE**

4 tablespoons/½ stick/
60 grams unsalted butter,
at cool room temperature

¼ cup firmly packed/
55 grams light brown sugar

1 large egg (about **50 grams**),
at room temperature

¼ cup/**85 grams** unsulfured
molasses

1 cup/**140 grams**
all-purpose flour

1¼ teaspoons ground ginger

½ teaspoon ground cinnamon

½ teaspoon kosher salt

¼ teaspoon baking powder

¼ teaspoon baking soda

⅛ teaspoon ground cloves

⅛ teaspoon freshly ground
black pepper

2 tablespoons chopped
semisweet chocolate, for
decorating the people
(optional)

In a stand mixer fitted with a paddle attachment, cream 3 tablespoons/45 grams of the butter and the brown sugar together on medium speed until light and fluffy, about 3 minutes. Add the egg and molasses and beat for 30 seconds to combine well. Scrape down the bowl and the paddle a few times to make sure the butter gets fully mixed in. In a large bowl, stir together the flour, ginger, cinnamon, salt, baking powder, baking soda, cloves, and pepper. Add the flour mixture to the butter mixture and beat on low until totally combined. Divide the dough in half and wrap both pieces in plastic wrap. Refrigerate for at least 1 hour so the dough stiffens enough so that you can roll it out.

Preheat the oven to 325°F and place a rack in the center of the oven. Line a baking sheet with parchment paper and set it aside.

To make the crust: Remove both pieces of dough from the fridge. Generously flick flour over the work surface and roll out one piece of dough until it is about ⅛ inch thick. Place it on the prepared baking sheet and bake for 18 to 20 minutes, rotating the baking sheet midway through the baking time, until it is baked through and firm.

Remove from the oven and let cool completely on the baking sheet on a wire rack. When cool, grind the cookie in a food processor into fine crumbs. You should get about 1½ cups/190 grams crumbs.

Butter and flour a 9-inch spring-form pan or spray it with pan spray. Melt the remaining 1 tablespoon butter and add it to the cookie crumbs. Stir together until the cookie crumbs are well coated with butter. Press the crumbs evenly over the bottom of the prepared pan. Turn the oven back on to 325°F. Bake the crust for about 20 minutes, rotating the pan midway through the baking time, until set. Remove from the oven and set aside.

The crust can be stored, well wrapped, at room temperature for up to 3 days.

To make the gingerbread people: Preheat the oven to 325°F and place a rack in the center of the oven. Line a baking sheet with parchment paper and set it aside.

On a well-floured surface, roll out the second piece of dough until it is about ⅛ inch thick. Using a 2-inch gingerbread person cutter, cut out people; lay them on the prepared baking sheet. Reroll the scraps and keep cutting out people. Bake for 15 to 20 minutes, rotating the baking sheet midway through the baking time, until the people are baked through and firm to the touch. Remove from the oven and let cool on the baking sheet on a wire rack. If you like, melt the chocolate in the microwave or in a bain-marie and spoon it into a parchment cornet (see page 25). Pipe eyes and mouths onto the people.

Gingerbread people can be stored in an airtight container at room temperature for up to 1 week.

Orange-Almond Pudding Cake

with Chocolate Ganache

MAKES ONE 8-INCH CAKE, TO SERVE 8 TO 10

Candied Oranges
(page 318)

5 large eggs (about
250 grams), at room
temperature

1 cup/**200 grams** sugar

½ teaspoon pure
vanilla extract

2¼ cups/**225 grams**
almond flour

1 teaspoon baking powder

½ teaspoon kosher salt

Chocolate-Orange Ganache
(page 318), melted and cooled
but still pourable

I first fell in love with this cake while spending an unforgettable weekend in the Ottolenghi pastry kitchens in London with two of my pastry chefs. Yotam Ottolenghi's talented army of pastry cooks churned out endless platters of stunning pastries, each of which looked more delectable than the last. This supremely moist and orangey cake was sitting on a counter half eaten, and Paula, one of the pastry chefs, saw me eyeing it. "Oh my, eat it, eat it all!" She grabbed a few forks for me and my team, we descended on this cake, and it disappeared in seconds. Not only is this cake gluten-free, but it's also made without any butter or oil. Yotam generously shared his recipe; I dress it up by double-glazing it with an orange-infused chocolate ganache to create a shiny mirrored surface.

—

Make and drain the candied oranges. Set aside 2 or 3 pretty slices for garnish on the cake. Finely chop the rest and set aside separately.

Preheat the oven to 300°F and place a rack in the center of the oven. Line the bottom of an 8-inch cake pan with a parchment paper circle (see page 23), or butter the pan liberally. Set it aside.

In a stand mixer fitted with a whisk attachment, whip the eggs and sugar on medium-high speed until frothy, about 2 minutes. Add the chopped candied oranges and vanilla and whip to combine. Stop the mixer and scrape the sides and bottom of the bowl, as well as the whisk. Whip again for a few seconds.

Add the almond flour, baking powder, and salt and whip on low to combine. Stop the mixer and scrape again. Continue to mix until the batter is homogeneous.

Scrape the batter into the prepared pan. Bake for 1 hour 20 minutes to 1 hour 30 minutes, rotating the cake pan midway through the baking time, until the cake springs back when you poke it in the middle and is firm to the touch, and a cake tester inserted into the middle of the cake comes out clean. Remove the cake from the oven and place the pan on a wire rack to cool.

While the cake is baking, make the ganache and set it aside to cool.

When the cake is entirely cool, run a knife around the edges of the cake, pop the cake out of the pan onto a flat plate, and remove the parchment. Turn the cake right side up on a wire rack placed over a baking sheet. Pour about half the ganache over the entire cake, using an offset spatula to coat the sides evenly. Place the cake in the fridge, still on the wire rack, to allow the ganache to set for at least 15 minutes.

Pour a second coat of ganache over the cake. Let the ganache set for at least 30 minutes. Place the cake on a serving platter. Cut into the orange slices and twist them into spirals; decorate the center of the cake with them. Serve.

The cake can be stored in an airtight container at room temperature for up to 3 days.

Candied Oranges

MAKES ABOUT 1½ CUPS/ 340 GRAMS

2 navel oranges

3 cups/**600 grams** sugar

—

Slice the ends off the oranges, then slice the oranges crosswise about ¼ inch thick.

In a medium saucepan, combine the sugar and 4 cups/960 grams water and bring to a boil. Add the orange slices to the sugar syrup and reduce the heat to very low.

Let the oranges simmer in the syrup for 2 to 3 hours, until they are translucent and the syrup has the consistency of maple syrup, gently stirring occasionally to move the top slices to the bottom of the syrup. Test for doneness by removing an orange slice from the syrup and biting into it; careful — it will be hot! The rind should be completely soft and sweet and the syrup should be very thick. Remove the saucepan from the heat and let the oranges cool completely in their syrup.

The oranges can be stored in their syrup in an airtight container in the refrigerator for up to 2 weeks. Drain before using.

Chocolate-Orange Ganache

MAKES ABOUT 1¼ CUPS

¾ cup/**180 grams** heavy cream

1 tablespoon grated orange zest (about 1 large orange)

6 ounces /**170 grams** semisweet or bittersweet chocolate, roughly chopped

—

In a small saucepan, heat the cream and orange zest over medium-high heat until just before it comes to a boil, when small bubbles collect along the sides of the pan. Turn off the heat and let the cream sit for 30 minutes to allow the orange to infuse into it.

Place the chocolate in a medium metal or heatproof glass bowl. Return the cream to just under a boil, then strain it through a fine-mesh strainer directly over the chocolate. Let it stand for 30 seconds. Slowly whisk the chocolate and cream together until the chocolate is completely melted and the ganache is smooth.

The ganache can be stored in an airtight container in the refrigerator for up to 2 weeks.

Funfetti

Angel Food Cake

MAKES ONE 9-INCH CAKE, TO SERVE 8 TO 10

12 large egg whites
(about 1½ cups/**360 grams**),
at room temperature

1 teaspoon pure vanilla extract

Pinch of cream of tartar

1½ cups/**300 grams** sugar

1 cup/**100 grams** sifted cake
flour (sift the flour first,
before measuring)

⅓ cup/**60 grams** store-bought
rainbow sprinkles

⅛ teaspoon kosher salt

Fluffy Marshmallow Frosting
(page 290)

We go rainbow crazy every June when Pride Week is celebrated in Boston and around the country. Every color of the rainbow is baked into cupcakes, folded into Oreo filling, even mixed through rice crispy treats. For over a week it looks like a carnival let loose on the pastry counter at Flour. I don't know what it is about rainbow sprinkles, but put them on a cake or in a cookie and you have an instant hit. This Funfetti angel food cake covered in toasted meringue is one of the prettiest—and for me tastiest—rainbow specials we offer. The meringue helps keep the cake tender by protecting it from drying out, but I doubt you'll have a lot of leftovers. We never do!

Preheat the oven to 350°F and place a rack in the center of the oven.

Place the egg whites, vanilla, 1 teaspoon water, and the cream of tartar in a stand mixer fitted with a whisk attachment (or in a large bowl, using a whisk). Whip on medium speed for 2 to 3 minutes (or 5 to 6 minutes by hand) until you can see the wires of the whisk leaving a slight trail in the whites.

With the mixer still on medium, or while continuing to whip vigorously by hand, slowly add ¾ cup/150 grams of the sugar, a few tablespoons at a time. After adding a little sugar, let it whip into the whites for 10 seconds or so, then add more sugar, then again wait about 10 seconds. Continue this way until all the sugar is added; that should take at least 1 minute. Once all the sugar

is added to the whites, whip on medium-high for 2 to 3 minutes more (5 to 6 minutes by hand), until the whites are glossy and shiny and hold a peak when you slowly lift the whisk straight up and out of them.

Stir together the cake flour, the remaining ¾ cup/150 grams sugar, the sprinkles, and salt in a small bowl. Carefully sprinkle the flour mixture on top of the whites and gently and quickly fold it in. When the everything is entirely mixed in, scrape the batter into an ungreased 9-inch angel food cake pan. Use a spoon or offset spatula to even off the top of the batter.

Bake for 30 to 40 minutes, rotating the cake pan midway through the baking time, until the entire top of the cake is light golden brown and the cake springs back when you press it lightly, and a cake tester inserted into the middle of the cake comes out clean. Immediately remove the cake from the oven and turn the pan upside down. (This ensures that the cake does not deflate and compact onto itself; since the cake pan is not greased, the cake won't fall out.) Leave the cake upside down until it is entirely cooled, at least 2 hours.

When the cake is cool, make the frosting.

Turn the cake pan right side up. Remove the cake from the pan by first running a knife around the outer edge of the cake and then around the inner tube of the pan; pop out the removable bottom along with the cake, then run a knife along the bottom of the cake to separate it from the pan. Turn the inner tube and pan bottom upside down and remove the cake carefully and quickly, then turn the cake right side up again onto a serving plate. Frost the sides, top, and inner tube with the frosting. Use an offset spatula or knife to smooth the frosting. Use a blowtorch to carefully torch the frosting all over to create a golden brown surface. If you do not have a torch, place the frosted cake on a baking sheet under the broiler and rotate it every few minutes until the sides and top are toasted, 8 to 12 minutes total. Serve immediately, or store at room temperature and serve within 6 hours at the very longest. (The frosting will not last for more than 6 hours at room temperature, and the cake itself does not store well in the fridge.)

Lamingtons

MAKES 16 INDIVIDUAL BITE-SIZE CAKES

Vanilla Genoise
(page 324)

1 cup/**125 grams** fresh or frozen raspberries

2 tablespoons superfine sugar

3¾ cups/**450 grams** confectioners' sugar

¾ cup/**90 grams** Dutch-processed cocoa powder

1 cup/**240 grams** whole milk

3 cups/**270 grams** unsweetened shredded coconut

Pretty much every night before falling asleep I cruise around Instagram, traveling the world, looking at what other pastry chefs in Korea, Australia, Mexico, California, Paris, and all other corners of the globe are creating. Christopher teases me about how easily I go down the rabbit hole of cupcakes and pies and croissants but I've learned a tremendous amount from those who generously post videos of various recipes and techniques. For some reason I've not yet figured out, Australia is home to many of my favorite Instagram bakeries. The pastries coming from Down Under are creative and enticing, and it's on my bucket list to make the trip someday. In the meantime I have been inspired to try to replicate some of the more drool-worthy pastries I've seen. Lamingtons are a popular snack cake in Australia; they are so beloved that Australians celebrate National Lamington Day every year in July. They are bite-size sponge cakes filled with jam, covered in chocolate, and rolled in coconut. I have no idea how close to or far from the real thing I am, but I think I've made something pretty darn delicious.

Make the vanilla genoise and set it aside. Place the raspberries and superfine sugar in a small bowl and stir to combine. Set aside.

In a large bowl, combine the confectioners' sugar and cocoa powder. Heat the milk in a small saucepan or in the microwave until there are small bubbles around the side of the saucepan and the milk is not quite at a boil. Pour the milk over the sugar-cocoa mixture and whisk until entirely smooth. Set the chocolate dipping sauce aside.

Remove the genoise from the cake pan by running a knife along the sides of the pan and then quickly inverting the pan onto a cutting board. The cake will pop out of the pan. Peel off the parchment on the bottom and flip the cake right side up, still on the cutting board. Even off the top using a long serrated knife. Carefully split the cake evenly in half horizontally (see page 28). Remove the top half of the cake and set it aside. Stir the raspberries and mash them a bit with a spoon. Drain off any excess liquid and spoon the raspberries onto the bottom half of the cake;

spread them evenly with the spoon or an offset spatula. You should have a thin layer of raspberries covering the whole cake layer. Replace the top of the cake and press down gently. Trim all four sides of the cake to square it off. Cut the cake into 16 squares by cutting it in 4 strips lengthwise and then widthwise.

Arrange your cake dipping station: Place the cake sandwich squares on one side, the chocolate dipping sauce in a deep bowl in the center, the coconut in a shallow bowl on the other side, and a wire rack beyond that. Pick up a cake sandwich square with a fork underneath it and carefully dip it entirely into the chocolate dipping sauce. Use a second fork or spatula to move the cake around so all sides get covered. Lift it out of the sauce with the fork and tap it on the side of the bowl to let any extra sauce drip down. Place the cake in the coconut and use the fork or your hands to toss coconut over the cake. Gently roll the cake around until it is covered on all sides. At this point you should be able to pick up the cake with your hands without getting too messy; place the lamington on the wire rack. Repeat with the rest of the squares, using up the chocolate and coconut.

Transfer the lamingtons to a serving plate and serve within a day of making them, or else they'll get dry.

Vanilla Genoise

MAKES ONE 8 X 8-INCH SQUARE CAKE

5 large eggs (about **250 grams**),
at room temperature

1 cup/**200 grams** sugar

1⅓ cups/**185 grams** all-purpose flour

¼ teaspoon kosher salt

½ cup/1 stick/**115 grams** unsalted butter,
melted and cooled

1 teaspoon pure vanilla extract

Preheat the oven to 350°F and place a rack in the center of the oven. Line the bottom of an 8 x 8-inch square baking pan with parchment paper. Spray the pan sides with pan spray or butter them, and set aside.

In a stand mixer fitted with a whisk attachment, beat the eggs and sugar on high speed until thick and light and voluminous, at least 4 or 5 minutes. When you lift the whisk out of the bowl the mixture should fall back onto itself in ribbons. Remove from the mixer and sprinkle the flour and salt over the egg-sugar mixture. Gently fold until most of the flour is mixed in.

Place the melted butter in a medium bowl and stir in the vanilla. Scoop 2 or 3 large scoops of the egg mixture into the butter and fold to lighten the butter. Pour the lightened butter into the egg mixture and fold until everything is combined. The batter will deflate a bit but will still be light and lovely. Scrape the batter carefully into the prepared pan and gently even it out with an offset or rubber spatula, taking care not to deflate the batter by being too aggressive with the spatula.

Bake for 35 to 45 minutes, rotating the cake pan midway through the baking time, until the cake is light golden brown on top and springs back when you press it in the middle, and a cake tester inserted into the middle of a cake comes out clean. Remove from the oven and let cool in the pan on a wire rack.

The genoise can be made up to 1 day in advance and stored, well wrapped, at room temperature.

Stone Fruit and Berry Financier Cake

with Toasted Meringue

MAKES ONE 9-INCH CAKE, TO SERVE 10

1 cup/**100 grams** sliced almonds

1⅓ cups/**135 grams** almond flour

1⅓ cups/**160 grams** confectioners' sugar

½ cup/**75 grams** whole wheat flour

½ teaspoon kosher salt

1 cup/2 sticks/**225 grams** unsalted butter, melted and cooled

7 large egg whites (about ⅞ cup/**210 grams**), at room temperature, for the cake

1 teaspoon pure vanilla extract

2½ cups assorted ripe but not mushy stone fruit and/or berries (weight will vary; use 2 or 3 of the following: raspberries; blackberries; strawberries, halved if large; pitted cherries; thinly sliced pitted peaches, plums, apricots, nectarines)

6 large egg whites (about ¾ cup/**180 grams**), at room temperature, for the meringue

1¼ cups/**250 grams** superfine sugar

A financier is an almond cake that is traditionally baked in small rectangular loaf pans that resemble gold bars—hence the name. While visiting the tremendously gorgeous Ottolenghi bakeries in London I fell in love with their financier cakes. These were no longer unassuming golden-brown bars but instead were transformed into dramatic fruit- and meringue-topped loaf cakes. I spent a day in the kitchen with the generous Ottolenghi bakers learning how to assemble these. I use their recipe as a jumping-off point to make a soft almond–whole wheat cake filled with jammy ripe fruit and piled high with an almond meringue that browns dramatically in the oven. It's a bit of a mess to cut, so I suggest presenting the cake whole first and then using a sharp serrated knife to slice it.

Preheat the oven to 375°F and place a rack in the lower third of the oven. Toast the almonds on a baking sheet for 5 to 7 minutes, until pale golden brown like maple wood. Set aside, but leave the oven on.

Butter the bottom and sides of a 9-inch springform pan or spray it with pan spray. If you don't have a springform pan, you can use an 8- or 9-inch round cake pan as long as it is at least 3 inches high; butter the bottom and sides and line it with a parchment paper circle (see page 23) on the bottom. It will be a little trickier to remove the cake from the pan, but not impossible.

In a large bowl, use a whisk to stir together the almond flour, confectioners' sugar, whole wheat flour, and salt. Add the melted butter, the 7 egg whites for the cake, and the vanilla and whisk until the batter is smooth and has no lumps. Pour into the prepared pan. Bake for 20 minutes, rotating the pan midway through the baking time, until the batter just sets and the top is not tacky when you touch it lightly.

Remove the cake from the oven and arrange the fruit in a single layer on top of the batter. Set it aside, leaving the oven on.

In a stand mixer fitted with a whisk attachment, whip the 6 egg whites for the meringue on medium speed until the wires of the whisk start to leave a trail in the whites, 2 to 3 minutes. Add the superfine sugar ¼ cup/50 grams at a time, whipping for about 15 seconds before adding the next quarter cup; repeat until all the sugar has been added. Increase the mixer speed to high and whip for 1 to 2 minutes, until the meringue is stiff and glossy. Fold in the toasted almonds. Scrape the meringue into the pan on top of the fruit and use an offset spatula to spread it evenly across the fruit. It should come about level to the top of the cake pan; discard any extra meringue. Make swirly patterns in the meringue with the offset spatula.

Place the cake on a baking sheet to catch any drips and place it in the oven. (The meringue puffs and grows so you want plenty of room above the cake to allow for it to grow.) Bake the cake for 50 to 60 minutes, rotating the cake midway through the baking time, until the meringue is toasty brown on top.

Remove the cake from the oven and the baking sheet and let it cool completely in the pan on a wire rack. Run a knife around the sides of the springform pan and remove the sides. Transfer the cake from the pan bottom to a serving plate.

If you did not bake the cake in a springform pan, run a knife around the edge of the cake and have a flat plate and the serving plate ready.

Place the flat plate on top of the cake and flip the cake over. Tap the pan to release the cake and remove the pan, then peel off the parchment circle. Immediately place the serving plate on top of the cake and flip the whole thing back over so the meringue is back on top. If you do this quickly enough, the meringue won't get too beat up and you'll still have a glorious cake to present.

Use a serrated knife to cut the cake. The meringue will crumble a bit and be a little messy to cut but it's so delicious no one will care once they eat it.

Leftover cake can be stored, well wrapped, at room temperature for up to 2 days.

whisk. Add half the remaining flour mixture; mix on low until it's mostly mixed in, then stop and scrape. Add the rest of the milk and mix again on low until it is mostly mixed in. Remove the bowl from the mixer, add the last of the flour mixture, and gently fold by hand with a rubber spatula until all of it is incorporated into the batter. Divide the batter between the prepared cake pans.

Bake for 30 to 35 minutes, rotating the cake pans midway through the baking time, until the cakes spring back when you poke them in the middle and a cake tester comes out clean when you insert it into the middle of a cake. Remove the cakes from the oven and let cool in the baking pans on a wire rack.

While the cakes are baking and cooling, make the frosting and vanilla syrup and set them aside.

When the cakes are completely cool, run a small paring knife around the edges of the cakes and remove them from the pans. Peel off the parchment circles. Trim the tops of the cakes to level them (they will have rounded a bit in the oven, and the scraps are your reward for your hard work so far). Place one cake on a large flat plate or serving platter, or a rotating cake stand (if you have one) and use a pastry brush to brush and soak the cake with about half the vanilla syrup. Spoon about 1 cup of

Malted Milk Frosting

MAKES ABOUT 5 CUPS

⅔ cup/**135 grams** superfine sugar

2 large egg whites (about ¼ cup/**60 grams**), at room temperature

2 cups/4 sticks/**455 grams** unsalted butter, at room temperature

3½ cups/**420 grams** confectioners' sugar

¾ cup/**105 grams** malted milk powder

2 tablespoons whole milk

2 teaspoons pure vanilla extract

Pinch of kosher salt

———

In a medium metal or heatproof glass bowl, whisk together the superfine sugar and egg whites to make a thick slurry. Place the bowl over a small pot of simmering water; make sure the pot is small enough that the bowl sits above the water and not directly touching it, or you may end up with scrambled egg whites. Cook, whisking occasionally, until the mixture is hot to the touch, 6 to 8 minutes. (When you stick your finger in the mixture it should be so hot you immediately remove your finger.) It will thin out a bit as the sugar melts.

Pour the sugar–egg white mixture into a stand mixer fitted with a whisk attachment, or use a handheld electric mixer. Whip on medium-high speed for 4 to 6 minutes, until the mixture cools. Add the butter bit by bit and whip on medium until the butter is thoroughly incorporated. Add the confectioners' sugar, malted milk powder, milk, vanilla, and salt and whip on medium until the frosting is smooth and satiny.

The frosting can be stored in an airtight container in the refrigerator for up to 2 weeks. Before using, let it sit out at room temperature for at least 6 hours or ideally overnight. Place the frosting in a stand mixer fitted with a paddle attachment and mix until it smooths out again. It will look broken (curdled and very lumpy, possibly even separated with some liquid seeping out) for a while until it warms up, but don't panic — just keep beating it and be patient.

the frosting on top; use an offset spatula to spread it evenly to the edges of the cake. Carefully place the second cake upside down (for even, sharp edges on the final cake) on top of the first cake and soak with the remaining vanilla syrup. Spoon another 1 cup of the frosting on top of the cake. Spread the frosting to the edges of the cake and then down the sides, smoothing it as well as you can and covering the entire cake with a thin layer of frosting. This is called a crumb coat (see page 23); it will keep loose crumbs from migrating to the surface of the finished cake. Refrigerate the cake for about 15 minutes to set the crumb coat completely.

If you would like to dye the remaining frosting blue, do so at this point by beating in a few drops of food coloring. Fit a pastry bag with a star tip and fill it with all but about 1 cup of the frosting; set it aside.

Remove the cake from the fridge and spoon the remaining frosting on the cake; spread it evenly over the top and sides. This is the final finishing layer of frosting. Smooth the surface with an offset spatula dipped in hot water and dried off before using.

Make the chocolate speckle, if using. When you speckle the cake, be sure to place the cake on a turntable or flat plate, and place that on a large, empty work surface covered in plastic or parchment paper so cleanup is easier. Dip four fingers into the speckle and use a pastry brush to quickly and firmly flick and hit the chocolate off your fingers in the direction of the cake to create random spots, to mimic a robin's egg. (Test this in the kitchen sink at first so you get the movement down.)

If the cake is not already on a serving platter, carefully transfer it to one. Pipe a border of frosting along the top or the bottom edge of the cake, or both.

The frosted cake can be stored in an airtight container at room temperature for up to 2 days.

Vanilla Syrup

MAKES 1 CUP

½ cup/**100 grams** sugar

½ teaspoon pure vanilla extract

—

In a small saucepan, combine the sugar with ½ cup/120 grams water, bring to a boil, and stir until the sugar is dissolved. Remove from the heat and stir in the vanilla extract. Let cool before using.

The syrup can be made in advance and stored in an airtight container in the fridge indefinitely.

Chocolate Speckle

MAKES ABOUT ¼ CUP, ENOUGH TO PRACTICE SPECKLING AND ALSO SPECKLE 1 CAKE

2 tablespoons Dutch-processed cocoa powder, sifted after measuring

—

In a small bowl, whisk the cocoa powder with 2 tablespoons water until smooth. The speckle will be a thin paste — not quite runny and not thick like spackle, but somewhere in between. You don't want it too wet or it will look like you spilled coffee on the cake. You don't want it too thick or it will look like blobs on the cake.

Speckle can be stored in an airtight container in the fridge indefinitely. It is easiest to use when chilled. Rewhisk before using.

Ashley's Birthday Cake

MAKES ONE 8-INCH CAKE, TO SERVE 8 TO 12

Homemade Sprinkles
(page 347)

Chocolate Pudding
Buttercream (page 345)

Coffee Syrup (page 347)

½ cup/**60 grams** Dutch-
processed cocoa powder

1 ounce/**30 grams**
unsweetened chocolate, finely
chopped (about 3 tablespoons)

1 cup/**240 grams** boiling water

1½ cups firmly packed/
330 grams light brown sugar

1 cup/**120 grams** cake flour,
sifted after measuring

1 cup/**120 grams** light rye flour

1 teaspoon baking soda

½ teaspoon kosher salt

1 cup/2 sticks/**225 grams**
unsalted butter, at warm
room temperature

¼ cup/**60 grams** crème fraîche

2 large eggs (about **100 grams**),
at room temperature

2 large egg yolks (about
40 grams), at room
temperature

At Myers+Chang our dessert menu is filled with mostly traditional American desserts with an Asian twist: We have coconut cream pie with lime whipped cream; a matcha cookies-and-cream ice cream sundae with chile-chocolate sauce and tamarind caramel; lemon-ginger mousse with a housemade ginger fortune cookie; and more. Our dear friend Ashley Stanley, who has been coming to the restaurant since we opened (and in fact started her nonprofit food rescue organization, Lovin' Spoonfuls, while sitting at our food bar), begged for a good old-fashioned birthday cake every time she came in. Christopher, too, pined for a straightforward, classic slice of cake. "So how do I make chocolate cake with chocolate frosting Asian?" I asked him. "Easy," he told me. "You don't. We'll put it on our menu for Ashley and it will be so good no one will wonder why it's on the menu." I think we accomplished that with this cake: a soft chocolate cake made with a mix of cake and rye flours, frosted with a chocolate pudding frosting you loved as a kid (and still do as an adult). The cake mixing method is my favorite way to mix a butter cake; I learned this technique from one of my baking mentors, Rose Levy Beranbaum, who preaches this method in her many excellent cookbooks. The cake is topped with homemade rainbow sprinkles that are as fun to make as they are to eat. The sprinkles recipe scales up easily and keeps indefinitely if you want to make enough for several cakes.

Make the sprinkles, buttercream, and coffee syrup and set them aside.

Combine the cocoa powder and chocolate in a small bowl. Pour the boiling water on top and whisk until the mixture is completely combined and smooth. (Tip: Start by bringing more than 1 cup water to a boil, then measure out 1 cup. If you boil exactly 1 cup water, it will end up being less than 1 cup once it starts to boil.) Set aside and let cool to room temperature, about 4 hours, or 1 hour in the refrigerator; whisk every 15 minutes if refrigerating.

Preheat the oven to 350°F and place a rack in the center of the oven.

In a stand mixer fitted with a paddle attachment, combine the brown sugar, cake flour, rye flour, baking soda, and salt on low speed for about 20 seconds, until there are no longer any sugar lumps. With the mixer on low, add the butter and continue to mix until the butter is just barely incorporated, 20 to 25 seconds, and the mixture resembles dough. Turn off the mixer. In a separate bowl, whisk together the crème fraîche, whole eggs, and egg yolks. Pour the crème fraîche mixture into the butter-flour mixture and gradually turn the mixer back on to medium-high. Beat for 2 minutes, until the batter is fluffy and light. Stop the mixer a few times and scrape down the sides and bottom of the bowl and the paddle. Turn the mixer to low and slowly pour in the cooled chocolate mixture. Mix for about 10 seconds to combine. Scrape the sides and bottom of the bowl and the paddle, then mix on medium for about 30 seconds, until the chocolate is thoroughly incorporated.

Line the bottoms of two 8-inch cake pans with parchment paper circles (see page 23) and spray the pans generously with pan spray or butter them generously.

Scrape one-third of the batter into one of the prepared pans and the remaining batter into the second pan. Bake the cakes, rotating the cake pans midway through the baking time, until the centers of the cakes spring back when you poke them and a cake tester inserted into the middle of a cake comes out clean. The shallower cake will take 25 to 35 minutes and the thicker cake will take 40 to 50 minutes.

Remove the cakes from the oven as they are done and let them cool in the pans on a wire rack.

When the cakes are completely cool, run a knife around the edge of the cakes and remove them from the pans. Trim the tops with a serrated knife to level them (they will have rounded a bit in the oven — these scraps make for great nibbling). Again using a serrated knife, split the thicker cake in half horizontally (see page 28). Place the bottom layer on a large flat plate, serving platter, or rotating cake stand (if you have one). Use a pastry brush to brush about one-third of the coffee syrup evenly over the top and sides of the cake. Spoon ¾ cup of the buttercream on top; use an offset spatula to spread the buttercream evenly to the edges of the cake.

Carefully place the second split layer upside down on top of that and brush with another third of the syrup. Spoon on ¾ cup of the buttercream and spread it to the edges of the cake. Place the single cake layer upside down on top of that (for even, sharp edges on the final cake). Brush with the rest of the syrup. Spoon about 1 cup of the buttercream on the top of the cake and spread it across the top and down the sides, smoothing it as well as you can and covering the entire cake with a thin layer of buttercream. (This is called a crumb coat — see page 23 — and it will keep any loose crumbs from migrating to the surface of the finished cake.) Refrigerate the cake for at least 1 hour to allow the buttercream to firm up.

Remove the cake from the fridge and beat the remaining buttercream with a wooden spoon to fluff it up again. Spoon a heaping cup or more of the buttercream on the cake. Spread it evenly across the top and down the sides. This is the final finishing layer of frosting. Use the remainder of the buttercream to pipe an edge along the top and/or the bottom edge of the cake, if desired. (If you have any buttercream left, it can be stored in an airtight container in the fridge for up to 1 week.) Place the cake back in the fridge for about 30 minutes to allow the buttercream to firm up.

Remove the cake from the fridge and sprinkle the top with the sprinkles right before serving.

The cake can be stored in an airtight container at cool room temperature for up to 2 days.

Continues...

Chocolate Pudding Buttercream

MAKES ABOUT 4½ CUPS

1½ cups/**300 grams** sugar

6 tablespoons/**50 grams**
all-purpose flour

¼ cup/**30 grams** Dutch-
processed cocoa powder

1½ cups/**360 grams**
whole milk

5 ounces/**140 grams**
bittersweet chocolate,
chopped into small pieces
(about ¾ cup)

3 ounces/**85 grams**
unsweetened chocolate,
chopped into small pieces
(about ½ cup)

1½ cups/3 sticks/
340 grams unsalted butter,
cut into cubes, at cool
room temperature

1 teaspoon pure vanilla extract

¼ teaspoon kosher salt

Whisk together the sugar, flour, and cocoa powder in a medium bowl. (It's really important to whisk all the dry ingredients together thoroughly before adding the milk, or the pudding will be lumpy.) Whisk in the milk. Scrape the pudding base into a medium saucepan and cook over medium heat, whisking constantly, until it comes to a boil, 4 to 6 minutes. Count to 30 while continuously whisking once it boils. It will be a smooth, thick mixture that coats the back of a spoon. Remove the pudding base from the heat, scrape it into a shallow container, and cover with plastic wrap, pressing it directly against the surface of the pudding base to prevent a skin from forming. Let cool to room temperature, about 1 hour.

Combine the bittersweet and unsweetened chocolates in a small heatproof glass bowl and microwave on medium power until completely melted (see page 26) or place over a small pot of simmering water and whisk occasionally until completely melted. Set aside to cool to room temperature, about 45 minutes.

Place the butter in a stand mixer fitted with a paddle attachment and beat on medium-high speed until smooth and light, about 1 minute. Reduce the speed to medium-low and add the pudding base a few tablespoons at a time. Add the vanilla and salt. Add the melted chocolate.

Turn the speed up to medium and mix for 6 to 8 minutes. The buttercream will look curdled and clumpy at first, then gradually it will start to look creamy. When the buttercream is entirely smooth, it is ready to use.

Buttercream can be stored in an airtight container in the refrigerator, for up to 1 week. Before using, transfer to a stand mixer fitted with a paddle attachment and beat to bring it back to a silky consistency; this will take a long time. It's best to remove it from the refrigerator up to 8 hours in advance so when you beat it, it doesn't separate.

Homemade Sprinkles

MAKES ABOUT 1 CUP

1½ cups/**180 grams** confectioners' sugar,
sifted after measuring

1½ tablespoons/**25 grams** egg white
(just under 1 large egg white; slightly whipping
the white makes measuring much easier)

¾ teaspoon kosher salt

¼ teaspoon pure vanilla extract

At least 3 different liquid or gel food colorings

Line three or four baking sheets with parchment paper and set them aside. If you don't have that many baking sheets, you can place sheets of parchment on a work surface in an area of your kitchen that you can leave undisturbed for 24 hours.

Combine the confectioners' sugar, egg white, salt, and vanilla in a small bowl and whisk until smooth. Whisk in up to 1 tablespoon water, a teaspoon at a time, until the paste has the consistency of peanut butter. Divide the paste evenly among smaller bowls and cover them with plastic wrap.

Working with one bowl at a time, stir 2 or 3 drops of food coloring into the paste, adding more drops as desired for brighter color. (Keep the other bowls covered with plastic wrap; this prevents the paste from drying out.) Leave one bowl untinted to make white sprinkles. Spoon one tinted paste into a pastry bag fitted with a tiny round tip (#5) or into a large parchment paper cornet (see page 25). Pipe straight, long lines onto a prepared baking sheet, using up all the paste. Wash out the bag and tip (if using), or make more cornets, and repeat with the remaining pastes. Let dry overnight, uncovered, at room temperature.

The next day, cut the long lines of paste into ¼-inch-long sprinkles using a pizza cutter.

Sprinkles can be stored indefinitely in an airtight container at room temperature. Note that sprinkles will start to bleed on a cake after a few hours, so it's best to decorate the cake shortly before serving.

Coffee Syrup

MAKES ABOUT 1 CUP

¾ cup/**180 grams** strong hot
brewed coffee

¾ cup/**150 grams** sugar

In a small bowl, whisk together the coffee and sugar until the sugar is dissolved. Store in an airtight container in the fridge for up to 2 months.

Passion Fruit Crêpe Cake

MAKES ONE 9-INCH CAKE, TO SERVE 10 TO 12

Crêpes (page 350)

1 recipe Master Pastry Cream
(page 434)

Passion Fruit Curd for Crêpe
Cake (page 351)

½ cup/**120 grams** heavy cream

2 tablespoons confectioners'
sugar, for garnish

A crêpe cake is layers and layers of thin, tender crêpes topped with cream and stacked one on top of the other to make a magical, ethereal stunner of a dessert. It is not hard to make; like most pastries it just takes a lot of patience and the willingness to follow through on a lot of different components, each with many steps. But the result will knock you out. The good thing is that pretty much every component can be made in advance and the cake itself is best after sitting for 4 hours at a minimum. Plan carefully (you'll need to start the recipe at least 2 days in advance) and have fun assembling!

At least 1 day before you'll be assembling the cake, make the crêpes.

Make the pastry cream and passion fruit curd and set aside.

In a stand mixer fitted with a paddle attachment, whip the heavy cream until it is stiff. Gently fold in the pastry cream until the mixture is homogeneous. You should have about 3½ cups of the pastry cream mixture.

Go through the crêpes and find the prettiest one; set it aside for the top. Place a crêpe on a flat serving plate and spoon 2 level tablespoons of the pastry cream mixture on top. Spread the cream out to the edge of the crêpe in a very thin, even layer. Spoon 1 level tablespoon of the passion fruit curd on top of the cream and spread it evenly in a thin layer. Center a second crêpe on top

and repeat until all the crêpes, pastry cream, and curd are used up, using the saved beauty crêpe for the final layer (don't top this one with cream or curd!). You should have a nice even stack of 18 to 20 crêpes with layers of cream and curd in between. For stability, cut a bamboo skewer to just under the exact height of the cake and poke it straight down into the center of the cake all the way through so it is not visible. Refrigerate the crêpe cake overnight so the cream has time to firm up.

Before serving, use a fine-mesh sieve to generously cover the top with confectioners' sugar. Use a serrated knife to carefully cut slices of cake.

Continues...

Crêpes

**MAKES 22 TO 24 CRÊPES,
ALLOWING FOR MESS-UPS AND SNACKING**

1½ cups/**210 grams**
all-purpose flour

1 tablespoon sugar

½ teaspoon kosher salt

6 large eggs (about
300 grams), at room
temperature

½ cup/1 stick/**115 grams**
unsalted butter, melted and
cooled, plus 1 to 2 tablespoons,
at room temperature,
for the pan

2⅔ cups/**640 grams**
whole milk, at room
temperature

The day before you'll be cooking the crêpes, mix the flour, sugar, and salt in a large bowl. In a medium bowl, whisk together the eggs, melted butter, and milk. Make a well in the flour mixture and pour in the egg mixture. Whisk them together until entirely combined and no lumps remain. Alternatively, place all the ingredients in a blender and blend for 30 seconds, until well combined. Transfer the crêpe batter to an airtight container and refrigerate overnight.

The next day, remove the crêpe batter from the fridge and whisk it well. Heat a 9-inch nonstick skillet over medium heat. Add a few teaspoons of the room temperature butter and tilt the skillet from side to side to cover the bottom with butter. Starting at one end of the skillet, use your right hand (if you are right-handed) to pour in a scant ¼ cup of the crêpe batter at around two o'clock on the pan; immediately lift up and tilt the skillet with your left hand and move it in a circle to distribute the batter evenly across the bottom of the skillet. Cook for 1 to 2 minutes, until the edges of the crêpe start to curl up and look dry. The bottom of the crêpe should start to look golden brown. When you can pull up the crêpe from the edge,

carefully flip it over with a spatula and cook for another 25 to 30 seconds, until the bottom is lightly browned. Remove the crêpe from the skillet and place it on a plate. Repeat with the remaining batter, stacking the crêpes one on top of the other (no parchment or waxed paper needed in between). If the crêpes start to stick to the skillet, add a few teaspoons more butter to the skillet to reseason it.

The first crêpe usually tears and is wonky as you are figuring out the heat and the right way to move the skillet. Some people prefer to pour with their left hand and control the skillet with their right hand — it's up to you, so play around with what works.

The crêpes can be stored in the fridge, well wrapped in plastic wrap, for up to 2 days.

Passion Fruit Curd for Crêpe Cake

MAKES ABOUT 2 CUPS

¾ cup/1½ sticks/**170 grams** unsalted butter, cut into small pieces

½ cup/**100 grams** passion fruit puree (either purchase or make by pureeing the inside of about 10 passion fruits with a few tablespoons water and straining the resulting mixture through a fine-mesh sieve)

3 tablespoons/**45 grams** fresh lemon juice (about ¾ large lemon)

¾ cup/**150 grams** sugar

5 large egg yolks (about **100 grams**), at room temperature

¼ teaspoon pure vanilla extract

¼ teaspoon kosher salt

In a medium saucepan, combine the butter, passion fruit puree, and lemon juice and heat over medium-high heat to just under a boil. In a medium bowl, whisk together the sugar and egg yolks. Remove the passion fruit mixture from the heat and gradually whisk about ½ cup of it into the sugar–egg yolk mixture to temper the eggs (see page 29). Continue whisking the hot liquid into the eggs about ½ cup at a time until it is all incorporated.

Return the curd to the saucepan and set it over medium heat. Cook, stirring continuously with a wooden spoon, making sure to scrape the bottom of the saucepan frequently to prevent the egg yolks from scrambling, until the curd thickens and coats the spoon with a thick enough layer that you can draw your finger through it and it holds a line, 5 to 8 minutes.

Remove the curd from the heat and strain it through a fine-mesh sieve into a medium bowl or pitcher. Whisk in the vanilla and salt. Cover with plastic wrap, pressing it directly on the surface of the curd (to prevent a skin from forming), and let cool to room temperature. Refrigerate for at least 4 hours before using.

The curd can be stored in an airtight container in the fridge for up to 1 week.

The wow factor

Almond Panna Cotta with Stone Fruit Cocktail / 355

Pumpkin-Pecan Bread Pudding / 357

Summer Blueberry-Peach Cobbler / 361

Rum Butterscotch Pudding Parfait
with Ginger-Molasses Crumble / 364

Dulce de Leche Brioche Buns / 367

Matcha Cream Puffs / 371

Vietnamese Espresso Profiteroles
with Spicy Chocolate Ganache / 375

Coconut Sticky Rice with Mango-Lime Curd
and Mango Snow / 379

Passion Fruit and Raspberry Pavlovas / 383

Marvelous Vanilla Caramel Merveilleux / 385

Swedish Napoleon / 388

CHAPTER 6

Time to Show Off

Almond Panna Cotta
with Stone Fruit Cocktail

MAKES 6 CUSTARDS

2 cups/**480 grams** whole milk

1 tablespoon plus 1 teaspoon unflavored granulated gelatin (measure what you need from two ¼-ounce packets of gelatin)

2 cups/**480 grams** half-and-half

¾ cup/**150 grams** sugar

1 teaspoon pure almond extract

½ teaspoon kosher salt

¼ teaspoon pure vanilla extract

Stone Fruit Cocktail (page 356)

When I was a little girl, my mother was notorious (in my eyes) for never letting us have dessert. Unless you count orange slices. Which I didn't. A few times a year for very special occasions she would break out her recipe box and make "White Almond Jell-O." I adored this Asian dessert of milk and almond extract set with enough gelatin that you could bounce a penny off it and topped with canned fruit cocktail. To me, this was fine dining at its very best. Years later as a professional pastry chef, I learned to make custards of all kinds. Panna cotta was and continues to be my favorite: milk and/or cream set with a little gelatin and simply flavored with vanilla or coffee.

Looking back at Mom's trusty recipe I realized hers is essentially a classic panna cotta flavored with almond. Armed with what I knew about what makes a great dessert, I fiddled with her recipe by reducing both the gelatin and the sugar and adding some half-and-half to create a really soft, silky, creamy custard. Topped with a fresh stone fruit compote, this panna cotta takes every taste memory I have of White Almond Jell-O and makes it even better than I remember.

As with any gelatin dessert, you will need to start this the day prior to serving to allow the gelatin ample time to set, so please plan accordingly.

Pour about 1 cup/240 grams of the milk into a medium bowl. Evenly sprinkle the gelatin across the surface of the milk. (Don't dump the gelatin in a pile onto the milk, or it will not dissolve properly.) Stir gently to expose all the gelatin to the milk and let it soften for a few minutes.

In a small saucepan, warm the rest of the milk with the half-and-half until it is hot to the touch, but don't bring it to a boil. (If the liquid is too hot the gelatin won't gel.) Whisk the hot milk-cream mixture into the milk-gelatin mixture until the gelatin fully dissolves. Whisk in the sugar, almond extract, salt, and vanilla until the sugar is totally dissolved. Carefully pour the mixture into six 6-ounce ramekins. Place them in the fridge overnight to fully set up. (At this point the panna cotta can be covered well with plastic wrap and stored in the fridge for up to 3 days.)

Make the stone fruit cocktail.

When you're ready to serve, run a knife around the edge of the ramekins and invert the panna cottas onto individual serving plates. Spoon the stone fruit cocktail over the top and alongside them. Serve immediately.

Stone Fruit Cocktail

MAKES ABOUT 3 CUPS

1 ripe red or black plum

1 ripe peach

2 ripe apricots

10 to 12 ripe fresh cherries

1 tablespoon sugar

6 to 8 fresh basil leaves

Slice the plum, peach, and apricots into thin slices and place in a medium bowl; discard the pits. Pit and halve the cherries and add to the stone fruits. Sprinkle the sugar over the fruits. Stack the basil leaves, roll them like a cigar, and slice them crosswise into very thin ribbons (this is known as chiffonade). Add the basil to the fruits and toss to combine. Let sit at room temperature for at least 10 minutes to draw out some of the juices of the fruits.

Stone fruit cocktail can be made up to 6 hours in advance and stored in the fridge. It will reduce in volume as it sits and the fruits let out more juice. Stir gently before using.

Pumpkin-Pecan
Bread Pudding

SERVES 10 TO 12

One 15-ounce/**425-gram** can pumpkin puree (NOT pumpkin pie mix with spices and sugar in it)

1 teaspoon ground ginger

1 teaspoon ground cinnamon

½ teaspoon freshly grated nutmeg

½ teaspoon kosher salt

Large pinch of ground cloves

⅔ cup/7 ounces/**200 grams** sweetened condensed milk

One 5-ounce/**140-gram** can evaporated milk

6 large eggs (about **300 grams**), at room temperature

2½ cups/**600 grams** half-and-half

1 teaspoon pure vanilla extract

8 slices stale white crusty bread, cut into 1-inch cubes (about 8 cups)

1 cup/**100 grams** pecan halves

¾ cup firmly packed/ **165 grams** light brown sugar

1 quart vanilla ice cream, for serving

This bread pudding was the happiest accident to ever occur at Flour. We had just finished a super-successful Thanksgiving season . . . except for the fact that we had overshot by a loooooong way how many pumpkin pies we would be baking off. We had a humongous vat of creamy, rich pumpkin custard left over and no more pie shells. "What about pumpkin bread pudding?" one of our bakers asked. Genius! We took leftover sticky buns, chopped them up, and soaked them in the pie base. We baked off the bread puddings the next day and drizzled them with some of the caramel goo that we bake the sticky buns in. It was so good that we sometimes make pumpkin pie base just so we can make this bread pudding.

If you happen to have 6 to 8 leftover sticky buns (unlikely!) then feel free to use those; however, here I modify the recipe using plain white bread, toasted pecans, and brown sugar. To give ample time for the bread to soak up the spiced custard you need to start the recipe a day in advance of serving.

Scrape the pumpkin puree into a medium saucepan and cook over medium-low heat, stirring occasionally with a wooden spoon, for 15 to 20 minutes, until it reduces into a somewhat thick paste and darkens in color. Remove the pumpkin from the heat and whisk in the ginger, cinnamon, nutmeg, salt, and cloves. Whisk in the condensed milk and evaporated milk.

In a large bowl, whisk the eggs together, then slowly whisk in the half-and-half and vanilla. Gradually add the pumpkin mixture and whisk until thoroughly mixed.

Generously butter a 9 x 13-inch baking pan or spray it with pan spray. Place the bread in the pan and pour the pumpkin custard over it. Push the bread down into the liquid, making sure all the bread is covered. Cover the pan with plastic wrap and let it sit overnight in the fridge. (This allows the bread to fully soak up all the pumpkin custard.)

The next day, preheat the oven to 350°F and place a rack in the center of the oven. Roughly chop the pecans and place on a baking sheet. Toast for 8 to 10 minutes, until they are light golden brown and fragrant. Remove from the oven and let cool for a few minutes.

Remove the bread pudding from the fridge and use a rubber spatula or wooden spoon to give the whole thing a few gentle folds to get the bread underneath on top and the stuff on top on the bottom. The bread will have soaked up a lot of the custard. Sprinkle about ½ cup/110 grams of the brown sugar and all the pecans evenly over the pudding. Gently fold the sugar and pecans into the pudding; you don't need to mix it together thoroughly, just enough to get some of the pecans and sugar into the pudding. Sprinkle the remaining ¼ cup/55 grams brown sugar evenly over the top.

Bake the bread pudding for 1 hour 10 minutes to 1 hour 20 minutes, rotating the pan midway through the baking time, until the pudding is browned on top and set in the middle. Test the pudding by pushing a paring knife into the center — it should come out dry.

Remove from the oven and let cool for at least 30 minutes before serving. The pudding will puff up in the oven, then deflate a bit as it cools. Serve warm with vanilla ice cream.

Leftover bread pudding can be stored, well wrapped, in the fridge for up to 5 days. You can serve it cold, or warm it in a 300°F oven for about 15 minutes.

Blueberry-Peach Cobbler

SERVES 8 TO 10

Cobbler Biscuits
(page 362)

8 cups/**1,000 grams**
fresh blueberries

3 cups thinly sliced unpeeled
ripe peaches (about
1½ pounds/**680 grams**
whole peaches)

¾ cup/**150 grams**
superfine sugar

3 tablespoons plus
2 teaspoons/**30 grams**
cornstarch

1 tablespoon grated lemon zest
(about 1 large lemon)

¼ teaspoon kosher salt

1 large egg yolk (about
20 grams), for egg wash

2 teaspoons sanding sugar

When you have a recipe you love, like I do my blueberry-lemon pie that I've perfected for Christopher, you pull it out of your back pocket for as many occasions as you can. I've used the blueberry pie filling for mini hand pies (see page 249), and I love to mix a few spoonfuls into hot grain cereal. In the height of summer I use the recipe as a jumping-off point to make a jammy, juicy cobbler with honey-sweet peaches. About half the blueberries and all the peaches are first cooked down until the juices are released, then the rest of the blueberries are tossed in to give the filling some body. The cream biscuits bake into the filling so they are crunchy on top and soft and tender underneath. The ratio of fruit to biscuit is about one to one, so you have enough biscuit with every bite of luscious fruit.

Make the biscuit dough and set the cut biscuits aside unbaked.

Preheat the oven to 350°F and place a rack in the center of the oven.

In a medium saucepan, combine about half the blueberries, all the peaches, the superfine sugar, cornstarch, lemon zest, and salt. Cook over medium heat, stirring occasionally, until the fruit, sugar, and cornstarch melt into a gooey mass, 3 to 5 minutes. Remove from the heat and stir in the remaining berries. Pour the fruit filling into a 9 x 13-inch baking pan and top with the biscuits.

Whisk the egg yolk in a small bowl with a fork. Use a pastry brush to brush the tops of the biscuits evenly

with the egg wash. Sprinkle the biscuits evenly with the sanding sugar.

Bake for about 1 hour, rotating the pan midway through the baking time, until the biscuits are golden brown and the fruit is bubbling.

Remove from the oven and let cool for at least 30 minutes before serving so no one burns the roof of their mouth.

Cobbler can be served warm or at room temperature. It is best eaten the day it's baked, but you can store leftover cobbler at room temperature, well wrapped, for up to 2 days. Refresh in a 300°F oven for about 10 minutes before serving.

Continues...

Cobbler Biscuits

MAKES 12 BISCUITS

2½ cups/**350 grams**
all-purpose flour

6 tablespoons/**75 grams** sugar

2½ teaspoons baking powder

½ teaspoon kosher salt

10 tablespoons/1¼ sticks/
140 grams unsalted butter,
cold, cut into 8 to 10 pieces

1 large egg (about **50 grams**),
at room temperature

1 large egg yolk (about
20 grams), at room
temperature, plus 1 yolk
(about **20 grams**) for egg wash,
if baking the biscuits
on their own

½ cup/**120 grams** heavy cream

¼ cup/**60 grams** whole milk

1 teaspoon pure vanilla extract

In a stand mixer fitted with a paddle attachment, briefly mix the flour, sugar, baking powder, and salt. Add the butter and paddle for about 30 seconds on low speed until the butter is somewhat broken down but there are still pieces about the size of lima beans.

In another bowl, whisk together the whole egg, 1 egg yolk, the cream, milk, and vanilla until thoroughly mixed. With the mixer running on low, pour the egg-milk mixture into the flour-butter mixture and paddle for 15 to 20 seconds, until the dough just comes together. There will probably still be a little loose flour mixture at the bottom of the bowl.

Remove the bowl from the mixer. Gather and lift the dough with your hands and turn it over in the bowl so that it starts to pick up the loose flour at the bottom. Turn the dough several times until all the loose flour is mixed in.

Flick flour over the work surface. Dump out the dough onto it and pat the dough into an 9-inch circle, ½ to ¾ inch thick. Use a 3-inch circle cutter to cut out biscuits. Gather and reroll the scraps, then cut out more biscuits. You should get 12 biscuits total.

Unbaked biscuits can be stored, well wrapped, in the fridge for up to 2 days or in the freezer for up to 2 weeks.

If you would like to bake the biscuits on their own (they are delicious in their own right), preheat the oven to 350°F and place a rack in the center of the oven. Line a baking sheet with parchment paper. Place the biscuits on the prepared baking sheet, at least 1 inch apart. Whisk the egg yolk for the egg wash in a small bowl with a fork. Use a pastry brush to brush the tops of the biscuits evenly with the egg wash. Bake for 40 to 45 minutes, rotating the baking sheet midway through the baking time, until the biscuits are entirely golden brown on top. Remove from the oven and let cool on the baking sheet on a wire rack.

Leftover baked biscuits can be stored in an airtight container at room temperature for up to 3 days. Refresh in a 300°F oven for 6 to 8 minutes before serving.

Rum Butterscotch Pudding Parfait

with Ginger-Molasses Crumble

MAKES 8 PARFAITS

Ginger-Molasses Cookie Crumble (page 366)

6 large egg yolks (about **120 grams**), at room temperature

6 tablespoons/**50 grams** cornstarch

1 teaspoon kosher salt

3⅓ cups/**800 grams** whole milk

2 tablespoons unsulfured molasses

2¼ teaspoons pure vanilla extract

2 tablespoons dark rum or Scotch

1 cup/**200 grams** superfine sugar

¾ cup/1½ sticks/**170 grams** unsalted butter, at cool room temperature

1 cup/**240 grams** heavy cream

½ cup/**120 grams** crème fraîche

3 tablespoons/**20 grams** confectioners' sugar

I make a mean butterscotch pudding, with lots of brown sugar and butter, finished with a hefty amount of salt and vanilla to accent the toasted caramel flavors. You can find the recipe in my first book, *Flour*. I make it over and over, especially when I am craving something unapologetically sweet. When Mike, one of our pastry chefs, presented me with his version, I made sure to keep a very open mind with the first bite. I had no need to worry—that first taste was so good I immediately asked for the recipe so I could add it to my repertoire. The main difference is that there's a swig of rum cooked into the pudding. It adds a fruity, bright note that helps cut through the rich custard. I like this pudding dressed up as a layered parfait with whipped crème fraîche and a spicy ginger cookie crumble. Make these ahead of time in small lidded cups and bring them in a cooler to your next picnic or outdoor event.

Make the crumble and set it aside.

In a medium bowl, whisk together the egg yolks, cornstarch, and salt. Whisk in about half the milk, the molasses, 2 teaspoons of the vanilla, and the rum. Set aside.

In a medium saucepan, combine the superfine sugar and about ¼ cup/ 50 grams water to moisten all of the sugar. Brush the sides of the pan with a pastry brush dipped in water if there are any sugar crystals clinging to the pan. Place the saucepan on high heat and bring to a boil. Don't stir the mixture and don't jostle the pan (you want to avoid crystallization of the syrup, which can happen if the pan is disturbed while the syrup is coming to a boil). Boil rapidly without moving the pan until the syrup starts to caramelize, 1 to 2 minutes. The sugar syrup will boil furiously at first, then slowly thicken as the water boils off. Some of the syrup around the edge will start to color to a golden yellow like a butterscotch candy — at this point swirl the pan to even out the coloring and caramelization. Keep swirling gently until the caramel is deep golden brown. Turn the heat down to low and slowly and carefully whisk in the remaining milk. Be very careful, as the caramel will sputter and spit and possibly seize up — use a long-handled whisk and stand away from the pot until it settles. Whisk until the milk is completely incorporated into the caramel and any hardened caramel bits have melted.

Ladle a few spoonfuls of the hot caramel milk into the egg yolk mixture and whisk to combine and temper the eggs (see page 29). Keep ladling and whisking until about half the caramel milk has been added to the egg yolk mixture. Scrape all the egg yolk–caramel milk mixture into the pot with the rest of the caramel milk.

Cook the pudding over medium heat, stirring constantly with a rubber spatula, for 6 to 8 minutes, until it thickens and coats the back of the spatula. (The pudding will start out liquid and sloshy and then start to steam as it gets thicker.) Immediately remove the pudding from the stove and pour it through a fine-mesh sieve into a heatproof container. Let the pudding cool to room temperature for 1 hour or so, stirring occasionally.

Scrape the pudding into a blender or a food processor, or if you have an immersion blender you can use that right in the container. With the blender running on low, add the butter in small chunks until all of the butter is added. Scrape the pudding into a container and cover with a piece of plastic wrap, pressing it directly against the surface (to prevent a skin from forming). Refrigerate the pudding for at least 6 hours or up to overnight, until fully chilled. (At this point the pudding can be stored in

an airtight container in the fridge for up to 4 days.)

When you are ready to make the parfaits, remove the pudding from the fridge and peel off the plastic. In a stand mixer fitted with a whisk attachment, whip together the heavy cream, crème fraîche, confectioners' sugar, and remaining ¼ teaspoon vanilla until soft and billowing. Spoon a heaping ½ cup of the pudding into each of eight rocks

glasses or other straight-sided, wide-mouthed 8-ounce glasses. Add a few tablespoons of cookie crumble on top of the pudding, sprinkling it evenly across the surface. Top with about ⅓ cup of the whipped crème fraîche. Garnish with more cookie crumble. Serve immediately, or keep chilled and serve within 5 hours.

Ginger-Molasses Cookie Crumble

**MAKES ABOUT 6 COOKIES, ENOUGH
CRUMBLE FOR 8 PARFAITS**

6 tablespoons/¾ stick/**85 grams** unsalted butter, melted and cooled until cool to the touch

½ cup firmly packed/**110 grams** light brown sugar

2 tablespoons/**40 grams** unsulfured molasses

1 large egg (about **50 grams**), at room temperature

1 cup/**140 grams** all-purpose flour

½ teaspoon baking soda

½ teaspoon ground ginger

¼ teaspoon ground cinnamon

¼ teaspoon kosher salt

⅛ teaspoon freshly ground black pepper

Preheat the oven to 350°F and position a rack in the center of the oven. Line a baking sheet with parchment paper and set it aside.

In a stand mixer fitted with a paddle attachment, combine the butter, brown sugar, molasses, and egg and mix on medium-high speed for about 20 seconds, until well combined. Paddle in 1 tablespoon water. In a separate bowl, stir together the flour, baking soda, ginger, cinnamon, salt, and pepper. With the mixer on low, paddle the flour mixture into the butter-sugar mixture until well combined. (At this point, the unbaked dough can be stored in an airtight container in the refrigerator for up to 1 week.)

Scoop out ¼-cup balls of dough and place them on the prepared baking sheet about 2 inches apart. Bake for 22 to 24 minutes, rotating the baking sheet midway through the baking time, until the cookies are crackly on top and firm to the touch.

Remove the cookies from the oven and let them cool on the baking sheet on a wire rack for 5 to 10 minutes. Transfer the cookies to the rack to cool completely.

Use a sharp chef's knife to chop the cookies into tiny pieces. You can also crumble the cookies by hand. The crumble will be a little soft and piece-y.

The crumble can be stored in an airtight container at room temperature for up to 3 days.

Dulce de Leche
Brioche Buns

MAKES 12 BUNS

One 14-ounce/**400-gram** can sweetened condensed milk (from whole milk, not skim or fat-free)

1 recipe Master Brioche Dough (page 444)

1 large egg (about **50 grams**), for egg wash

2 tablespoons sugar

Large pinch of ground cinnamon

Dulce de leche is a completely decadent concoction made of milk mixed with sugar that is cooked long and slow until it caramelizes and becomes thick and deep golden brown. It's like eating the richest caramel candy you can imagine: so sweet it hurts your teeth but so rich you really don't mind. A shortcut method of making dulce de leche is to simmer an unopened can of sweetened condensed milk for about 3 hours. It slowly caramelizes in the can; you can use it in cakes, frostings, pies, and cookies. One of our pastry chefs, Miguel, who hails from Mexico, where dulce de leche is popular, filled our fluffy buttery brioche with this gooey caramel for a monthly special. It was a knockout combination. It also makes for a spectacular presentation when you cut into the brioche and the dulce de leche oozes out. Prepare this when you want to show off for a special brunch.

Because the various components need to be prepared ahead, be sure to plan accordingly.

Make the dulce de leche: Place the unopened can of condensed milk in a pot tall enough that you can cover it with a few inches of water. Fill the pot with water and make sure it covers the can all the way to the top and then some. Bring the water to a boil. Lower the temperature to medium so that the water is at a steady simmer. Cover the pot and simmer for 3 hours, keeping an eye on the water level and adding more if necessary. The entire can should be underwater at all times.

After 3 hours of simmering, turn off the heat and let the can sit in the water until it is cool enough to handle. Remove the can from the water and let sit at room temperature for at least 2 hours. (The unopened can of dulce de leche can be stored in the fridge for up to 1 month.)

Pro tip: VERY IMPORTANT! This has never happened to us or anyone we know, but we have heard stories that if the water is not completely covering the can, it could explode, and the same if you don't let the can cool completely before opening. So please be careful! Again, we have never seen it, but better to be safe than sorry.

Mix the brioche dough and let it proof for 6 hours or up to overnight in the fridge as directed.

Line a 12-cup jumbo muffin tin with muffin papers and set it aside. (You can also make these without a muffin tin and bake them free form on a baking sheet lined with parchment paper.)

Divide the brioche dough into 12 pieces, each roughly 3½ ounces/100 grams. Place the dough pieces on the work surface and one by one round each piece into a ball. To do this, cup the dough in your hand, making a cage for the dough with your palm and fingers. Press the dough into the work surface while simultaneously moving the dough and your hand in a circular motion. (Rounding buns is sort of like tying your shoe — it is a very easy motion once you get it but first learning it takes some practice. Keep practicing and you will get it! The purpose of rounding the dough is to create a taut ball of dough that allows the brioche to grow and proof evenly and bake nicely.) Place the brioche balls in the muffin tins or on the prepared baking sheet. Cover with plastic wrap and let proof at room temperature for about 1 hour, until the brioches are soft and relaxed.

Open the can of dulce de leche and stir it with a spoon — it should have the same consistency as uncooked sweetened condensed milk, like very thick, viscous honey. If the dulce de leche has cooked too much, it will have a consistency more like sour cream; in that case you need to thin it out by mixing in a few drops of milk or water. Fill a pastry bag fitted with a ½-inch round tip with the dulce de leche. Using a chopstick or a small paring knife, poke a hole in the center on the top of a brioche ball and push into the dough; you want to poke deep into the brioche but not so deep you go to the bottom. Place the tip of the pastry bag deep into the hole and slowly pull up, angling the pastry bag forward and backward and left and right as you pipe. The goal is to pipe the dulce evenly throughout the ball and not just in the center. Continue with all the brioche balls and all the dulce de leche. The dulce de leche may leak out the top of the brioche, which is normal; do your best to keep it all inside, and if needed, wipe off any rogue dulce de leche with your finger. Cover again with the plastic wrap and let the brioches continue to proof for 30 to 45 minutes, until the brioches are wobbly and feel a bit like water balloons when you poke them.

Preheat the oven to 350°F and place a rack in the center of the oven. Whisk the egg for the egg wash in a small bowl with a fork. Use a pastry brush to brush the tops of the brioches evenly with the egg wash. Stir together the sugar and cinnamon and sprinkle evenly and generously across the tops of the brioches. Bake for 30 to 35 minutes, rotating the pan midway through the baking time, until the brioches are golden brown all over.

Remove from the oven and let cool in the pan on a wire rack.

Dulce de leche brioches are best served the same day you bake them so the dulce de leche is soft and the brioches are fresh.

Vietnamese Espresso Profiteroles

with Spicy Chocolate Ganache

MAKES ABOUT 20 PROFITEROLES

Vietnamese Espresso Ice Cream (page 377)

½ cup/1 stick/**115 grams** unsalted butter

1 tablespoon sugar

½ teaspoon kosher salt

1 cup plus 1 tablespoon/ **150 grams** all-purpose flour

4 large eggs (about **200 grams**), at room temperature

Spicy Ganache (page 377), warmed

Profiteroles were one of the first "fancy" desserts I ever made before I became a professional pastry chef. I had a book on pastry fundamentals and I remember starting at page one with *pâte à choux* (cream puff dough). *Choux* means "cabbage" in French, and these little puffs look a bit like cabbages if you squint. (You have to squint a lot.) You can pipe pastry cream into the round puffs for bakery cream puffs, or fill them with ice cream and drizzle them with chocolate for the classic bistro dessert profiteroles. Here I jazz up the French tradition by whipping up a quick ice cream that tastes like the popular Vietnamese coffee drink made with sweetened condensed milk and strong espresso. The chocolate ganache drizzle echoes the Asian flavor of the ice cream with hint of cayenne pepper. All the components can be made ahead of time (and in fact you must make the ice cream a day in advance to give it ample time to firm up) and assembled quickly right before serving, so it's a terrific dessert option for a dinner party.

Make the ice cream and store it in the freezer until you're ready to assemble the profiteroles.

Preheat the oven to 400°F and place racks in the center and bottom third of the oven. Butter two baking sheets or line them with parchment paper and set aside.

In a medium saucepan, heat the butter, sugar, salt, and 1 cup/240 grams water over medium heat until the butter is melted. Do not let the mixture come to a boil or the water will evaporate. Add the flour all at once and use a wooden spoon to stir the flour into the liquid until it is fully

incorporated. The mixture will look like a stiff pancake batter. Keep stirring vigorously over medium heat and the mixture will slowly start to get stiffer and look more like loose dough and less like batter. It will lose its shine and become more matte as well. Stir continuously for 3 to 4 minutes, until the dough starts to leave a film on the bottom of the pan.

Remove the dough from the heat and place it in a stand mixer. Using a paddle attachment, mix the dough for 1 minute on medium-low speed. Alternatively, beat the dough in a bowl by hand with a wooden spoon

for 2 to 3 minutes. (This will allow some of the steam to escape and the dough will cool slightly.)

Crack the eggs into a small pitcher or liquid measuring cup and whisk to break up the yolks. With the mixer on medium-low, gradually add the eggs to the dough. When the eggs are all added, turn the mixer up to medium and beat for about 20 seconds, until the dough is glossy and shiny and soft like gluey mashed potatoes.

Spoon the dough into a pastry bag fitted with a 1-inch round tip or cut the corner so that the hole is about 1 inch in diameter. Pipe out round puffs onto the prepared baking sheets about 2 inches in diameter, spacing the puffs a few inches away from each other.

Place the baking sheets in the oven, one on each rack. The heat of the oven will immediately start turning the liquid in the dough into steam and it will cause the puffs to inflate.

Bake for about 15 minutes, until the puffs have expanded and have started to turn golden brown, then turn the oven down to 325°F. Continue baking for another

20 to 30 minutes, rotating the baking sheets and switching their positions after 10 to 15 minutes, until the puffs are entirely golden brown like honey.

Remove from the oven and let cool completely on the baking sheets on a wire rack. (At this point the unfilled puffs can be stored in an airtight container at room temperature for up to 4 days or in the freezer for up to 1 month. Refresh in a 300°F oven for 3 to 4 minutes if at room temperature, 8 to 10 minutes if frozen, then let cool again before continuing.)

While the puffs are baking and cooling, make the ganache. If it has been refrigerated, melt it before using by placing it in a metal or heatproof glass bowl over a pot of simmering water and stirring until warm and melted.

If the ice cream is too hard to scoop, remove it from the freezer 10 minutes before assembling. Split the cooled puffs in half horizontally. Using a ½-cup measure or ½-cup ice cream scoop, place a large scoop of ice cream on the bottom half of each puff. Top with the top half and drizzle about 1 tablespoon of the warm ganache on top. Serve immediately.

Vietnamese Espresso Ice Cream

MAKES ABOUT 2 QUARTS

2 tablespoons instant espresso powder

1 tablespoon plus 1 teaspoon pure vanilla extract

½ teaspoon kosher salt

2½ cups/**600 grams** heavy cream

One 14-ounce/**400-gram** can sweetened condensed milk

In a small bowl, whisk together the espresso powder, vanilla, salt, and 2 tablespoons warm water until the espresso powder is dissolved. Stir the espresso mixture into the cream in a large bowl and whip by hand with a whisk or with a handheld electric mixer, or in a stand mixer fitted with a whisk attachment, until it thickens to soft peaks (i.e., it holds a soft peak when you lift a spoon out of the mixture). Pour in the sweetened condensed milk and whip until the ice cream base is thoroughly combined and again at soft peak stage. It will be billowing and mound gently on a spoon when you dip into it. Gently transfer the base to an airtight container and freeze until solid, at least 8 hours.

The ice cream can be stored in an airtight container in the freezer for up to 1 month.

Spicy Ganache

MAKES ABOUT 1½ CUPS

8 ounces/**225 grams** semisweet or bittersweet chocolate

1 cup/**240 grams** heavy cream

½ teaspoon cayenne pepper, or more to taste

Chop the chocolate and place it in a medium metal or heatproof glass bowl. Heat the cream in a small saucepan over medium-high heat until just before it comes to a boil, when small bubbles collect along the sides of the pan. Pour the cream over the chocolate and let stand for 30 seconds. Add the cayenne pepper. Slowly whisk everything together until the chocolate is completely melted and the ganache is smooth.

The ganache can be stored in an airtight container in the refrigerator for up to 2 weeks.

Coconut Sticky Rice

with Mango-Lime Curd and Mango Snow

MAKES 6 SERVINGS

1½ cups/**300 grams** sweet glutinous rice (sometimes called Thai sticky rice or Thai sweet rice)

Mango Ice (page 380)

Mango-Lime Curd (page 381)

One 13.5- to 14-ounce/ **375- to 390-gram** can full-fat coconut milk

¼ cup/**50 grams** sugar

½ teaspoon kosher salt

2 ripe Champagne mangos

1 teaspoon white sesame seeds, for garnish

1 teaspoon black sesame seeds, for garnish

Grated zest of 1 lime, for garnish

On a recent trip to Thailand, Christopher and I enjoyed the traditional Thai dessert of coconut sticky rice and mango at least once if not two or three times a day. I was so infatuated by it that some days it was my breakfast, my afternoon snack, and my after-dinner dessert. At the airport on our way back home I spent the last of my baht on—you guessed it—sticky rice and mango. Back in Boston I was determined to add this to our menu at Myers+Chang. Sticky or glutinous rice is translucent and chewy and highly addictive. The sticky rice pudding is simply sticky rice mixed into a slightly sweetened coconut milk custard; alongside we serve a tart tropical mango curd with juicy fresh mango folded in. Fluffy mango snow on top makes the dessert extra special.

Read through the recipe carefully: the sticky rice needs to soak overnight, and the mango ice needs to be made a day in advance. And then once you mix the rice with the coconut milk you need to serve it right away. Otherwise the rice continues to absorb the coconut over time and turns into a firm mass.

The day before serving, place the sticky rice in a bowl and add enough water to cover; set aside at room temperature to soak overnight. Make the mango ice.

At least 4 hours before serving, make the mango-lime curd.

If you have a rice cooker, drain the soaked rice and place it in the rice cooker, add 1½ cups/360 grams water, and turn the rice cooker on. When the rice is finished cooking, transfer it to a large bowl and let

it cool to room temperature, about 1 hour.

If you're not using a rice cooker, drain the soaked rice and place it in a large heatproof fine-mesh sieve that fits over a saucepan. Fill the saucepan with water, making sure it does not touch the bottom of the sieve when it is placed in the pan. Bring the water to a boil over high heat, then reduce the heat so the water is at a gentle simmer. Cover the pan and let the rice steam for

20 minutes. Remove the lid and turn the rice over in the sieve with a large spoon or rubber spatula (it might be stuck together as one piece). Add more water to the pan if necessary and keep steaming the rice, covered, for another 20 minutes. Check the rice — it should be translucent and soft with no hard bits. If it is still hard, steam it for another 10 minutes, until it fully cooks. Turn off the heat and let the rice continue to steam, covered, for another 10 minutes. Transfer the rice to a large bowl and let it cool to room temperature.

While the rice is cooling, whisk together the coconut milk, sugar, and salt in another large bowl. When the rice has cooled to room temperature, add it to the coconut milk mixture. Stir the rice into the coconut milk with a fork and smush the rice around until it is fully mixed into the coconut milk.

Remove the mango ice from the freezer and let it sit at room temperature for about 10 minutes. Peel the mangos. Cut half into thin slices for garnish and set aside. Cut the rest into cubes of about ½ inch. Fold the mango cubes into the mango-lime curd. Divide the mango curd mixture among six ice cream bowls or medium cups. Divide the coconut sticky rice among the bowls, piling it on top of the mango mixture.

Use a spoon to scrape at the mango ice to make shavings. Keep scraping until all the ice is shaved into soft fluffy snow. If you have bits of ice that don't scrape well, use the butt of a rolling pin or a wooden spoon to beat the ice so it smushes up. Divide the snow evenly among the bowls, covering the rice. Arrange the mango slices on top of the snow and sprinkle evenly with the white and black sesame seeds and the lime zest. Serve immediately.

Mango Ice

MAKES 1½ CUPS

1 cup/**200 grams** mango puree

2 tablespoons sugar

—

In a shallow metal pan or plastic container, stir together the mango puree, ¼ cup/ 60 grams water, and the sugar until the sugar is dissolved. Cover the container and freeze for at least 6 hours or up to overnight, until solid.

Mango ice can be stored in an airtight container in the freezer for up to 1 month.

Mango-Lime Curd

½ cup/**100 grams** mango puree

¼ cup/**60 grams** fresh lime juice
(4 to 5 limes)

3 tablespoons/**45 grams**
unsalted butter

¼ cup/**50 grams** sugar

2 large egg yolks (about **40 grams**),
at room temperature

⅛ teaspoon kosher salt

—

In a medium saucepan, heat the mango puree, lime juice, and butter over medium-high heat until the butter is melted and the mixture is almost at a boil. In a medium bowl, whisk together the sugar and egg yolks. Remove the mango mixture from the heat and gradually whisk a few tablespoons of it into the egg yolk mixture to temper the eggs (see page 29). Continue whisking the mango mixture into the egg yolk mixture a few tablespoons at a time until it is all incorporated.

Return the curd to the saucepan over medium heat. Cook, stirring continuously with a wooden spoon and making sure to scrape the bottom of the saucepan frequently to prevent the egg yolks from scrambling, until the curd thickens and coats the spoon with a thick enough layer that you can draw your finger through it and it holds a line, 4 to 6 minutes.

Remove the curd from the heat and strain it through a fine-mesh sieve into a medium bowl or pitcher. Whisk in the salt. Cover with plastic wrap, pressing it directly against the surface of the curd (to prevent a skin from forming), and let cool to room temperature. Refrigerate for at least 4 hours before using.

The curd can be stored in an airtight container in the fridge for up to 1 week.

Passion Fruit and
Raspberry Pavlovas

MAKES 8 INDIVIDUAL PAVLOVAS

6 large egg whites
(about ¾ cup/**180 grams**),
at room temperature

1¼ cups/**250 grams**
superfine sugar

2 tablespoons cornstarch,
sifted after measuring

⅛ teaspoon kosher salt

1 teaspoon pure vanilla extract

1 cup/**240 grams** heavy cream

2 teaspoons
confectioners' sugar

Passion Fruit Curd for
Pavlovas (page 384)

2 pints/**500 grams** fresh
raspberries

Pavlovas should be on every restaurant dessert menu: They are elegant, easy to put together, and ridiculously delicious. What's not to love about ethereal, crunchy meringue and soft cream and fruit? The dessert was created in New Zealand in honor of the famous Russian ballerina Anna Pavlova, who was visiting the country during a world tour. I make these for all occasions and holidays and sometimes just because. The passion fruit curd is so good you'll want to put it on everything. I love the combination of the tropical passion fruit with tart-sweet raspberries, but feel free to use your favorite fruit.

Preheat the oven to 175°F and place a rack in the center of the oven. Line a baking sheet with parchment paper and set it aside.

In a stand mixer fitted with a whisk attachment, beat the egg whites on medium speed for about 1 minute. The whites will start to froth and turn into bubbles and eventually the yellowy viscous part will disappear. Keep whipping until you can see the wires of the whisk leaving a slight trail in the whites, 2 to 3 minutes.

With the mixer still on medium, slowly add the superfine sugar in six to eight increments, whipping for about 20 seconds after each addition. (It should take about 3 minutes to add all the sugar.) When all the sugar has been incorporated into the egg whites, increase the speed to medium-high and beat for about 1 minute longer. The meringue

should be fluffy and look a bit like shaving cream. Remove the bowl from the mixer and, using a rubber spatula, fold in the cornstarch, salt, and vanilla. The meringue batter will be gloppy and sticky-looking.

Using a ½-cup ice cream scoop or ½-cup dry measuring cup, scoop 8 mounds of meringue onto the prepared baking sheet, spacing them about 3 inches apart. Use a large spoon to press a well into the center of each meringue mound, moving the spoon around in a circular motion to make a shallow depression in the meringue.

Bake for 3 hours, rotating the baking sheet a few times. Turn off the oven and let the meringues sit in the oven overnight.

The next day, remove the meringues from the oven and carefully peel them off the parchment. (At this

Passion Fruit Curd for Pavlovas

MAKES 1¼ CUPS

½ cup/1 stick/**115 grams** unsalted butter,
cut into small pieces

¼ cup/**50 grams** passion fruit puree
(either purchase or make by pureeing the inside
of about 5 passion fruits with a few tablespoons
water and straining the resulting mixture
through a fine-mesh sieve)

2 tablespoons fresh lemon juice
(about ½ large lemon)

½ cup/**100 grams** sugar

3 large egg yolks (about **60 grams**),
at room temperature

⅛ teaspoon kosher salt

—

In a medium saucepan, heat the butter, passion fruit puree, and lemon juice to just under a boil over medium-high heat. In a medium bowl, whisk together the sugar and egg yolks. Remove the passion fruit mixture from the heat and gradually whisk a few tablespoons of it into the egg yolk mixture to temper the eggs (see page 29). Continue whisking the hot liquid into the egg yolk mixture a few tablespoons at a time until it is all incorporated.

Return the curd to the saucepan over medium heat. Cook, stirring continuously with a wooden spoon and making sure to scrape the bottom of the saucepan frequently to prevent the egg yolks from scrambling, until the curd thickens and coats the spoon with a thick enough layer that you can draw your finger through it and it holds a line, 5 to 8 minutes.

Remove the curd from the heat and strain it through a fine-mesh sieve into a medium bowl or pitcher. Whisk in the salt. Cover with plastic wrap, pressing it directly against the surface of the curd (to prevent a skin from forming), and let cool to room temperature. Refrigerate for at least 4 hours before using.

Curd can be stored in an airtight container in the fridge for up to 1 week.

point the meringues can be stored in an airtight container at room temperature for up to 2 days.)

When you're ready to serve, whip the cream and confectioners' sugar in a medium bowl with a whisk until it is soft and billowing. Do not over-whip or the cream will get grainy. It should look similar to the meringue when it was fully whipped.

Place each meringue on an individual serving plate or all together on a large serving platter. Spoon about 2 tablespoons of the whipped cream into the center of each meringue. Make a depression in the cream, then spoon about 2 heaping table-spoons of the passion fruit curd on top of the cream. Crush some of the raspberries and keep some whole and scatter both evenly on top of the curd.

Passion fruit pavlovas should be served within 1 hour or so of assem-bling. (Once filled, the meringues get really soft after a few hours.)

Marvelous Vanilla Caramel

Merveilleux

MAKES 8 MERVEILLEUX

Vanilla Caramel Cream
(page 386)

8 large egg whites
(about 1 cup/**240 grams** egg
whites), at room temperature

1 cup/**200 grams**
superfine sugar

1 cup/**120 grams**
confectioners' sugar

¼ teaspoon kosher salt

One of the many things I love about New York City is that you can open up a restaurant selling one single menu item and there will be an audience for it. I've stumbled upon a rice pudding take-out shop, a mac-and-cheese restaurant, a bakery that sells chocolate cake and chocolate cake only. But only in New York can you open up a store that sells something that no one's even heard of and thrive. Christopher and I walked into Aux Merveilleux de Fred because it looked pretty and French and there were pastries in the window. When we got inside we realized that the pastries in the window were the only pastries in the shop: big and small merveilleux. We had no idea what these were, so the counter staff kindly explained how mounds of airy meringue are sandwiched with flavored whipped creams and rolled around in various toppings to make an ethereal treat. *Merveilleux* means "marvelous" in French, and showcasing this classic old-fashioned confection was the raison d'être of this jewelbox patisserie. We got one of each of five different flavors and sat outside on a park bench and inhaled them one by one. They were creamy and light, a little chewy where the meringue met the filling, and completely irresistible. They were perfectly named. Making these takes some planning ahead as you need to make the meringues at least a day in advance.

Make the caramel sauce for the caramel cream and set it aside. But don't whip and finish the cream yet.

Preheat the oven to 175°F and place racks in the center and bottom third of the oven. Line two baking sheets with parchment paper and set them aside.

In a stand mixer fitted with a whisk attachment, beat the egg whites on medium speed until soft peaks form, 3 to 4 minutes. The whites will start to froth and turn into bubbles and eventually the yellowy viscous part of the whites will disappear. Keep whipping until you can see the wires of the whisk leaving a slight trail in

Vanilla Caramel Cream

MAKES ABOUT 4 CUPS

½ cup/**100 grams** sugar

2 cups/**480 grams** heavy cream

Seeds scraped from ½ vanilla bean (see page 28)

⅛ teaspoon kosher salt

—

Combine the sugar with about ¼ cup/60 grams water in a medium saucepan and bring to a boil over high heat. Brush down the sides of the pan with a wet pastry brush. Continue boiling until the syrup starts to change color, about 2 minutes. (There is so little sugar, the whole process happens quickly once the sugar starts to color, so be aware.) Swirl the pan to help the syrup color evenly, and keep swirling gently until the caramel is deep golden brown.

Turn the heat down to low and, with a long-handled whisk, slowly and carefully whisk in 1 cup/240 grams of the cream and the vanilla seeds. Be careful, as the caramel will sputter and spit — stand away from the pot until it settles. Whisk until the cream is completely incorporated into the caramel and you have no more little bits of hardened sugar. Whisk in the salt.

Remove the caramel sauce from the heat, carefully transfer it to a heatproof container, and store in the fridge for at least 8 hours (ideally overnight) or up to 3 days so it chills enough to blend into the remaining cream and be whip-able.

When you're ready to use the caramel cream, whip the remaining 1 cup/240 grams cream in a large bowl by hand or with a handheld electric mixer, or in a stand mixer fitted with a whisk attachment, until the cream is fluffy and holds a stiff peak. Whip in the caramel sauce until well incorporated. Use immediately.

Using a ¼-cup measuring cup or a ¼-cup ice cream scoop, scoop 24 round mounds of meringue onto the prepared baking sheets.

Bake for about 4 hours, rotating the baking sheets and switching their positions a few times, until the meringues are firm to the touch and you can remove them easily from the parchment without them falling apart. (If it's particularly humid outside, you may need to bake them for up to 8 hours before they are firm enough.)

Turn off the oven but leave the meringues in the oven for at least 6 or up to 12 hours, until they are fully crispy inside. They should still be white or just have a tiny bit of color on them. If any sugar has pooled out of the meringues, snap it off when it cools.

Remove the 8 ugliest meringues from the baking sheets (they are all beautiful, but some are less pretty than others) and place them in a plastic or paper bag. Crush these meringues with your hands until you have a bag of finely crushed crumbs. Be careful not to overcrush them into powder — you want crumbs that are about the size of rice grains. Pour these into a medium bowl and set it aside.

Finish making the caramel cream.

Carefully remove the remaining 16 meringues from the baking sheets and pair them up so that like sizes are together. To assemble each merveilleux, scoop a rounded tablespoon of the whipped caramel cream onto the flat side of a meringue. Sandwich it with another meringue, flat side down, and use another 5 to 6 tablespoons of the caramel cream to cover the top and

the whites. Test for soft peak stage by stopping the mixer, removing the whisk from the whites, and lifting it up; the whites should peak and then droop.

With the mixer on medium, add the superfine sugar in three increments, whipping for 1 minute between additions. The mixture will start to get glossy and stiff. Meanwhile, sift the confectioners' sugar and salt together. Once you've beaten all of the superfine sugar into the egg whites, increase the mixer speed to medium-high and whip for about 30 seconds more. It will look like thick shaving cream. Remove the bowl from the mixer and fold in the confectioners' sugar and salt.

fill in the sides. Don't worry about it looking pretty — you just want to cover the entire meringue sandwich with cream. Place the whole thing in the bowl of crumbs and roll it around, using your hands or two spoons, until covered. Set it aside on a plate and repeat with the remaining meringues, cream, and crumbs until all the merveilleux have been assembled. Refrigerate for at least 1 hour or up to 8 hours before serving so all the flavors can meld and the merveilleux can firm up a bit.

Merveilleux should be eaten the same day they are made. (Though I'll admit to having held them overnight and still enjoying them the next day; they are just a little squishier and less crunchy. Still amazing.)

Swedish Napoleon

MAKES ONE 10-INCH CAKE, TO SERVE 10 TO 12

1 recipe Master Pastry Cream (page 434)

Apple Jam (page 390)

Raspberry Topping (page 391)

1 recipe Master Puff Pastry Dough (page 442) or Master Quick Puff Pastry Dough (page 440), or 1½ pounds/**680 grams** store-bought all-butter puff pastry

1¼ cups/**300 grams** heavy cream

3 tablespoons/**22 grams** confectioners' sugar

½ cup/**150 grams** thick raspberry jam

When I was in high school, I spent a summer as an exchange student in Switzerland to better my French. My host family was Swedish and within a week of my arrival we jetted off to Stockholm to spend the summer. So while my *Comment allez-vous?* didn't get much better, by the end of the summer my Swedish *Hur mår du?* was pretty perfect. Fast-forward many years later, and *Roy Bakes*, a popular pastry show in Sweden, reached out to film at Flour. I couldn't wait to show off my linguistic skills with the host! When Roy arrived, charming as can be, the only word I could remember was *jordgubbe* (strawberry).

Thankfully, we filmed in English. I taught Roy the ins and outs of our Boston cream pie, and in return he shared with me one of his favorite classic Swedish pastries, a Nafoleonbakelse or Napoleonskake. As he was explaining it to me both of our mouths were watering, and he invited me to Sweden to try the real thing. "First you have a layer of crispy puff pastry and then spread some homemade apple jam on top; layer two is more puff pastry and some vanilla custard with whipped cream; the third layer is more puff pastry and some raspberry jam and fondant. You must come and try it!" I have yet to take him up on his offer but I was so taken by his description that I came up with my own version. I think he would love this.

—

Make the pastry cream, apple jam, and raspberry topping and set them aside. Make the puff pastry and let it chill in the fridge, or thaw the store-bought puff pastry in the fridge.

Preheat the oven to 400°F and place a rack in the top third of the oven. Line two baking sheets with parchment paper and set aside; if you have a full-size (18 x 26-inch) baking sheet and your oven is big enough to hold it, line just the one sheet.

Generously flick flour over the work surface and, using a lot of strength

Apple Jam

6 small or 4 large Granny Smith apples, peeled, cored, and finely chopped (about 6 cups)

¾ cup/**150 grams** sugar

2 tablespoons/**30 grams** unsalted butter

1 teaspoon pure vanilla extract

¼ teaspoon kosher salt

Place the apples, sugar, butter, and about ½ cup/ 120 grams water in a small saucepan and cook over medium-low heat, stirring occasionally, until most of the apples have broken down and the mixture becomes a thick chunky jam, 1½ to 2 hours. Add more water as needed to keep the apples from drying out or burning. Stir in the vanilla and salt. Transfer to an airtight container and let cool.

Apple jam can be stored in an airtight container in the fridge for up to 1 week.

and firmness, roll out the puff pastry to a long rectangle, about 12 x 22 inches. Cut the puff pastry into thirds, each third measuring about 12 x 7 inches. Place the puff pastry rectangles on the prepared baking sheets. If you're using a full-size baking sheet, put all the puff pastry rectangles on the one sheet; if not, place one rectangle on one sheet and two on the second. Place a sheet of parchment directly on top of the puff pastry, then place another baking sheet directly on top of that. (The puff pastry is so puffy that you need to weight it down while you bake it so it doesn't get too tall. If you don't have enough baking sheets, you can bake the puff pastry in batches; just let the baking sheets cool fully between batches.)

Bake until the puff pastry is totally golden brown throughout, rotating the baking sheets and switching their positions after about 15 minutes. Check the puff pastry after around 25 minutes by carefully removing the top sheet and peeling off the parchment to take a peek; reduce the heat to 350°F. Total baking time should be 30 to 35 minutes. When the puff pastry is fully golden, remove the baking sheets from the oven, carefully remove the top baking sheets and parchment, and let the puff pastry cool completely on the baking sheets on wire racks.

While the puff pastry is cooling, in a large bowl by hand or using a handheld electric mixer, or in a stand mixer with a whisk attachment, whip the cream with the confectioners' sugar until it is stiff; set aside. Warm the raspberry jam gently in the microwave or on the stove in a small skillet until it is loose and spreadable; set aside.

To assemble the napoleon, have all your components on hand: a serrated knife, an offset spatula, the cooled puff pastry rectangles, apple jam, whipped cream, pastry cream, warmed raspberry jam, and raspberry topping. Place one puff pastry rectangle on a cutting board and spread it evenly with the apple jam. Using the offset spatula, spread the whipped cream on top of the apple jam. Place another puff pastry rectangle on top of the cream and gently press down to adhere. Spread the pastry cream evenly on top of the puff pastry rectangle. Thinly spread the top of the last puff pastry rectangle with the raspberry jam until evenly covered. Turn the puff pastry rectangle upside down so that the jam is facing the pastry cream and press it down gently to adhere. Cover the entire top with the raspberry topping; spread quickly so you have a smooth surface. Using a serrated knife, very carefully trim all four edges of the napoleon to expose the sides. Carefully transfer the napoleon to a flat plate or serving platter and place it in the fridge for at least 4 hours before serving to allow the whole thing to meld together a bit.

The napoleon can be stored in an airtight container or well wrapped in plastic in the fridge for up to 1 day.

Raspberry Topping

MAKES 1½ CUPS

2 teaspoons raspberry jam

2 cups/**240 grams** confectioners' sugar, sifted after measuring

—

Heat the jam in a tiny skillet or in the microwave until it thins out. Push it through a fine-mesh sieve into a small bowl to remove any seeds. Add the confectioners' sugar and 2 tablespoons water and whisk until well combined. It should be thick but spreadable, so add a few drops more water if needed to make it spreadable. Cover until needed.

Raspberry topping can be stored in an airtight container at room temperature for up to 1 week.

Sweets for my sweet

Sticky Bun Popcorn / 394

Butter Mochi / 396

Maple Pecan Tassies / 398

Brown Butter–Peanut Rice Crispy Treats
with Peanut Butter Ganache / 401

Billionaire's Shortbread / 402

Peppermint Kisses / 405

Vanilla-Mint Marshmallows / 408

Christopher's Honeycomb / 411

Brown Butter Butterscotch Caramels / 413

Apple Cider–Miso Caramels / 416

Salted Almond English Toffee / 419

Chocolate Almond Cocoa Nib Caramels / 421

Chocolate–Peanut Butter Buttercrunch / 425

Almond Pistachio Cherry Honey Nougat / 427

CHAPTER 7

I Made This
for You

Sticky Bun Popcorn

MAKES 16 TO 18 CUPS

About six years after Flour opened, we were featured on a popular Food Network show called *Throwdown! with Bobby Flay* in which Chef Bobby challenged me and Flour in a competition to see who could make the better sticky buns. (I'm proud to say we won!) Our sticky buns are made with buttery, soft brioche dough and baked in a butter-cream–brown sugar–honey concoction that we call Goo. I'm convinced you could pour this goo on pretty much anything and it would make it shine. This recipe tests my theory: We mix popcorn with toasted pecans and a light goo coating, then bake it all together to make it extra crispy and caramelized. Sharing a big bowl of this with Christopher while watching TV, lying on the couch, is the best way I know to spend a lazy Sunday afternoon.

3 tablespoons/**45 grams** vegetable oil (such as canola)

¾ cup/**165 grams** unpopped popcorn kernels

2 cups/**200 grams** pecan halves, toasted (see page 29)

¾ cup firmly packed/**165 grams** light brown sugar

¾ cup/1½ sticks/**170 grams** unsalted butter

¾ cup/**255 grams** honey

½ teaspoon pure vanilla extract

½ teaspoon kosher salt

¼ teaspoon baking soda

¼ teaspoon ground cinnamon

Preheat the oven to 350°F and place racks in the center and bottom third of the oven. Line two baking sheets with parchment paper and set them aside.

In a very large pot with a lid, heat the oil over high heat until hot. Add the popcorn kernels, cover the pot, and reduce the heat to medium-high. Shake the pot every few seconds until you start to hear the popping. As soon as you can hear it popping, shake the pot constantly. When the popping slows down to one pop every few seconds, turn off the heat but keep shaking. When you hear one pop every 5 or 6 seconds, remove the pot from the stove and dump the popcorn into a large bowl. Remove and discard any unpopped kernels. Add the pecan halves to the popcorn.

These next few steps go quickly, so be sure to have all the ingredients and equipment at hand. Return the pot to the stove and add the brown sugar and butter. Heat over high heat until the butter melts. The mixture will get foamy and start to color bit by bit. Cook, stirring constantly with a wooden spoon or silicone spatula, for 3 minutes — the color will deepen a shade and it will smell rich and delicious. Add the honey and bring back to a boil. Remove from the heat and stir in the vanilla, salt, baking soda, and cinnamon. (The caramel goo will bubble up and foam a bit from the reaction of the baking soda with the sugar.)

Drizzle the caramel goo over the popcorn-pecan mixture and toss to distribute well, until the popcorn is evenly colored. Spread on the prepared baking sheets. Bake for 15 to 20 minutes, rotating the baking sheets and switching their positions midway through the baking time, until the nuts are deeply toasted and the popcorn smells fragrant.

Remove from the oven and let cool on the baking sheets on a wire rack. When the popcorn cools, it will be crunchy and crispy. Break up the popcorn into bite-size clusters after it cools.

Sticky bun popcorn can be stored in an airtight container at room temperature for up to 1 week.

Butter Mochi

MAKES ABOUT 24 SQUARES

4½ cups/1 pound/**455 grams** mochiko (glutinous rice flour or sweet rice flour)

One 13.5- to 14-ounce/ **375- to 390-gram** can full-fat coconut milk

1½ cups/**360 grams** whole milk, at room temperature

1⅔ cups/**335 grams** sugar

½ cup/1 stick/**115 grams** unsalted butter, melted

3 large eggs (about **150 grams**), at room temperature

1 tablespoon baking powder

1 teaspoon kosher salt

1 teaspoon pure vanilla extract

¾ cup/**90 grams** sweetened shredded coconut

Every few years Christopher and I take an extended work vacation in Hawaii. It started about a decade ago when we were invited by the Hawaii Culinary Education Foundation to teach restaurant business classes and baking classes to culinary students and professionals in Honolulu. The director of the foundation, Hayley, and her husband, Mike, have since become dear friends; we continue the friendship by finding any reason we can to travel back to teach more classes and spend time enjoying the unparalleled hospitality of the Hawaiian people. While teaching how to make our famous sticky buns at the Halekulani Hotel one year, I tasted an unusual and delicious Hawaiian pastry called butter mochi. The hotel pastry chef, Mark, had baked off an impressive spread of desserts for the students to enjoy during break and these plain-looking treats were displayed on a large platter alongside standard blueberry muffins and tropical fruit tarts. I loved them so much I took a goody bag of them back to my room and nibbled on them for the rest of the trip, trying to make them last. I knew I had to make these when I got back home and asked Chef Mark for the recipe. He generously shared, and I created my own version of this classic Hawaiian pastry. The mochi is super chewy and fun to eat and very easy to make.

—

Preheat the oven to 350°F and place a rack in the center of the oven. Generously butter a 9 x 13-inch baking pan. Set aside.

In a large bowl, combine the mochiko, coconut milk, milk, sugar, melted butter, eggs, baking powder, salt, and vanilla. Whisk together until smooth. Add the shredded coconut and whisk it in. Let the batter sit for about 15 minutes at room temperature for the rice flour to fully absorb the liquid.

Pour into the prepared pan and bake for 1 hour 10 minutes to 1 hour 20 minutes, rotating the pan midway through the baking time, until the top of the cake is golden brown and the mochi feels firm when you press it in the middle. Remove from

the oven and let cool in the pan on a wire rack.

Cut the mochi into small pieces, about 2 x 2 inches square, and use a small spatula to remove them from the pan. Place each piece in a small muffin paper or on a piece of parchment or waxed paper.

Butter mochi can be stored in an airtight container at room temperature for up to 4 days. You can also freeze them; put them in a 325°F oven for about 20 minutes to revive and get a little chewy and caramelized on top.

Maple Pecan Tassies

MAKES 24 TASSIES

Pecan Tassie Dough
(opposite)

1 cup/**100 grams** pecan halves

⅔ cup firmly packed/
150 grams light brown sugar

¼ cup/**85 grams** maple syrup

3 eggs (about **150 grams**),
at room temperature

3 tablespoons/**45 grams**
unsalted butter,
melted and cooled

1 teaspoon pure vanilla extract

¼ teaspoon kosher salt

Jonathan, our pastry chef at Flour Harvard, created this recipe for a monthly special at the start of maple-eating season in the fall. Even though maple-tapping season is in the spring when the sap starts running, the time to smother everything in maple syrup is when the weather gets cooler and the leaves start to turn color. A tassie is a mini pecan pie made with tender, flaky cream cheese dough. Jonathan wanted to highlight local maple syrup so he substituted maple for part of the sugar. The result is a buttery, mellow, nutty, bite-size treat. They are hard to stop eating, which to me is the definitive sign of a great pastry.

Make the pecan tassie dough and chill as directed. Shape the dough into 24 balls 1 inch in diameter and press them evenly over the bottoms and up the sides of the 24 cups of a mini muffin tin. Set aside.

Preheat the oven to 350°F and place a rack in the center of the oven. Toast the pecans on a baking sheet for 6 to 8 minutes, until they are lightly toasted inside; break a few open to check. Let cool, then roughly chop into small pieces. Set aside.

In a medium bowl, stir together the brown sugar, maple syrup, eggs, butter, vanilla, and salt. Add about half the chopped pecans and mix until well combined. Spoon the mixture evenly into the prepared shells (2 to 3 teaspoons per cup), filling them all the way. Sprinkle them generously and evenly with the remaining nuts.

Bake for 24 to 28 minutes, rotating the muffin tin midway through the baking time, until they are puffed and brown.

Remove from the oven and let cool for a few minutes in the tin on a wire rack. Pop them out of the pans and continue cooling on the wire rack.

Pecan tassies can be stored in an airtight container at room temperature for up to 2 days.

Pecan Tassie Dough

MAKES ENOUGH DOUGH FOR 24 TASSIES

½ cup/1 stick/**115 grams** unsalted
butter, at room temperature

6 tablespoons/3 ounces/**85 grams**
cream cheese, at warm room temperature

1 cup plus 3 tablespoons/**165 grams**
all-purpose flour

⅛ teaspoon kosher salt

In a small bowl with a wooden spoon, or in a stand mixer fitted with a paddle attachment, beat the butter and cream cheese together until smooth. Gradually add the flour and salt and mix until well combined. Wrap the dough in plastic wrap and refrigerate until firm enough to handle, at least 1 hour.

The dough can be stored, well wrapped, in the fridge for up to 3 days or frozen for up to 1 month. Let thaw overnight in the fridge before using.

Peanut Butter Ganache

MAKES ABOUT 2½ CUPS

10 ounces/**280 grams** semisweet or bittersweet chocolate, chopped (about 1⅔ cups)

1 cup/**260 grams** creamy peanut butter

1 teaspoon kosher salt

—

Melt the chocolate in a bain-marie or in the microwave (see page 26). Whisk in the peanut butter a few tablespoons at a time until the ganache is smooth. Whisk in the salt.

Peanut butter ganache can be stored in an airtight container at room temperature for up to 1 week. Beat with a wooden spoon, or in a stand mixer with a paddle attachment before using.

Brown Butter–Peanut Rice Crispy Treats

with Peanut Butter Ganache

MAKES 12 HUGE OR 24 MORE NORMAL-SIZE TREATS

1 cup/2 sticks/**225 grams** unsalted butter

Seeds scraped from ½ vanilla bean (see page 28)

Two 10-ounce bags/**560 grams** regular-size marshmallows

1 teaspoon kosher salt

6 cups/**160 grams** crisp rice cereal

2 cups/**300 grams** salted roasted peanuts, roughly chopped

Peanut Butter Ganache (opposite)

I'll let you in on a secret: I don't like peanut butter. I know, I know, WHO doesn't like peanut butter? Peanuts and peanut butter have an off taste to me, so I've always avoided the two. Until this treat. I adore our brown butter–rice crispy treats. When we make them at Flour and trim the edges, you can find me standing next to the pan waiting for the little scraps. Adding peanut butter and peanuts and covering the whole thing in peanutty ganache actually makes them taste better. I never thought I would love a peanut butter treat, but here you go. If you love our rice crispy treats, wait until you try these.

Butter a 9 x 13-inch baking pan, spray it with cooking spray, or line it with parchment paper. Set aside.

In a large saucepan, heat the butter over low heat. Add the vanilla seeds and heat until the butter is melted. Once it has melted it will start to bubble and crackle — if you lean in and listen it will sound like an audience of people clapping their hands politely (in anticipation of these treats!).

Watch the butter carefully and you'll see it slowly browning; as soon as the bubbling subsides, after about 5 minutes, the butter will be fully browned and it's ready for the addition of the marshmallows. Add the marshmallows right away at this point or the butter may burn, which

you don't want. Keeping the heat on low, use a wooden spoon to stir in the marshmallows and salt. Stir well until the marshmallows are completely melted and the vanilla seeds are evenly distributed.

Remove the pot from the heat and add the cereal and peanuts. Mix well with a wooden spoon. Pat the mixture into the prepared pan. Let cool to room temperature, about 1 hour.

While the treat is cooling, make the ganache. Spread the ganache evenly over the top. Let cool until firmed up. Cut into 12 or 24 pieces.

The treats can be stored in an airtight container at room temperature for up to 2 days.

Billionaire's Shortbread

MAKES 18 BARS

¾ recipe/1½ cups/**375 grams** Master Ganache (page 432)

1 recipe Rick's Master Shortbread (page 436)

1 cup/**200 grams** sugar

½ cup/**120 grams** heavy cream

½ cup/1 stick/**115 grams** unsalted butter, cut into 4 or 5 pieces

1 teaspoon pure vanilla extract

1 teaspoon kosher salt

¼ cup/**25 grams** cocoa nibs or chopped almonds

My husband is a junk food aficionado. There isn't a salty chip or nutty, chocolatey candy bar that is not on his list of favorite foods. High on that list of favorites is the almighty Twix bar: sweet caramel on top of a crunchy cookie, covered in milk chocolate. I wanted to re-create this for him and after some research discovered it is similar to the popular British cookie called millionaire's shortbread, made with the same components. I start with the most tender, buttery shortbread you can make, top it with a thick layer of slightly salty, chewy caramel, and cover the whole thing in dark chocolate ganache. It's so rich and luxurious I call it Billionaire's Shortbread.

Make the ganache and set it aside at room temperature. Make the shortbread dough and refrigerate it.

Preheat the oven to 350°F and place a rack in the center of the oven.

Remove the shortbread dough from the refrigerator and let it sit for about 30 minutes to soften. Roll it between two large sheets of parchment paper into a 9 x 13-inch rectangle. Trim the edges so you have a fairly neat squared-off rectangle. It should be about ⅓ inch thick. Carefully peel off the top sheet of parchment (place the whole thing back in the fridge for a few minutes if the dough sticks to the parchment). Transfer the dough, still on the bottom sheet of parchment, to a rimmed 9 x 13-inch quarter-sheet pan. Trim the parchment so that it fits the baking sheet.

Bake for about 20 minutes, rotating the baking sheet midway through the baking time, until the shortbread is light brown, about the same color as maple wood. Let cool completely in the pan on a wire rack.

While the shortbread is cooling, put the sugar in a medium saucepan and carefully add about ¼ cup/60 grams water to moisten it. Be sure the sides of the pan do not have any sugar crystals on them; if they do, use a pastry brush dipped in water to wash the sides down of any clinging sugar. (This helps prevent crystallization of the sugar as you are caramelizing it.) Bring the sugar syrup to a boil over high heat. Do not move the pan as the syrup is coming to a boil. (Sometimes when sugar syrup is jostled while caramelizing it causes enough disturbance that the sugar

starts to crystallize, and then you can't use it. If this does happen, you'll need to clean out the pot and start over again.) Once the syrup starts to color slightly to a pale brown, it is safe to gently swirl the pan to even out the caramelization. It will take 3 to 4 minutes for the sugar to start caramelizing and another 30 seconds or so for the color to even out. When the sugar is golden brown, turn the heat down to medium and carefully pour in the cream. It will sputter a bit and get clumpy; whisk occasionally with a long-handled whisk and continue to cook on medium heat until the clumps of caramel have entirely melted, about 1 minute. Whisk in the butter until melted and combined. Bring the heat back up to high and whisk constantly until the caramel reaches 230°F on a candy thermometer. Remove from the heat and whisk in the vanilla and salt. Pour the caramel directly on top of the shortbread and let cool to room temperature.

If the ganache is not liquid, warm it up gently on the stove or in the microwave until it is pourable. Pour it evenly on top of the caramel and let it cool at room temperature. Let stand until the ganache is completely firm, then cut the shortbread into 18 rectangles, about 2 x 3 inches. Sprinkle the cocoa nibs evenly on top.

The shortbread can be stored in an airtight container in the refrigerator or at cool room temperature for up to 5 days.

Peppermint Kisses

MAKES ABOUT 10 DOZEN KISSES

8 large egg whites
(about 1 cup/**240 grams**),
at room temperature

1 cup/**200 grams**
superfine sugar

1 cup/**120 grams**
confectioners' sugar

½ teaspoon kosher salt

1¼ teaspoons pure
peppermint extract

1 tablespoon red food
coloring gel

Every holiday season, one of my favorite things is walking into our production kitchen and watching an army of bakers piping tray after tray of these stunning, simple treats. Meringue is spiked with a touch of peppermint extract and then deftly piped into little kiss-shaped cookies. The pastry bag is striped with a touch of red food coloring, which streams down the sides of the cookies, creating a lovely striped kiss. Packaged in little plastic bags tied with ribbon, they will become your go-to holiday gift.

Preheat the oven to 175°F and place a rack in the center of the oven. Line a baking sheet with parchment paper and set it aside.

In a stand mixer fitted with a whisk attachment, whip the egg whites on medium speed until soft peaks form, 3 to 4 minutes. Whip until the wires of the whisk leave a slight trail in the whites. Test for soft peak stage by stopping the mixer and removing the whisk from the whites and lifting it up; the whites should peak and then droop.

With the mixer on medium, add the superfine sugar in three increments, whipping for about 1 minute between additions. Meanwhile, sift the confectioners' sugar and salt together and set aside. Once you've beaten all the superfine sugar into the egg whites, increase the mixer

speed to medium-high, add the peppermint extract, and beat for about 15 seconds more. Remove the bowl from the mixer and fold in the confectioners' sugar and salt.

Place a ¾-inch round pastry tip in an 18-inch pastry bag. Fold back the pastry bag about halfway down and cuff it over your hand. Dip a wooden skewer or chopstick into the red food coloring and paint 4 long stripes, starting as close to the tip as you can all the way up the side of the pastry bag. Fill the bag halfway with the meringue (don't ever fill a pastry bag more than halfway or you'll create a mess) and pipe kisses about 1 inch wide and 1 inch tall (around the same size as a Hershey's Kiss) onto the prepared baking sheet. To do this, hold the pastry bag about an inch above the baking sheet, squeeze the meringue out of the bag, release

1.

2.

pressure on the bag, and pull up to create the top of the kiss. Pipe kisses about an inch apart and fill up the baking sheet, piping onto a second baking sheet as needed. Add more red food coloring to the inside of the pastry bag as needed when you refill the bag with meringue and pipe until you have used up all the meringue.

Bake the kisses for about 4 hours, rotating the baking sheet a few times, until the kisses are completely dried out inside and out (break a few open to check). Turn off the oven but leave the kisses in the oven to dry out overnight.

The kisses can be stored in an airtight container. If the weather is not humid, you can store them for up to 1 month. Otherwise they are best eaten within a few days.

3.

Vanilla-Mint Marshmallows

MAKES ABOUT 25 JUMBO MARSHMALLOWS

6¾ teaspoons/**21 grams**
unflavored powdered gelatin
(three ¼-ounce packets)

1⅔ cups/**335 grams**
superfine sugar

1 cup/**320 grams** light
corn syrup

½ teaspoon kosher salt

Seeds scraped from 1 vanilla
bean (see page 28)

¼ teaspoon pure
peppermint extract

½ cup/**65 grams** cornstarch

½ cup/**60 grams**
confectioners' sugar

Marshmallows belong to that group of foods we typically purchase but that are really gratifying to make from scratch. If you've never made homemade mayonnaise, butter, ricotta cheese, or puff pastry, give them a whirl and show off your skills to your friends and family. These marshmallows will earn you the crown of DIY Wizard. They are fluffy and airy and have cleaner, purer flavors than any marshmallow you'll find on the grocery shelves. Once you get the hang of making marshmallows, play around with different fruits and extracts and come up with your own signature flavors. They take about a day to dry before you can start eating them, so plan ahead.

Pour ½ cup/120 grams cold water into a stand mixer fitted with a whisk attachment. Sprinkle the gelatin evenly over the water and set it aside to bloom (i.e., absorb the water and soften).

In a small heavy-bottomed saucepan, combine the superfine sugar, corn syrup, ½ cup/120 grams water, and salt and stir together to moisten the sugar. Bring to a boil over high heat. Using a candy thermometer, cook the sugar syrup to 240°F, soft ball stage (see "Cooking Sugar," page 21).

As soon as it reaches 240°F, remove the syrup from the heat and slowly stream it into the softened gelatin with the mixer on high speed. Drizzle the syrup down the side of the bowl; be careful not to drizzle it in the

middle of the bowl or it will hit the whisk and be flung all around.

Once all the syrup has been whipped in, add the vanilla seeds and peppermint extract. Whip on high until cool to the touch, 10 to 15 minutes. It will go from a milky white mixture to a fluffy, voluminous marshmallow.

While the marshmallow is whipping, sift the cornstarch and confectioners' sugar together into a small container or bowl.

Line the bottom of a 8 x 8-inch square baking pan with parchment paper and spray the sides generously with cooking spray or rub them with a little vegetable oil. Sprinkle a few tablespoons of the cornstarch–confectioners' sugar mixture evenly across the parchment.

Apple Cider–
Miso Caramels

MAKES ABOUT 32 CARAMELS

4 cups/**960 grams** apple cider

½ cup/1 stick/**115 grams**
unsalted butter, cut
into chunks

¾ cup/**150 grams**
superfine sugar

½ cup firmly packed/
110 grams light brown sugar

½ cup/**120 grams** heavy cream

1 tablespoon plus 2 teaspoons
red miso paste

½ teaspoon ground cinnamon

½ teaspoon ground ginger

Christopher loves these caramels so much that whenever I make them I literally have to hide them so he doesn't eat them all at once. Sometimes I forget my hiding places and happen upon a rogue caramel when cleaning out a cabinet. It's like hitting the jackpot! I'm sure right now I have a few caramels tucked away in a purse or drawer, waiting to be discovered at some future date. The inspiration for this recipe came from the prolific and uber-talented Deb Perelman, who is the author of the blog *Smitten Kitchen* and *The Smitten Kitchen Cookbook*. Her caramels are bright and chewy and taste a little like caramel apples. I add rich miso paste to contrast with the tangy cider, as well as ground ginger to introduce a warm, spicy note. Making caramels might seem tricky but all you really need is a reliable candy thermometer. Invest in one and you'll open the door to a whole new category of baking and confections.

Line the sides and bottom of an 8 x 8-inch square metal baking pan with parchment paper. The easiest way to do this is to line the pan with two strips of parchment, one widthwise and one lengthwise, so there is overhang on all sides. If the parchment isn't sticking, dab a little butter on the sides of the pan so it does. Spray the parchment with cooking spray and set the pan aside.

Place the cider in a large heavy-bottomed saucepan and bring it to a rolling boil over high heat. Boil until it reduces to ½ cup, 30 to 40 minutes. You don't need to watch it for the first 20 minutes or so, but

once it starts to boil down and thicken, keep an eye on it and give it an occasional stir to make sure it doesn't go too far and burn. It will start to foam up and get darker and thicker and a touch viscous as it gets closer to being reduced to the right amount.

Once it reduces to ½ cup, remove it from the heat and stir in the butter, superfine sugar, brown sugar, and cream. Return the pan to the stove and bring it to a boil over high heat. Use a candy thermometer to keep track of the temperature and boil until the thermometer reads 250°F, (the start of hard ball stage), 6 to 10

minutes. This is the point at which the caramel will be firm enough to hold its shape when it cools. It's almost ready at this point.

Keep boiling until it gets to 252°F, about another 2 minutes, then immediately remove it from the heat. Watch it carefully, as you don't want it to go over 255°F. If you don't have a candy thermometer, set a glass of ice water near the pot and spoon a little of the caramel into the water to test the consistency. If you can

gather it in your fingers and roll it into a hard ball, it is the right temperature.

Immediately stir in the miso paste, cinnamon, and ginger until well distributed. Carefully pour the caramel into the prepared pan and let it sit at room temperature for 2 to 3 hours, until cool.

Pop the caramel out of the pan, peel off the parchment, and place it on a cutting board. Use a sharp chef's knife to cut the caramel into 4 strips

one way and 8 the other way so you have 32 pieces. (Dip the knife in hot water and dry it off with a paper towel before every slice for easiest slicing.)

Cut parchment or waxed paper into 3 x 4-inch pieces. Wrap each caramel in a piece of paper and twist the ends. Store in an airtight container at room temperature for softer caramels, or in the fridge for chewy ones, for up to 2 months.

Salted Almond
English Toffee

MAKES ENOUGH FOR 4 OR 5 NICE-SIZE GIFT PACKETS

Everyone has their movie candy of choice—for me it was always a toss-up between a box of Raisinets and a Skor candy bar. I loved the chewiness of the Raisinets and how a box could last at least through the first quarter of the movie. The crunchy, buttery milk chocolate–covered toffee of the Skor usually got devoured during previews and I always wanted more. You might think that making something like a candy bar is complicated and out of reach. But far from it—as with most baking recipes, as long as you read the recipe carefully and have some patience, you can pretty much make any kind of candy bar you want. I played with the basic flavors of my childhood Skor bar and added a hefty dose of salt, lots of candied brown sugar almonds, and bittersweet chocolate to contrast with the sweet, rich toffee. Packed in little tins or cellophane bags, it makes an excellent gift.

3 tablespoons firmly packed/**40 grams** light brown sugar

2¼ teaspoons kosher salt

1½ cups/**210 grams** whole almonds

2 cups/**400 grams** superfine sugar

1½ cups/3 sticks/**340 grams** unsalted butter, cut into chunks, at room temperature

2 teaspoons pure vanilla extract

6 ounces/**170 grams** bittersweet chocolate, shaved fine (about 1 cup)

½ teaspoon flaked salt (optional)

Preheat the oven to 350°F and place a rack in the center of the oven.

In a medium bowl, combine the brown sugar and 1 teaspoon of the salt. Mix in 1 tablespoon water and stir until you get a soupy glaze. Stir in the almonds until well covered. Spread them out on a baking sheet and toast for 8 to 10 minutes, until light golden brown and shiny. Remove from the oven and let cool. Roughly chop the almonds and set them aside.

Line a rimmed baking sheet with a silicone baking mat or butter it generously. Set it aside.

Combine the superfine sugar and about ½ cup/120 grams water in a medium heavy-bottomed saucepan. Stir to moisten the sugar with the water. Add the butter. Place on the stove over high heat and bring to a boil without moving the pan or stirring. When it comes to a boil, watch it carefully until it starts to take on a little color, 8 to 12 minutes. As soon as you see it starting to color, you can stir it; whisk the syrup to even out the caramelization. Reduce the heat to medium-high, keeping the syrup at a rolling boil, and swirl the pan to keep the caramelization even, watching the color as it darkens and deepens.

Cook and whisk until the syrup is a deep rich amber, the color of cherrywood; it will take 4 to 6 minutes from the time it first starts to color to reach the right color.

Remove the syrup from the heat and whisk in the remaining 1¼ teaspoons salt and the vanilla. The vanilla will cause the toffee to sputter and spit, so stand back!

Immediately pour the toffee onto the prepared baking sheet. Tilt the sheet back and forth to even out the toffee and fill most of the pan. Let it sit at room temperature until it is firm to the touch but still hot, 5 to 8 minutes.

Sprinkle the chocolate evenly over the toffee. The chocolate will start to melt on contact. Use an offset spatula to evenly spread the chocolate on the toffee. Sprinkle evenly with the chopped almonds and the flaked salt, if you're using it.

Let sit at room temperature for at least 8 hours, until firm. Break into bite-size pieces to serve.

The toffee can be stored in an airtight container at room temperature for up to 2 weeks.

Chocolate Almond
Cocoa Nib Caramels

MAKES ABOUT 32 CARAMELS

1 cup/**100 grams** sliced
almonds

10 ounces/**280 grams**
bittersweet chocolate

2 cups/**480 grams**
heavy cream

1¾ cups/**350 grams** sugar

½ cup/**160 grams** light
corn syrup

3 tablespoons/**40 grams**
unsalted butter

1 cup/**130 grams** cocoa nibs

2 teaspoons pure
vanilla extract

1 teaspoon kosher salt

I grew up reading *James and the Giant Peach* and fantasizing about living inside a juicy, fragrant peach and having to eat my way out to survive. The plot of this popular children's book is actually a bit different from my memory, but when you are a food-obsessed girl you focus on the things that matter—and for me that was always anything edible. Fast-forward many years later, to 2016: That year marked the centenary of Roald Dahl, the author of *James and the Giant Peach*. We were invited to take part in a campaign called Dahlicious Delights to celebrate his birthday. We would create a confection to sell at Flour and part of the proceeds would go to Partners in Health, an incredible nonprofit cofounded by Dahl's daughter Ophelia. As a huge PIH supporter and admirer of Ophelia, I jumped at the chance to be a part of this celebration. We created these "hornets stewed in tar" as a nod to the line in the book: "I've eaten many strange and scrumptious dishes . . . [like] scrambled dregs and stinkbugs' eggs and hornets stewed in tar." The almonds and cocoa nibs look like the bits and pieces of a hornet strewn throughout the dark caramel tar. Dahl calls hornets stewed in tar among the "finest foods in the world." We think these caramels taste like the best Tootsie Roll in the world.

Preheat the oven to 350°F and place a rack in the center of the oven. Place the almonds on a baking sheet and toast for 6 to 8 minutes, until light golden brown. Remove from the oven and let cool.

Line a 9 x 13-inch baking pan with parchment paper, making sure the parchment hangs over the edges of

the pan; you may need two sheets of parchment, one widthwise and one lengthwise, to cover the sides completely.

Chop the chocolate into small pieces and place in a medium metal or heatproof glass bowl. Place the cream in a small saucepan and bring to just under a boil over high heat.

Pour the cream over the chocolate and whisk until the chocolate is totally melted. Set aside.

In a medium heavy-bottomed saucepan, stir together the sugar and about ½ cup/120 grams water, enough to moisten all the sugar. Add the corn syrup and bring to a boil over high heat. Don't stir or jostle the pot at all once the syrup comes to a boil. Let it boil until the mixture starts to caramelize, 8 to 10 minutes. Usually one part of the pot will start to color a bit; at this point you can safely swirl the pan to even out the caramelization. Swirl and continue to cook until the sugar is a deep, dark golden brown (if you are a beer aficionado, the color is the same as Sam Adams lager), another 3 to 4 minutes.

Whisk in the chocolate-cream mixture all at once and stir to combine. Bring back to a boil. Use a candy thermometer to keep track of the temperature. Boil until the mixture reaches 255°F, whisking constantly. This will take another 5 to 8 minutes. If you don't have a candy thermometer, set a glass of ice water near the pot and spoon a little of the caramel into the water to test the consistency. If you can gather it in your fingers and roll it into a hard ball, it is the right temperature.

When it reaches 255°F, whisk in the butter all at once until well incorporated. Remove the mixture from the stove and stir in the sliced almonds, cocoa nibs, vanilla, and salt.

Pour the candy into the prepared baking pan and spread it out with a wooden spoon or spatula. Let the candy cool for 2 to 3 hours or up to overnight at room temperature, until firm. If the caramel is not firm enough to cut, place it in the fridge for a few hours.

Pop the caramel out of the pan, peel off the parchment, and place it on a cutting board. Using a sharp knife greased with a little vegetable oil (such as canola), divide the caramel into 8 strips, then cut across into 4 rows, resulting in 32 individual caramels. Wrap each caramel in a piece of waxed or parchment paper about 4 x 4 inches square.

Store in an airtight container at room temperature for soft caramels, or in the fridge for firmer, chewier caramels, for up to 1 month.

Chocolate–Peanut Butter

Buttercrunch

MAKES 15 TO 20 CANDIES

2¼ cups/**600 grams** extra-crunchy peanut butter

2 teaspoons kosher salt

½ teaspoon baking soda

1 teaspoon pure vanilla extract

1 cup/**200 grams** sugar

¾ cup/**240 grams** light corn syrup

6 ounces/**170 grams** semisweet chocolate

Basically a homemade Butterfinger, this buttercrunch is the perfect balance of peanut butter and chocolate in a light crunchy candy bar. Rachael, our production pastry chef, first shared her buttercrunch recipe with me when we were looking for a garnish for a chocolate–peanut butter cheesecake special. We crumbled it on top and it made a super peanut buttery dessert even more wonderfully peanut buttery. After making it a few times and chopping it all up into little pieces I realized that if I kept it whole and covered it with chocolate it makes an incredible candy bar. You can dip the pieces entirely in chocolate if you like (double the amount of chocolate in the recipe) but I prefer it on one side only to make sure the peanut butter flavor is not overwhelmed by the chocolate. Try both and see which you prefer.

Place the peanut butter in a medium metal or heatproof glass bowl over a pot of simmering water. Stir for a few minutes to melt the peanut butter so it becomes liquidy. Alternatively, heat the peanut butter in the microwave at 50% power for 30 to 45 seconds, until it warms up and becomes soft and somewhat pourable. Keep it nearby and warm.

Combine the salt and baking soda. Have the baking soda–salt mixture and the vanilla nearby.

Line a rimmed baking sheet with parchment paper; gather a whisk and a silicone spatula or wooden spoon and have them all nearby.

Combine the sugar, corn syrup, and about ½ cup/120 grams water in a

small heavy-bottomed saucepan. Make sure the sugar is moistened with the water and bring to a boil over high heat. Clip a candy thermometer on the sides of the pan and cook without stirring until the sugar syrup reaches 285°F. (If you don't have a candy thermometer, set a glass of ice water near the pot and spoon a little of the caramel into the water to test the consistency. If it separates into hard but pliable threads, it is the right temperature.)

As soon as the syrup reaches 285°F, remove the pot from the heat and immediately whisk in the baking soda–salt mixture and the vanilla. Whisk vigorously and the syrup will turn opaque and foamy. Immediately scrape this out into the liquid peanut mixture.

Switch to the silicone spatula and quickly fold the peanut mixture into the foamy syrup. You don't have to thoroughly fold it, and it's okay to have striations of the syrup in the peanut butter. It will start to turn into a solid mass and look like brown taffy. Quickly scrape it out onto the prepared baking sheet, spreading the mixture with an offset spatula so it is about an inch thick and shaping it so it is a somewhat rectangular shape. Let cool at room temperature for a few hours until completely cool.

When the buttercrunch is cool, chop the chocolate fine. Place about two-thirds of the chocolate in a metal or heatproof glass bowl and place the bowl over a pot of simmering water. Stir the chocolate from time to time to melt, until it is hot to the touch. Alternatively you can melt the chocolate in the microwave, stirring it every 20 seconds or so to melt it evenly (see page 26).

Once the chocolate is entirely melted and hot, add the rest of the unmelted chopped chocolate. Stir slowly and carefully until this chocolate is melted by the heat of the already-melted chocolate. When all the chocolate is completely melted, the temperature of the chocolate should be just under body temperature. The best way to test is to place a little bit of chocolate right underneath your lip. If you can't feel it or it is a bit cool, it is perfect. If it feels warm, you need to add a bit more unmelted chocolate and keep stirring to cool it down. (By introducing the unmelted chocolate to the melted chocolate, you are encouraging the melted chocolate to become tempered. This means that when you cover the buttercrunch in it, it will cool into a snappy, firm, shiny coating for the candy instead of a streaked, soft, unattractive coating.)

Spread the tempered chocolate evenly across the surface of the buttercrunch. Let the chocolate set for about 1 hour at room temperature.

Use a sharp chef's knife to cut the buttercrunch into rectangular pieces about 2 inches across.

Buttercrunch can be stored in an airtight container at room temperature for up to 3 weeks.

Almond Pistachio Cherry

Honey Nougat

MAKES 24 PIECES

2 cups/**280 grams** whole raw almonds

2 cups/**280 grams** whole shelled unsalted pistachios

½ cup/**60 grams** confectioners' sugar, sifted after measuring

1 cup/**340 grams** honey

2 large egg whites (about ¼ cup/**60 grams**), at room temperature

1½ teaspoons kosher salt

2 teaspoons pure almond extract

1 teaspoon pure vanilla extract

2½ cups/**500 grams** superfine sugar

½ cup/**160 grams** light corn syrup

1 cup/**200 grams** dried cherries

This might sound blasphemous since I've made my name as a pastry chef, but I don't typically like really sweet things. I rarely had sweets growing up other than fruit (and an apple is still my favorite afternoon snack), and my palate is geared toward desserts and pastries that don't scream SUGAR!! This nougat is a distinct exception. It's so sweet it almost hurts my teeth but it's so good I keep reaching for more. Packed full of nuts and dried cherries, it is both super chewy and super crunchy. It is also really beautiful and makes a gorgeous gift when wrapped individually in clear cellophane so you can see all the different colors. It takes a full day to set, so be sure to plan in advance when making this recipe.

Preheat the oven to 350°F and place a rack in the center of the oven. Place the almonds and pistachios on a baking sheet and toast for 8 to 10 minutes, until the insides of the nuts are light golden brown and fragrant; break a few open to check. Set aside.

Line a 9 x 13-inch rimmed baking sheet with a silicone baking mat and dust it generously with about half the confectioners' sugar; set it aside.

Bring the honey to a boil in a small heavy-bottomed saucepan and cook until it reaches 250°F, about 3 minutes. It will get pretty foamy while it is boiling. While the honey is cooking, place the egg whites in a stand mixer fitted with a whisk attachment.

As soon as the honey reaches 250°F, remove it from the stove. Turn the mixer on high speed and slowly drizzle the honey down the side of the mixer bowl into the whites. (Don't drizzle it into the center or the whisk will fling it every which way except into the whites.) Add the salt and the almond and vanilla extracts and reduce the speed to medium. Whip for 6 to 8 minutes, until the mixture turns light and fluffy. If the sugar syrup has not reached the proper temperature by then, turn the mixer to its lowest speed.

While the mixture is whipping, place the superfine sugar, corn syrup, and ¾ cup/180 grams water in a small heavy-bottomed saucepan and stir carefully to moisten the sugar. Turn the heat on high and bring the mixture to a boil. Reduce the heat to medium and cook the sugar syrup until it reaches 310°F, a little less than 15 minutes. Switch out the whisk attachment of the mixer for the paddle, and keep the mixer running on low. When the syrup comes to 315°F, remove it from the heat and slowly drizzle the syrup down the side of the mixer bowl into the honey–egg white mixture with the mixer on medium. Again, be sure to drizzle down the side of the bowl and not in the center of the bowl. Paddle for 5 to 6 minutes on medium to allow the mixture to thicken and aerate. You want it to be cool enough to touch but still hot and pliable enough that you can add the nuts and fruit. Add the toasted nuts and the cherries and paddle just long enough to incorporate them into the nougat. Don't paddle too long, or the cherries will stain the white nougat.

Scrape the nougat out onto the prepared baking sheet. It will be extremely sticky and gooey and hard to handle. Do the best you can to scrape it all out of the bowl. The easiest way to flatten it on the baking sheet is to wet your hands and press down with the palms of your hands on the nougat and flatten and fill the sheet. Dust the top of the nougat with the remaining confectioners' sugar and use a rolling pin to roll across the top of the nougat and smooth it out. Cover the nougat with plastic wrap and let it sit overnight at room temperature to firm up.

The next day, use a long sharp serrated knife sprayed with cooking spray or wiped with a little vegetable oil (such as canola) to cut along the edges of the pan to release the nougat. Invert onto a cutting board and peel off the baking mat. Using the knife in a sawing motion,

spraying it or wiping it with oil from time to time, cut the nougat into 8 strips about 1½ inches wide, then cut each strip into 3 pieces about 2½ inches long, to make 24 pieces of nougat total. Let the nougat sit at room temperature, either on the cutting board or on a flat plate or platter, uncovered, for at least 8 hours to dry the sides.

Wrap each piece of nougat in a little piece of wax paper or cellophane to keep it from spreading and softening. Store in an airtight container at room temperature for up to 2 weeks.

The special sauce

Master Ganache / 432

Master Frangipane / 433

Master Pastry Cream / 434

Master Lemon Curd / 435

Rick's Master Shortbread / 436

Master Pâte Sucrée / 437

Master Single-Crust Pâte Brisée / 438

Master Double-Crust Pâte Brisée / 439

Master Quick Puff Pastry Dough / 440

Master Puff Pastry Dough / 442

Master Brioche Dough / 444

CHAPTER 8

Master of Your Pastry Domain

Master

Ganache

8 ounces/**225 grams**
semisweet or bittersweet
chocolate

1 cup/**240 grams**
heavy cream

Chop the chocolate into small pieces and place in a medium metal or heatproof glass bowl. Heat the cream in a small saucepan until just before it comes to a boil, when small bubbles collect along the sides of the pan. Pour the cream over the chocolate and let it sit for about 30 seconds. Slowly whisk the chocolate and cream together until the chocolate is completely melted and the mixture is smooth.

Ganache can be stored in an airtight container in the refrigerator for up to 1 week.

Master

Frangipane

⅔ cup/**100 grams** whole blanched raw almonds, or 1 cup/**100 grams** almond flour

½ cup/1 stick/**115 grams** unsalted butter, at room temperature

½ cup/**100 grams** sugar

2 large eggs (about **100 grams**), at room temperature

1 tablespoon plus 1 teaspoon all-purpose flour

¼ teaspoon pure vanilla extract

⅛ teaspoon kosher salt

If using whole almonds, grind them in a food processor as finely as you can without turning them into a paste. Set aside.

In a stand mixer fitted with a paddle attachment, beat the butter with the sugar on medium speed for 1 to 2 minutes, until light. Or use a wooden spoon to beat the butter and sugar until light. Add the ground almonds or almond flour and beat on medium for another minute, until the almonds are incorporated. Stop the mixer and scrape the bottom and sides of the bowl.

Turn the mixer to low and beat in the eggs. Add the all-purpose flour, vanilla, and salt and mix until combined. The frangipane will be soft and spreadable.

Frangipane can be used immediately or stored in an airtight container in the refrigerator for up to 1 week or in the freezer for up to 1 month. If frozen, thaw it in the refrigerator overnight before using. Remove from the refrigerator a few hours before using to allow it to come to room temperature, and beat it with a wooden spoon to soften it enough to spread.

Master
Pastry Cream

MAKES ABOUT 2 CUPS/675 GRAMS

1⅔ cups/**400 grams** whole milk

¾ cup/**150 grams** sugar

3 tablespoons/**25 grams** cornstarch

½ teaspoon kosher salt

6 large egg yolks (about **120 grams**), at room temperature

2 teaspoons pure vanilla extract

In a medium saucepan, heat the milk on medium-high heat until just before it comes to a boil, when bubbles start to form around the edge of the pan. In a small bowl, thoroughly mix together the sugar, cornstarch, and salt. (Mixing the cornstarch into the sugar will prevent it from clumping when you add it to the egg yolks.) Whisk the egg yolks in a medium heatproof bowl until blended. Slowly whisk in the sugar-cornstarch mixture until completely incorporated. Remove the milk from the heat and slowly add it to the egg yolk mixture, whisking constantly, to temper the eggs (see page 29).

When the milk is all whisked into the egg yolk mixture, return everything to the saucepan and heat it over medium heat. Whisk continuously and vigorously for about 1 minute. At first the mixture will be very frothy and liquid; as it cooks more, it will slowly start to thicken until the frothy bubbles disappear, the mixture starts to steam, and the whole thing become more viscous. After 1 minute, stop whisking every few seconds to see if the mixture has come to a boil. If not, keep whisking vigorously. As soon as you do see it boiling, whisk vigorously for about 10 seconds, then immediately pour the pastry cream into an airtight container. Stir in the vanilla. Cover with plastic wrap pressed directly against the surface of the pastry cream (to prevent a skin from forming) and let cool to room temperature. Refrigerate for at least 4 hours, until cold, before using.

The pastry cream can be stored in an airtight container in the refrigerator for up to 3 days.

Master

Lemon Curd

MAKES ABOUT 2½ CUPS/750 GRAMS

1 cup/**240 grams** fresh lemon juice (about 8 large lemons)

4 tablespoons/½ stick/ **60 grams** unsalted butter

2 tablespoons/**30 grams** heavy cream

4 large eggs (about **200 grams**), at room temperature

2 large egg yolks (about **40 grams**), at room temperature

1 cup/**200 grams** sugar

½ teaspoon kosher salt

½ teaspoon pure vanilla extract

In a small saucepan, combine the lemon juice, butter, and cream and heat over medium-high heat to just under a boil.

Whisk together the whole eggs and egg yolks in a small heatproof bowl; slowly whisk in the sugar until combined. Remove the cream mixture from the heat and gradually whisk a little bit of it into the egg mixture to temper the eggs (see page 29). Continue whisking the hot liquid into the eggs a little at a time until all of it is added.

Return the mixture to the saucepan. Over medium heat, stir the mixture continuously with a wooden spoon, making sure to scrape the bottom of the saucepan frequently to prevent the eggs from scrambling at the bottom. Cook the mixture until it thickens and coats the spoon with a layer of curd thick enough that you can draw your finger through it and it holds a line. This will take 3 to 4 minutes, depending on the heat of your stove.

Remove the curd from the heat and strain it through a fine-mesh sieve into an airtight container. Whisk in the salt and vanilla. Cover with plastic wrap pressed directly against the surface of the curd (to prevent a skin from forming) and let cool to room temperature. Refrigerate for 1 to 2 hours, until cold, before using.

The curd can be stored in an airtight container in the refrigerator for up to 5 days.

Rick's Master Shortbread

MAKES 1¼ POUNDS/600 GRAMS DOUGH

1 cup/2 sticks/**225 grams** unsalted butter, at room temperature

6 tablespoons/**75 grams** superfine sugar

2 tablespoons confectioners' sugar

1 teaspoon pure vanilla extract

1 large egg yolk (about **20 grams**), at room temperature

1 cup/**140 grams** all-purpose flour

1 cup/**120 grams** cake flour, sifted after measuring

½ teaspoon baking powder

½ teaspoon kosher salt

In a stand mixer fitted with a paddle attachment, by hand with a wooden spoon, or with a handheld electric mixer, cream together the butter, superfine sugar, and confectioners' sugar on medium speed until the mixture is light and fluffy, about 5 minutes. Beat in the vanilla and egg yolk until thoroughly combined. Scrape the bowl and paddle with a rubber spatula to make sure all the yolk is thoroughly mixed in.

In a small bowl, stir together the all-purpose flour, cake flour, baking powder, and salt. With the mixer on low, slowly add the flour mixture to the butter-sugar mixture. Mix on low until the flour is totally blended in and the dough is homogenous, about 15 seconds. Stop the mixer and scrape the bowl and paddle again to make sure the flour mixture is entirely incorporated.

Scrape the dough out of the bowl onto a sheet of plastic wrap. Wrap the dough entirely with the plastic and press down to form a flat disk about 6 inches wide and 1 inch thick. Refrigerate for about 30 minutes, until the dough has firmed up but is still somewhat pliable, before using.

Shortbread dough can be stored, well wrapped, in the refrigerator for up to 5 days or in the freezer for up to 1 month. If frozen, thaw overnight in the refrigerator, then let it soften at room temperature for about 20 minutes before using.

Master
Pâte Sucrée

**MAKES ENOUGH DOUGH FOR
ONE 8- TO 10-INCH TART SHELL (325 GRAMS)**

½ cup/1 stick/**115 grams** unsalted butter, at cool room temperature

¼ cup/**50 grams** sugar

½ teaspoon kosher salt

1 cup/**140 grams** all-purpose flour

1 large egg yolk (about **20 grams**), at room temperature

In a stand mixer fitted with a paddle attachment, cream the butter, sugar, and salt together for 2 to 3 minutes, until pale and light. Scrape down the sides and bottom of the bowl and the paddle with a rubber spatula. Add the flour and paddle on low speed for about 30 seconds, until the flour is entirely incorporated. The mixture will look like wet sand. Add the egg yolk and mix until the dough comes together, about 30 seconds. Remove the dough from the bowl, wrap it tightly in plastic wrap, and let it rest in the refrigerator for about 1 hour before using.

The dough can be tightly wrapped in plastic and stored in the freezer for up to 2 weeks, or in the refrigerator for up to 5 days. If frozen, thaw it in the refrigerator overnight before using.

Master
Single-Crust Pâte Brisée

**MAKES ENOUGH DOUGH FOR
ONE SINGLE-CRUST 9-INCH PIE (220 GRAMS)**

1 cup/**140 grams**
all-purpose flour

2 teaspoons sugar

½ teaspoon kosher salt

9 tablespoons/1⅛ sticks/
130 grams unsalted
butter, cold

1 large egg yolk
(about **20 grams**),
at room temperature

2 tablespoons/**30 grams**
whole milk

In a stand mixer fitted with a paddle attachment, paddle together the flour, sugar, and salt for 10 to 15 seconds. Cut the butter into about 12 pieces and add it to the flour mixture. Paddle slowly until the flour is no longer bright white and the mixture holds together when you clump it, and there are still lumps of butter the size of pecans throughout, 30 to 45 seconds.

Whisk together the egg yolk and milk in a small bowl and add them all at once to the flour-butter mixture. Paddle very briefly, just until it barely comes together, about 30 seconds. It will look really shaggy and more like a mess than a dough.

Dump the dough out onto a clean work surface and gather it together into a tight mound. Using the heel of your hand, smear the dough, starting at the top of the mound and sliding your hand down the sides of the mound along the work surface, until most of the butter chunks are smeared into the dough and the whole thing comes together. (This technique is called fraisage — see page 25 — and makes for a very flaky pie dough.)

Wrap the dough tightly with plastic wrap and press down to make a disk about 1 inch thick. Refrigerate for at least 1 hour before using.

The dough can be stored in the refrigerator for up to 4 days or in the freezer for up to 4 weeks. Wrap in another layer of plastic if storing for more than 1 day.

Master

Double-Crust Pâte Brisée

**MAKES ENOUGH DOUGH FOR
ONE DOUBLE-CRUST 9-INCH PIE (555 GRAMS)**

1¾ cups/**245 grams**
all-purpose flour

1 tablespoon sugar

1 teaspoon kosher salt

1 cup/2 sticks/**225 grams**
unsalted butter, cold

2 large egg yolks
(about **40 grams**),
at room temperature

3 tablespoons/**45 grams**
whole milk

In a stand mixer fitted with a paddle attachment, paddle together the flour, sugar, and salt for 10 to 15 seconds. Cut the butter into about 12 pieces and add it to the flour mixture. Paddle slowly until the flour is no longer bright white and the mixture holds together when you clump it, and there are still lumps of butter the size of pecans throughout, 60 to 90 seconds.

Whisk together the egg yolks and milk in a small bowl and add them all at once to the flour-butter mixture. Paddle very briefly, just until it barely comes together, about 30 seconds. It will look really shaggy and more like a mess than a dough.

Dump the dough out onto a clean work surface and gather it together into a tight mound. Using the heel of your hand, smear the dough, starting at the top of the mound and sliding your hand down the sides of the mound along the work surface, until most of the butter chunks are smeared into the dough and the whole thing comes together. (This technique is called fraisage — see page 25 — and makes for a very flaky pie dough.)

Wrap the dough tightly in plastic wrap and press it down to make a disk about 1 inch thick. Refrigerate for at least 1 hour before using.

The dough can be stored in the refrigerator for up to 4 days or in the freezer for up to 4 weeks. Wrap in another layer of plastic if storing for more than 1 day.

Master

Quick Puff Pastry Dough

MAKES ABOUT 1½ POUNDS/680 GRAMS DOUGH

1¾ cups/**245 grams** all-purpose flour

5 tablespoons/**40 grams** cake flour, sifted after measuring

1 teaspoon kosher salt

1½ cups/3 sticks/**340 grams** unsalted butter, cold

6 tablespoons/**90 grams** ice-cold water

Combine the all-purpose flour, cake flour, and salt in a stand mixer fitted with a paddle attachment, or use a handheld electric mixer. Cut up the butter into ½-inch cubes and toss it all into the flour. Pulse the mixer on and off on the lowest speed until the butter is broken down into pieces the size of lima beans, 45 seconds to 1 minute. Pour in the water and mix just until everything comes together in a shaggy and rough-looking dough, 10 to 15 seconds.

Generously flick flour over the work surface. Dump out the dough onto the work surface and pat it into a rough square, around 8 x 8 inches. Using a rolling pin, roll the dough from left to right as well as you can into a rectangle 18 inches wide from side to side, 8 inches long from top to bottom, and ½ inch thick. Flick the dough with flour as needed to prevent the rolling pin from sticking. Don't worry if it seems really messy and not at all smooth. Just do your best to roll the square into a rectangle.

Lightly score the rectangle in thirds with a bench scraper or knife. Each third should be 6 inches wide and 8 inches long from top to bottom. Brush off any loose flour from the dough. Take the right third of the dough and, as best you can, flip it over onto the middle third. Then take the left third of the dough and, again as best you can, flip that on top of the middle and right third (like folding a business letter). You should now have a pile of dough about 6 inches wide from side to side, 8 inches long from top to bottom, and 2 inches thick. Rotate the dough pile 90 degrees (a quarter-turn) clockwise so that now it is 8 inches wide and 6 inches long. (This process — folding the dough in thirds and then rotating it 90 degrees — is called giving the dough a trifold and turn.) The dough should still be rough-looking, and you'll see bits of butter throughout.

Using the rolling pin, once again roll this out into a rectangle about 18 inches wide and 8 inches long. This time the dough should be a little more cohesive, and you should find it a little easier to roll out. Make sure the work surface and dough are well floured. Do your best to roll the dough into as even a rectangle as

When rolling out a laminated dough like puff pastry, your goal is to keep the layers directly on top of one another and lined up evenly to preserve the layering. In between turns, you have three layers of dough, one on top of the another. Rather than immediately rolling these out again with a back-and-forth motion, first flatten the dough with the rolling pin by firmly pressing down on it and then moving the pin up and down and pounding along the length of the dough — use the rolling pin to create ridges as it compacts the dough. Once the dough is pressed down all over, use the pin to roll back and forth, smoothing out the ridges while flattening and rolling the dough into the shape you want. By pressing down first before rolling, you preserve the layers. If you were to start rolling immediately after folding the dough, the very top layer would take all the pressure from the rolling pin and stretch out way over the very bottom layer. Using this technique to compress the dough first helps to keep the layers even, making for a more flaky end product. You also want to flip the dough over occasionally during the rolling process to make sure the top and bottom layers are getting equal attention from the rolling pin.

you can, with sharp corners. Again, divide the dough into thirds, flipping the right third into the middle and the left third on top of that, and turning the entire piece of dough 90 degrees. Dust off any loose flour in between folds.

Repeat this process twice more, rolling out the dough to an 18 x 8-inch rectangle, for a total of four trifolds and turns. By the time you get to the fourth turn, the dough should be a 6 x 8-inch rectangle, completely cohesive and almost smooth. There may be small chunks of butter in it but it should no longer be shaggy and difficult to work with.

Place the dough on parchment paper on a baking sheet and cover it completely with plastic wrap, tucking the plastic under the dough as if tucking it into bed. Refrigerate the dough for at least 1 hour or up to 2 hours.

Generously flick flour over the work surface. Remove the dough from the refrigerator, unwrap it, and place it on the work surface with the long side of the rectangle closest to you. Give the dough a trifold and turn

(fold it in thirds, then rotate it 90 degrees). Flip the dough over occasionally during the rolling process to make sure the top and bottom layers are getting equal attention from the rolling pin. Give it one more trifold and turn for a total of 2 trifolds and turns after it has rested in the fridge. The final packet will be about 6 x 8 inches.

The quick puff pastry dough is now finished, but needs to rest before you can use it. Wrap the dough in plastic wrap and let it rest in the refrigerator for at least 1 hour.

The dough can be stored in the refrigerator for up to 2 days, or frozen, well wrapped in plastic, for up to 1 month. Pull the dough out of the freezer the night before you plan to use it and thaw in the refrigerator.

Master
Puff Pastry Dough

MAKES ABOUT 1½ POUNDS/680 GRAMS DOUGH

1¾ cups/**245 grams** all-purpose flour

1 teaspoon kosher salt

6 tablespoons/¾ stick/**85 grams** unsalted butter, at room temperature

1 cup/2 sticks/**225 grams** unsalted butter, cold

½ cup/**120 grams** ice-cold water

In a stand mixer fitted with a paddle attachment, mix together the flour, salt, and room temperature butter on low speed for 6 to 8 minutes, until the butter is completely incorporated into the flour and the mixture resembles damp sand. Add the water and mix on low until the dough is combined, 1 to 2 minutes. It will be somewhat damp and sticky, with some drier spots. Remove the dough from the mixer bowl, shape it into a rough square about 5 x 5 inches, place it on a parchment paper–lined baking sheet, and cover it loosely with plastic wrap. (This dough block is called the détrempe.) Place the détrempe in the refrigerator for about 20 minutes.

While the détrempe is chilling, place the cold butter in the mixer and beat it on medium speed for 2 to 3 minutes to soften it entirely. Scrape the butter onto a sheet of parchment or plastic wrap and press it into a flat rectangle, about 4 x 5 inches. Leave it out in a cool part of the kitchen — between 66° and 68°F — until the détrempe is done resting.

Generously flick flour over the work surface. Remove the détrempe from the fridge, unwrap it, and place it on the work surface. Press the détrempe with your hands into a rectangle about 8 inches wide from side to side and 5 inches long from top to bottom. Unwrap the butter rectangle and place it on the right half of the détrempe so the butter covers the entire right half. Fold the left half of the détrempe over the butter and press down on the edges to seal in the butter. Rotate the dough 90 degrees (a quarter-turn) clockwise so that the rectangle is 5 inches wide from side to side and 4 inches long from top to bottom, and generously flour underneath and on top of the dough.

Press the dough down with the palms of your hands, flattening it out before you start to roll it out. Slowly begin rolling the dough out from side to side into a long rectangle about 15 inches wide from side to side and 10 inches long from top to bottom. The dough might be a little sticky, so again be sure to flour the dough and the work surface as needed to prevent the rolling pin from sticking. Using a bench scraper or knife, lightly score the rectangle into thirds; each third will be 5 inches wide from side to side and 10 inches long from top to bottom. Brush any loose flour off the dough. Flip the right third of the dough over onto the middle third. Then flip the left third of the dough on top of the stacked middle and right thirds. (This is like folding a business letter.) The dough should now be about 5 inches wide from side to side, 10 inches long from top to bottom, and about 1 inch thick. Rotate the dough pile counterclockwise 90 degrees; it will now be 10 inches wide from side to side and 5 inches long from top to bottom, and the folded seam will be at the top, facing away from you. (The process of folding and rotating is called giving the dough a trifold and turn.)

Repeat the process once more, rolling out the dough into a long rectangle, again about 15 inches wide from side to side and 10 inches long from top to bottom, and proceeding as directed above to

give it another trifold and turn. This time the dough will be a bit tougher to roll out and a bit more elastic. Try to keep the dough in a nice rectangle, flipping it upside down as needed as you roll it back and forth.

Place the dough back on the parchment-lined baking sheet from the détrempe and cover it completely with plastic wrap, tucking the plastic under the dough as if tucking it into bed. Refrigerate the dough for about 1 hour to rest.

Generously flick flour over the work surface. Remove the dough from the refrigerator, unwrap it, and place it on the work surface, with the long side of the rectangle facing you and the seam of the dough on top, facing away. This time roll out the dough into a rectangle about 27 inches wide from side to side and 8 inches long from top to bottom. Be firm with the dough; it will be a bit tough to roll out and you'll need to have patience. Once again score it lengthwise into thirds, give it another trifold (fold the right third onto the middle third, and fold the left third on top of that), and rotate it counterclockwise.

Give it another trifold and turn. Return the dough to the baking sheet and again cover it with plastic wrap. Let it rest in the refrigerator for 1 hour more.

Repeat rolling it out, and giving it another trifold and another turn. Return the dough to the baking sheet and again cover it with plastic wrap. Let it rest in the refrigerator for another hour.

Again, place the dough on a well-floured work surface with the long side facing you. Roll it into a rectangle 27 inches wide from side to side and 8 inches long from top to bottom, score it into thirds, give it one last trifold to 9 x 8 inches, and give it a turn counterclockwise for good measure.

Give the dough a final rest in the fridge for at least 1 hour before using.

The dough can be stored, tightly wrapped in plastic wrap, in the fridge for up to 5 days or in the freezer for up to 3 months. If frozen, let the dough thaw overnight in the fridge before using.

Master

Brioche Dough

MAKES ABOUT 2½ POUNDS/1,200 GRAMS DOUGH

1¾ cups/**245 grams** all-purpose flour

2 cups/**300 grams** high-gluten bread flour

2¼ teaspoons/**7 grams**/ 1 (¼-ounce) packet active dry yeast

⅓ cup/**65 grams** sugar

2½ teaspoons kosher salt

4 large eggs (about **200 grams**), at room temperature

18 tablespoons/2¼ sticks/ **255 grams** unsalted butter, cut into 10 to 12 pieces, at room temperature

In a stand mixer fitted with a dough hook attachment, combine the all-purpose flour, bread flour, yeast, sugar, salt, ½ cup/120 grams cold water, and the eggs. Mix on low speed until the ingredients have come together, 3 to 4 minutes. Scrape the bowl as necessary to make sure all the flour is incorporated into the wet ingredients. Mix on low for another 3 to 4 minutes once the dough has come together. It will be very stiff.

Add the butter to the dough piece by piece and continue mixing on low for about 10 minutes. The butter needs to mix completely into the dough, so stop the mixer occasionally to scrape the sides of the bowl and break up the dough with your hands if necessary to help the butter mix in.

Once the butter is completely incorporated into the dough, mix on medium for another 15 minutes, until the dough becomes sticky and soft and somewhat shiny. Turn the mixer up to medium-high and mix for

about 1 minute — you should hear a slap-slap-slap sound as the dough hits the sides of the bowl. Test the dough by pulling at it — it should stretch a bit and have a little give. If it seems wet and loose and more like a batter than a dough, add a few tablespoons of either all-purpose or bread flour and mix until it comes together. If it breaks off into pieces when you pull at it, continue to mix it on medium for another 2 to 3 minutes, until it develops more strength and stretches when you grab it. When it's ready you should be able to gather it all together and pick it up all as one piece.

Place the dough in a large bowl or plastic container and cover the top with plastic wrap pressed directly against the surface of the dough to prevent a skin from forming. Let the dough proof in the refrigerator for at least 6 hours or up to overnight. The dough is now ready to use.

Index

NOTE: PAGE REFERENCES IN *ITALICS* INDICATE PHOTOGRAPHS

A

Adams, Jody, 14–15

Alina's Milk Bread, *132*, 133–34

Almond flour

Gluten-Free Apple Spice Pecan Muffins, 58–59, *59*

Master Frangipane, 433

Mixed Nut and Honey Whole Grain Biscotti, 180–81, *181*

Olive Oil Cake with Fresh Grapes, *296*, 297

Orange-Almond Pudding Cake with Chocolate Ganache, *316*, 317–18

Persian Love Cookies, 174–75, *175*

Stone Fruit and Berry Financier Cake with Toasted Meringue, 325–27, *326*

Almond(s)

Billionaire's Shortbread, 402–4, *403*

Candied, Brown Sugar Meringues, 205–7, *206*

Chocolate Cocoa Nib Caramels, 421–22, *423*

Croissants, 86–87, *87*

Flour Power Bars, *168*, 169–70

Joy Tart, 233–35, *234*

Macaroons, Vegan, 166, *167*

Master Frangipane, 433

Mixed Nut and Honey Whole Grain Biscotti, 180–81, *181*

-Orange Pudding Cake with Chocolate Ganache, *316*, 317–18

Ossa dei Morti, 185–86, *187*

Panettone, 139–40, *141*

Panna Cotta with Stone Fruit Cocktail, *354*, 355–56

Pistachio Cherry Honey Nougat, 427–28, *429*

Salted, English Toffee, *418*, 419–20

Stone Fruit and Berry Financier Cake with Toasted Meringue, 325–27, *326*

Angel Food Cake, Funfetti, 319–20, *321*

Anise seeds

Mixed Nut and Honey Whole Grain Biscotti, 180–81, *181*

Anzacs, 182–84, *183*

Apple Cider

Apple Glaze, 59

-Miso Caramels, 416–17, *417*

Sticky Buns, 93–94, *95*

Apple(s)

Apple Cider Sticky Buns, 93–94, *95*

Butter, Vanilla, 272

Chaussons aux Pommes, *270*, 271–72

Compote, 336

fresh, for recipes, 36

Jam, 390

Pie, Old-Fashioned Double-Crust, 273–74, *274*

Sarah's Adult Spice Cake, *332*, 333–36

Spice Pecan Muffins, Gluten-Free, 58–59, *59*

Tarte Tatin (variation), 276

-Vanilla Pound Cake, 62–63, *63*

Apricot(s)

Almond Panna Cotta with Stone Fruit Cocktail, *354*, 355–56

Walnut Raisin Loaf, Henry's, 123–24, *125*

Ashley's Birthday Cake, *342*, 343–47

B

Babka, Housemade Nutella, *154*, *155–57*

Bacon and Gorgonzola Drop Biscuits, *42*, 43–44

Bain-marie, 31

Baker's Dozen

    adjusting recipes, 19

    being present, 20

    cleaning as you go, 19–20

    don't give up, 20

    having fun, 20

    having patience, 20

    ingredient temperatures, 18–19

    kitchen scales, 18

    mise en place, 18

    oven temperature, 18

    reading the recipe, 18

    salt, 19

    tests for doneness, 19

Baking mats, silicone, 33–34

Baking pans, 31

Baking sheets

    rotating in oven, 27

    types of, 31

Banana(s)

    -Chocolate Muffins, Vegan, 52, *53*

    Cream Pie with Salted Caramel and Dark Chocolate, 264–66, *265*

    Hummingbird Cupcakes, 283–84, *285*

    Nutty Seedy Breakfast Cookies, 78–79, *79*

    ripe, for recipes, 36–37

Bars

    Billionaire's Shortbread, 402–4, *403*

    Brown Butter–Peanut Rice Crispy Treats with Peanut Butter Ganache, *400*, 400–401

    Butter Mochi, 396–97, *397*

    Flour Power, *168*, 169–70

    Gluten-Free Double Chocolate–Walnut Brownies, 171–72, *173*

Bench scraper, 32

Bentonwood Bakery, 14

Berry(ies)

    Blackberry-Buttermilk Muffin Cakes, *60*, 61

    Blueberry Hand Pies, 249–51, *250*

    Cranberry-Pecan Bread, 146–48, *147*

    Fresh, Spring Ricotta Pie with, 227–28, *229*

    Fresh Fruit Tart, 224, *225–26*

    Gluten-Free Lemon Raspberry Chia Muffins, 56, *57*

    Hazelnut-Raspberry Rugelach, 211–13, *212*

    Homemade Rhubarb-Strawberry Spoon Jam, 76, *77*

    individually quick frozen (IQF), for recipes, 37

    Lamingtons, *322*, 323–24

    Nutty Seedy Breakfast Cookies, 78–79, *79*

    Passion Fruit and Raspberry Pavlovas, *382*, 383–84

    Raspberry Swirl Meringues, 202–4, *203*

    Rhubarb-Strawberry Jam-n-Butter Biscuits, 75–76, *77*

    ripe, for recipes, 37

    and Stone Fruit Financier Cake with Toasted Meringue, 325–27, *326*

    Strawberries and Cream Chiffon Cake, *328*, 329–31

    Strawberry Slab Pie, 252, *253–54*

    Summer Blueberry-Peach Cobbler, *360*, 361–62

    Whole Wheat Maple-Blueberry Scones, 69–70, *71*

Biba, 14

Billionaire's Shortbread, 402–4, *403*

Birthday Cake, Ashley's, *342*, 343–47

Biscotti, Mixed Nut and Honey Whole Grain, 180–81, *181*

Biscuits

    Cobbler, 362

    Gorgonzola and Bacon Drop, *42*, 43–44

    Rhubarb-Strawberry Jam-n-Butter, 75–76, *77*

Bittersweet Chocolate–Orange Truffle Tart with Salted Caramel, 245–248, *247*

Blackberry(ies)

    -Buttermilk Muffin Cakes, *60*, 61

    Fresh Fruit Tart, 224, *225–26*

    Spring Ricotta Pie with Fresh Berries, 227–28, *229*

Black Sesame–Tahini Spiral Shortbreads, *218*, 219–21

Blind baking, 21

Blueberry(ies)

    Fresh Fruit Tart, *224*, 225–26

    Hand Pies, 249–51, *250*

    individually quick frozen (IQF), for recipes, 37

    -Maple Whole Wheat Scones, 69–70, *71*

    -Peach Cobbler, Summer, *360*, 361–62

    Spring Ricotta Pie with Fresh Berries, 227–28, *229*

Bourbon

    Eggnog Cheesecake with Gingerbread People, 312–15, *313*

Bowls, 32

Bowl scraper, 32

Bread Pudding, Pumpkin-Pecan, 357–58, *359*

Breads

    Apple Cider Sticky Buns, 93–94, *95*

    Brown Butter Cinnamon Rolls with Cream Cheese Frosting, *96*, 97–98

    Challah, *110*, 111–12

    Ciabatta, *136*, 137–38

    Cranberry-Pecan, 146–48, *147*

    Dulce de Leche Brioche Buns, 367–68, *369*

    Fig-Walnut, 149–50

    Garlicky Cheesy Monkey, 126–27, *127*

    Gluten-Free Focaccia, *108*, 109

    Henry's Apricot Walnut Raisin Loaf, 123–24, *125*

    Honey Whole Wheat, 151–52, *153*

    Hot Cross Buns, *128*, 129–31

    Housemade Nutella Babka, *154*, 155–57

    Irish Soda, 66–68, *67*

    Milk, Alina's, *132*, 133–34

    Mushroom and Thyme Brioches, 49–51, *50*

    My Rye, 114–15, *115*

    Panettone, 139–40, *141*

    scoring and slashing, 27–28

    Sticky Bun Kouigns Amann, 99–102, *101*

    Vinal Bakery Multigrain English Muffins, *142*, 143–45

    Whole Grain Pull-Apart Rolls, *116*, 117–18

    Whole Wheat Brioches à Tête, 119–22, *120*

Breakfast

    Almond Croissants, 86–87, *87*

    Apple Cider Sticky Buns, 93–94, *95*

    Apple-Vanilla Pound Cake, 62–63, *63*

    Blackberry-Buttermilk Muffin Cakes, *60*, 61

    Brown Butter Cinnamon Rolls with Cream Cheese Frosting, *96*, 97–98

    Choux Donuts with Mascarpone Cream, 103–5, *104*

    Country Feta Pies, 40–41, *41*

    Currant Spelt Oat Scones, 64–65, *65*

    Fresh Fig Danish, *88*, 89–92

    Gluten-Free Apple Spice Pecan Muffins, 58–59, *59*

    Gluten-Free Ham and Cheese Puffs, 47–48, *48*

    Gluten-Free Lemon Raspberry Chia Muffins, 56, *57*

    Gorgonzola and Bacon Drop Biscuits, 42, 43–44

    Irish Soda Bread, 66–68, *67*

    Mushroom and Thyme Brioches, 49–51, *50*

    Nutty Seedy Breakfast Cookies, 78–79, *79*

    Parmesan-Chive Scones, 45–46, *46*

    Rhubarb-Strawberry Jam-n-Butter Biscuits, 75–76, *77*

    Ricotta-Cherry Scones, 72, 73–74

    Spelt Croissants, *80*, 81–85

    Sticky Bun Kouigns Amann, 99–102, *101*

    Vegan Carrot-Ginger Muffins, *54*, 55

    Vegan Chocolate-Banana Muffins, 52, *53*

    Whole Wheat Maple-Blueberry Scones, 69–70, *71*

Brioche Buns, Dulce de Leche, 367–68, *369*

Brioche Dough, Master, 444

Brioches

    à Tête, Whole Wheat, 119–22, *120*

    Mushroom and Thyme, 49–51, *50*

Brownies, Gluten-Free Double Chocolate–Walnut, 171–72, *173*

Brown Sugar

    -Candied Almond Meringues, 205–7, *206*

    Graham Cracker Pie Shell, 238

    making your own, 35

    for recipes, 35

Buckwheat flour
    Gluten-Free Apple Spice Pecan Muffins,
      58–59, *59*
    Gluten-Free Double Chocolate–Walnut Brownies,
      171–72, *173*
Buns
    Dulce de Leche Brioche, 367–68, *369*
    Hot Cross, *128*, 129–31
    Sticky, Apple Cider, 93–94, *95*
    Sticky, Kouigns Amann, 99–102, *101*
Butter
    for cake pans, 21
    Crumbs, 244
    Mochi, 396–97, *397*
    Salted, 76
    and sugar, creaming, 23
    unsalted, for recipes, 35
Buttercream, Chocolate Pudding, 345
Buttercrunch, Chocolate–Peanut Butter, 424, 425–26
Buttermilk, for recipes, 37
Butterscotch
    Brown Butter Caramels, 413–14, *415*
    Rum Pudding Parfait with Ginger-Molasses
      Crumble, 364–66, *365*

C

Cake pans
    buttering and flouring, 21
    materials and sizes, 31
    rotating in oven, 27
Cakes
    Apple-Vanilla Pound, 62–63, *63*
    Birthday, Ashley's, *342*, 343–47
    crumb coating, 23
    Eggnog Cheesecake with Gingerbread People,
      312–15, *313*
    Funfetti Angel Food, 319–20, *321*
    Ginger-Peach Crumb, 306–7
    Hummingbird Cupcakes, 283–84, *285*
    Japanese Cotton Cheesecake, 300–302, *301*

    Keith's Homemade Devil Dogs, *208*, 209–10
    Lamingtons, *322*, 323–24
    Lemon Meringue Cupcakes, 289–90, *291*
    Malted Chocolate, 337–40, *338*
    Nutmeg, Syrian, 298, *299*
    Olive Oil, with Fresh Grapes, 296, 297
    Orange-Almond Pudding, with Chocolate
      Ganache, *316*, 317–18
    Passion Fruit Crêpe, *348*, 349–51
    Plum Upside-Down, 303–5, *304*
    Simple Lemon Spiral, *308*, 309–10
    Spice, Sarah's Adult, *332*, 333–36
    splitting into layers, 28
    Stone Fruit and Berry Financier, with Toasted
      Meringue, 325–27, *326*
    Strawberries and Cream Chiffon, *328*, 329–31
    Super Bowl Cupcakes, *286*, 287–88
    Vanilla Bean Cupcakes with Creamy Ginger
      Frosting, *280*, 281–82
    Vanilla Genoise, 324
    Vegan Hostess Cupcakes, *292*, 293–95
Cake stand, rotating, 33
Candies
    Almond Pistachio Cherry Honey Nougat,
      427–28, *429*
    Apple Cider–Miso Caramels, *416–17*, *417*
    Brown Butter Butterscotch Caramels, 413–14,
      415
    Chocolate Almond Cocoa Nib Caramels,
      421–22, *423*
    Chocolate–Peanut Butter Buttercrunch, *424*,
      425–26
    Christopher's Honeycomb, *410*, 411–12
    Salted Almond English Toffee, *418*, 419–20
Candy thermometer, 32
Caramel
    -Chocolate Oreos, Gluten-Free, *176*, 177–79
    Cream, Vanilla, 386
    making, 22–23
    Popcorn Cookies, Jessi's, 191–92, *193*
    Salted, and Dark Chocolate, Banana Cream Pie
      with, 264–66, *265*

Salted, Bittersweet Chocolate–Orange Truffle Tart
   with, 245–48, *247*
Salted, Sauce for Banana Cream Pie, 266
Salted, Sauce for Truffle Tart, 246
Sauce, 178
Vanilla Merveilleux, Marvelous, 385–87, *387*
Caramelized Onions, 44
Caramels
   Apple Cider–Miso, 416–17, *417*
   Brown Butter Butterscotch, 413–14, *415*
   Chocolate Almond Cocoa Nib, 421–22, *423*
Caraway seeds
   Irish Soda Bread, 66–68, *67*
   My Rye Bread, 114–15, *115*
Cardamom
   Persian Love Cookies, 174–75, *175*
Carrot-Ginger Muffins, Vegan, *54*, 55
Cashews
   Flour Power Bars, *168*, 169–70
Challah, *110*, 111–12
Chaussons aux Pommes, *270*, 271–72
Cheese. *See also* Cream Cheese
   Choux Donuts with Mascarpone Cream,
      103–5, *104*
   Country Feta Pies, 40–41, *41*
   Garlicky Cheesy Monkey Bread, 126–27, *127*
   Gorgonzola and Bacon Drop Biscuits, *42*, 43–44
   and Ham Puffs, Gluten-Free, 47–48, *48*
   Mushroom and Thyme Brioches, 49–51, *50*
   Parmesan-Chive Scones, 45–46, *46*
   Ricotta-Cherry Scones, *72*, 73–74
   Spring Ricotta Pie with Fresh Berries, 227–28, *229*
Cheesecakes
   Eggnog, with Gingerbread People, 312–15, *313*
   Japanese Cotton, 300–302, *301*
Cherry(ies)
   Almond Panna Cotta with Stone Fruit Cocktail,
      354, 355–56
   Almond Pistachio Honey Nougat, 427–28, *429*
   Crumb Pie, *242*, 243–44
   Nutty Seedy Breakfast Cookies, 78–79, *79*

Panettone, 139–40, *141*
   -Ricotta Scones, *72*, 73–74
Chia (seeds)
   Flour Power Bars, *168*, 169–70
   Lemon Raspberry Muffins, Gluten-Free, *56*, 57
Chiffon Cake, Strawberries and Cream, *328*, 329–31
Chive-Parmesan Scones, 45–46, *46*
Chocolate
   Almond Cocoa Nib Caramels, 421–22, *423*
   Almond Joy Tart, 233–35, *234*
   Ashley's Birthday Cake, *342*, 343–47
   -Banana Muffins, Vegan, 52, *53*
   Billionaire's Shortbread, 402–4, *403*
   bittersweet, about, 35
   Bittersweet, –Orange Truffle Tart with Salted
      Caramel, 245–48, *247*
   -Caramel Oreos, Gluten-Free, *176*, 177–79
   Chip Cookies, Thin, Crispy, 194–95, *195*
   choosing, 35
   Christopher's Honeycomb, *410*, 411–12
   Dark, and Salted Caramel, Banana Cream Pie
      with, 264–66, *265*
   Double, Rye Cookies, 196–98, *197*
   Double, –Walnut Brownies, Gluten-Free, 171–72,
      173
   Ganache, Orange-Almond Pudding Cake with,
      316, 317–18
   Ganache, Spicy, Vietnamese Espresso
      Profiteroles with, *374*, 375–77
   Housemade Nutella Babka, *154*, 155–57
   Keith's Homemade Devil Dogs, *208*, 209–10
   Lamingtons, *322*, 323–24
   Malted, Cake, 337–40, *338*
   Master Ganache, 432
   melting, 26
   milk, about, 35
   Milk, Graham Cracker Pie Shell, 262
   Mocha Chip Cookies, 199–200, *201*
   -Orange Ganache, 318
   –Peanut Butter Buttercrunch, *424*, 425–26
   Pudding Buttercream, 345
   Raspberry Swirl Meringues, 202–4, *203*

Chocolate (cont.)

    Salted Almond English Toffee, *418*, 419–20

    semisweet, about, 35

    S'mores Pie, 261–62, *263*

    Soy Ganache, 295

    Speckle, 340

    Spicy Ganache, 377

    Super Bowl Cupcakes, *286*, 287–88

    tempering, 28–29

    unsweetened, about, 35

    Vegan Hostess Cupcakes, *292*, 293–95

    white, buying, 35

Choux Donuts with Mascarpone Cream, 103–5, *104*

Christopher's Honeycomb, *410*, 411–12

Ciabatta, *136*, 137–38

Cinnamon Brown Butter Rolls with Cream Cheese Frosting, *96*, 97–98

Clove Glaze, 131

Cobbler Biscuits, 362

Cobbler, Summer Blueberry-Peach, *360*, 361–62

Cocoa Nib(s)

    Billionaire's Shortbread, 402–4, *403*

    Chocolate Almond Caramels, 421–22, *423*

Cocoa powder, Dutch-processed, about, 35–36

Coconut

    Almond Joy Tart, 233–35, *234*

    Anzacs, 182–84, *183*

    Butter Mochi, 396–97, *397*

    Lamingtons, *322*, 323–24

    Nutty Seedy Breakfast Cookies, 78–79, *79*

    Sticky Rice with Mango-Lime Curd and Mango Snow, *378*, 379–81

Coconut milk, for recipes, 37

Coffee

    Mocha Chip Cookies, 199–200, *201*

    Syrup, 347

    Vietnamese Espresso Ice Cream, *374*, 377

    Vietnamese Espresso Profiteroles with Spicy Chocolate Ganache, *374*, 375–77

Compote, Apple, 336

Cookie Crumble, Ginger-Molasses, 366

Cookies

    Anzacs, 182–84, *183*

    Baby Palmiers, 214, 215–16

    Breakfast, Nutty Seedy, 78–79, *79*

    Brown Sugar–Candied Almond Meringues, 205–7, *206*

    Caramel Popcorn, Jessi's, 191–92, *193*

    Chocolate Chip, Thin, Crispy, 194–95, *195*

    Double Chocolate Rye, 196–98, *197*

    Gingerbread People, *313*, 314–15

    Gluten-Free Chocolate-Caramel Oreos, *176*, 177–79

    Hazelnut-Raspberry Rugelach, 211–13, *212*

    Lemon-Polenta, *164*, 165

    Lemon Sugar, with Lemon Glaze, *188*, 189–90

    Mixed Nut and Honey Whole Grain Biscotti, 180–81, *181*

    Mocha Chip, 199–200, *201*

    Ossa dei Morti, 185–86, *187*

    Pecan Sandies, 160–61, *161*

    Persian Love, 174–75, *175*

    Raspberry Swirl Meringues, 202–4, *203*

    Tahini–Black Sesame Spiral Shortbreads, *218*, 219–21

    Vegan Almond Macaroons, 166, *167*

    Walnut Meltaways, 162–63, *163*

Cornet, making a, 25–26

Cornmeal

    Lemon-Polenta Cookies, *164*, 165

    My Rye Bread, 114–15, *115*

Coulis, Raspberry, 204

Cranberry(ies)

    Nutty Seedy Breakfast Cookies, 78–79, *79*

    -Pecan Bread, 146–48, *147*

Cream, scalding, 27

Cream Cheese

    Eggnog Cheesecake with Gingerbread People, 312–15, *313*

    Fresh Fig Danish, *88*, 89–92

    Frosting, Brown Butter Cinnamon Rolls with, *96*, 97–98

    Ginger Cream, 334

Hazelnut-Raspberry Rugelach, 211–13, *212*

Japanese Cotton Cheesecake, 300–302, *301*

Magic Sally Frosting, 284

Maple Pecan Tassies, 398–99, *399*

Sarah's Adult Spice Cake, *332*, 333–36

Cream Puffs, Matcha, *370*, 371–73

Crème fraîche

  about, 36

  making your own, 36

Crêpe Cake, Passion Fruit, *348*, 349–51

Croissants

  Almond, 86–87, *87*

  Spelt, *80*, 81–85

Crostatas, Fresh Peach, *258*, 259–60

Crumb Cake, Ginger-Peach, 306–7

Crumb coating a cake, 23

Crumbs, Butter, 244

Crust, Gingerbread, 314–15

Cupcakes

  Hummingbird, 283–84, *285*

  Lemon Meringue, 289–90, *291*

  Super Bowl, *286*, 287–88

  Vanilla Bean, with Creamy Ginger Frosting, *280*, 281–82

  Vegan Hostess, *292*, 293–95

Curd

  Lemon, Master, 435

  Mango-Lime, and Mango Snow, Coconut Sticky Rice with, *378*, 379–81

  Passion Fruit, 351, 384

Currant(s)

  Irish Soda Bread, 66–68, *67*

  Spelt Oat Scones, 64–65, *65*

D

Danish, Fresh Fig, *88*, 89–92

Dates

  Flour Power Bars, *168*, 169–70

Devil Dogs, Keith's Homemade, *208*, 209–10

Digital scale, 33

Donuts, Choux, with Mascarpone Cream, 103–5, *104*

Double-Crust Pâte Brisée, Master, 439

Dough

  blind baking, for pie and tart shells, 21

  docking, before baking, 24

  fraisage technique, 25

  Master Brioche, 444

  Master Double-Crust Pâte Brisée, 439

  Master Pâte Sucrée, 437

  Master Puff Pastry, 442–43

  Master Quick Puff Pastry, 440–41

  Master Single-Crust Pâte Brisée, 438

  Rick's Master Shortbread, 436

  rolling out, 26–27

Dulce de Leche Brioche Buns, 367–68, *369*

E

Eggnog Cheesecake with Gingerbread People, 312–15, *313*

Eggs

  Country Feta Pies, 40–41, *41*

  gram, volume, and weight measurements, 36

  large, for recipes, 36

  warming to room temperature, 36

  whipping whites of, 29–30

Electric mixer, handheld, 34

English Muffins, Vinal Bakery Multigrain, *142*, 143–45

English Toffee, Salted Almond, *418*, 419–20

Equipment

  bain-marie, 31

  baking pans, 31

  baking sheets, 31

  bench scraper, 32

  bowls, 32

  bowl scraper, 32

  candy thermometer, 32

  knives, 32

  measuring cups and spoons, 32

  Microplane zester, 32

  muffin tins, 32

Equipment (cont.)

    parchment paper, 32

    pastry bag and tips, 33

    rolling pins, 33

    rotating cake stand, 33

    scale, 33

    sifter, 33

    silicone baking mats, 33–34

    spatulas, 34

    stand mixer, 34

    whisk, 34

    wire rack, 34

Espresso

    Mocha Chip Cookies, 199–200, *201*

    Vietnamese, Ice Cream, *374*, 377

    Vietnamese, Profiteroles with Spicy Chocolate Ganache, *374*, 375–77

F

Feta Pies, Country, 40–41, *41*

Fig

    Fresh, Danish, *88*, 89–92

    -Walnut Bread, 149–50

Financier Cake, Stone Fruit and Berry, with Toasted Meringue, 325–27, *326*

Flour. *See also specific flour types*

    all-purpose, about, 36

    bread, about, 36

    cake, about, 36

    for cake pans, 21

    flicking, 24

    rye, about, 36

    spelt, about, 36

    whole wheat, about, 36

Flour (bakeries), 15–16

Flour Power Bars, *168*, 169–70

Focaccia, Gluten-Free, *108*, 109

Fontina

    Garlicky Cheesy Monkey Bread, 126–27, *127*

    Mushroom and Thyme Brioches, 49–51, *50*

Fraisage technique, 25

Frangipane

    in Almond Croissants, 86–87, *87*

    in Fresh Peach Crostatas, *258*, 259–60

    in Galette des Rois, 267–68, *269*

    Master, 433

    -Plum Tart, 230–32, *231*

Frostings

    Chocolate Pudding Buttercream, 345

    Cream Cheese, Brown Butter Cinnamon Rolls with, *96*, 97–98

    Creamy Ginger, Vanilla Bean Cupcakes with, *280*, 281–82

    Creamy Vanilla, 210

    Fluffy Marshmallow, 290

    Magic Sally, 284

    Malted Milk, 339

    Peanut Butter, 288

Fruit. *See also specific fruits*

    fresh, in-season, for recipes, 36–37

    Fresh, Tart, *224*, 225–26

    Stone, and Berry Financier Cake with Toasted Meringue, 325–27, *326*

    Stone, Cocktail, Almond Panna Cotta with, *354*, 355–56

Funfetti Angel Food Cake, 319–20, *321*

G

Galette des Rois, 267–68, *269*

Ganache

    Chocolate-Orange, 318

    Master, 432

    Peanut Butter, Brown Butter–Peanut Rice Crispy Treats with, *400*, 400–401

    Soy, 295

    Spicy, 295

Garlicky Cheesy Monkey Bread, 126–27, *127*

Genoise, Vanilla, 324

Ginger

    -Carrot Muffins, Vegan, *54*, 55

    Cream, 334

Eggnog Cheesecake with Gingerbread People, 312–15, *313*

Frosting, Creamy, Vanilla Bean Cupcakes with, *280*, 281–82

Gingerbread Crust and People, *313*, 314–15

-Molasses Crumble, Rum Butterscotch Pudding Parfait with, 364–66, *365*

-Peach Crumb Cake, 306–7

Sarah's Adult Spice Cake, *332*, 333–36

Glazes

    Apple, 59

    Clove, 131

    Lemon, 190

    Maple, 70

    Pomegranate, 175, *175*

Gluten-Free Apple Spice Pecan Muffins, 58–59, *59*

Gluten-Free Chocolate-Caramel Oreos, *176*, 177–79

Gluten-Free Double Chocolate–Walnut Brownies, 171–72, *173*

Gluten-Free Focaccia, *108*, 109

Gluten-Free Ham and Cheese Puffs, 47–48, *48*

Gluten-Free Lemon Raspberry Chia Muffins, 56, *57*

Gorgonzola and Bacon Drop Biscuits, *42*, 43–44

Graham Cracker

    Brown Sugar Pie Shell, 238

    Milk Chocolate Pie Shell, 262

Grapes

    Fresh, Olive Oil Cake with, *296*, 297

    Fresh Fruit Tart, *224*, 225–26

H

Half-sheet baking sheets, 31

Ham and Cheese Puffs, Gluten-Free, 47–48, *48*

Handheld electric mixer, 34

Hand Pies, Blueberry, 249–51, *250*

Hazelnut(s)

    Butter, 213

    Housemade Nutella Babka, *154*, 155–57

    -Raspberry Rugelach, 211–13, *212*

Henry's Apricot Walnut Raisin Loaf, 123–24, *125*

Honey

    and Mixed Nut Whole Grain Biscotti, 180–81, *181*

    Nougat, Almond Pistachio Cherry, 427–28, *429*

    Whole Wheat Bread, 151–52, *153*

Honeycomb, Christopher's, *410*, 411–12

Hostess Cupcakes, Vegan, *292*, 293–95

Hot Cross Buns, *128*, 129–31

Hummingbird Cupcakes, 283–84, *285*

I

Ice, Mango, 380

Ice Cream, Vietnamese Espresso, *374*, 377

Ingredients

    brown sugar, 35

    butter, 35

    chocolate, 35

    cocoa powder, 35–36

    crème fraîche, 36

    eggs, 36

    flour, 36

    folding, 24–25

    fruits, 36–37

    milk, 37

    salt, 37

    sugar, 37

    temperature for, 18–19

    tempering, 29

    vanilla beans and vanilla extract, 37

Irish Soda Bread, 66–68, *67*

J

Jam

    Apple, 390

    Homemade Rhubarb-Strawberry Spoon, 76, *77*

Japanese Cotton Cheesecake, 300–302, *301*

Jessi's Caramel Popcorn Cookies, 191–92, *193*

K

Katz, Rick, 14
Keith's Homemade Devil Dogs, *208*, 209–10
Kisses, Peppermint, 405–6, *407*
Kitchen scales, 18
Knives, 32
Kosher salt, 37
Kouigns Amann, Sticky Bun, 99–102, *101*

L

Lamingtons, *322*, 323–24
Lemon
    Curd, Master, 435
    Double, Cream Tart, 239–40, *241*
    Glaze, 190
    Meringue Cupcakes, 289–90, *291*
    -Polenta Cookies, *164*, 165
    Raspberry Chia Muffins, Gluten-Free, 56, *57*
    Spiral, Simple, *308*, 309–10
    Sugar Cookies with Lemon Glaze, *188*, 189–90
Lime
    Cream Pie with Brown Sugar Graham Crust, 236–38, *237*
    -Mango Curd and Mango Snow, Coconut Sticky Rice with, *378*, 379–81
Loaf pans, 31

M

Macaroons, Vegan Almond, 166, *167*
Magic Sally Frosting, 284
Malted Chocolate Cake, 337–40, *338*
Malted Milk Frosting, 339
Mammano, Jamie, 15
Mango
    Fresh Fruit Tart, *224*, 225–26
    Ice, 380
    -Lime Curd and Mango Snow, Coconut Sticky Rice with, *378*, 379–81

Maple
    -Blueberry Whole Wheat Scones, 69–70, *71*
    Glaze, 70
    Pecan Tassies, 398–99, *399*
Marshmallow, Vegan, 294
Marshmallow Frosting, Fluffy, 290
Marshmallow Meringue, 262
Marshmallows
    Brown Butter–Peanut Rice Crispy Treats with Peanut Butter Ganache, *400*, 400–401
    Vanilla-Mint, 408–9, *409*
Mascarpone Cream, Choux Donuts with, 103–5, *104*
Master Brioche Dough, 444
Master Double-Crust Pâte Brisée, 439
Master Frangipane, 433
Master Ganache, 432
Master Lemon Curd, 435
Master Pastry Cream, 434
Master Pâte Sucrée, 437
Master Puff Pastry Dough, 442–43
Master Quick Puff Pastry Dough, 440–41
Master Shortbread, Rick's, 436
Master Single-Crust Pâte Brisée, 438
Matcha
    Cream Puffs, *370*, 371–73
    Oreos (variation), 178
Measuring cups and spoons, 32
Meringue
    Marshmallow, 262
    Toasted, Stone Fruit and Berry Financier Cake with, 325–27, *326*
Meringues
    Brown Sugar–Candied Almond, 205–7, *206*
    Passion Fruit and Raspberry Pavlovas, *382*, 383–84
    Peppermint Kisses, 405–6, *407*
    Raspberry Swirl, 202–4, *203*
Merveilleux, Marvelous Vanilla Caramel, 385–87, *387*
Microplane zester, 32

Milk
    Bread, Alina's, *132*, 133–34
    coconut, for recipes, 37
    scalding, 27
    soy, for recipes, 37
    whole, for recipes, 37
Millet
    Nutty Seedy Breakfast Cookies, 78–79, *79*
Mise en place, 18
Miso–Apple Cider Caramels, 416–17, *417*
Mistral, 15
Mocha Chip Cookies, 199–200, *201*
Mochi, Butter, 396–97, *397*
Molasses
    Gingerbread Crust and People, *313*, 314–15
    -Ginger Crumble, Rum Butterscotch Pudding
       Parfait with, 364–66, *365*
    My Rye Bread, 114–15, *115*
Monkey Bread, Garlicky Cheesy, 126–27, *127*
Muffin Cakes, Blackberry-Buttermilk, *60*, 61
Muffins
    Apple Spice Pecan, Gluten-Free, 58–59, *59*
    Carrot-Ginger, Vegan, *54*, 55
    Chocolate-Banana, Vegan, 52, *53*
    English, Vinal Bakery Multigrain, *142*, 143–45
    Lemon Raspberry Chia, Gluten-Free, 56, *57*
Muffin tins
    lining with muffin papers, 32
    rotating in oven, 27
    sizes, 32
Mushroom and Thyme Brioches, 49–51, *50*
Myers, Christopher, 14–15

N

Napoleon, Swedish, 388–91, *389*
Nougat, Almond Pistachio Cherry Honey, 427–28,
    429
Nutella, Housemade, Babka, *154*, 155–57
Nutmeg Cake, Syrian, 298, *299*

Nut(s)
    Flour Power Bars, *168*, 169–70
    Mixed, and Honey Whole Grain Biscotti,
       180–81, *181*
    Nutty Seedy Breakfast Cookies, 78–79, *79*
    toasting, 29

O

Oat(s)
    Anzacs, 182–84, *183*
    Currant Spelt Scones, 64–65, *65*
    Flour Power Bars, *168*, 169–70
    Nutty Seedy Breakfast Cookies, 78–79, *79*
    Vinal Bakery Multigrain English Muffins, *142*,
       143–45
Offset spatula
    spreading with, 28
    uses for, 34
Olive Oil Cake with Fresh Grapes, *296*, 297
Onions
    Caramelized, 44
    Gorgonzola and Bacon Drop Biscuits, *42*, 43–44
Orange(s)
    -Almond Pudding Cake with Chocolate Ganache,
       316, 317–18
    Bittersweet Chocolate Truffle Tart with Salted
       Caramel, 245–48, *247*
    Candied, 131, 318
    -Chocolate Ganache, 318
    Hot Cross Buns, *128*, 129–31
    Panettone, 139–40, *141*
    Slices, Candied, 248
Oreos, Gluten-Free Chocolate-Caramel, *176*, 177–79
Ossa dei Morti, 185–86, *187*
Oven temperature, checking, 18

P

Palmiers, Baby, *214*, 215–16
Panettone, 139–40, *141*

Panna Cotta, Almond, with Stone Fruit Cocktail, *354*, 355–56

Pans, baking, 31

Parchment paper

cutting circle from, 23–24

making cornet with, 25–26

uses for, 32

Parfait, Rum Butterscotch Pudding, with Ginger-Molasses Crumble, 364–66, *365*

Parmesan

-Chive Scones, 45–46, *46*

Gluten-Free Ham and Cheese Puffs, 47–48, *48*

Passion Fruit

Crêpe Cake, *348*, 349–51

and Raspberry Pavlovas, *382*, 383–84

Pastry bags

cloth or plastic, 33

filling, 24

piping with, 26

sizes, 33

Pastry Cream, Master, 434

Pastry tips, 33

Pâte Brisée

Master Double-Crust, 439

Master Single-Crust, 438

Pâte Sucrée, Master, 437

Pavlovas, Passion Fruit and Raspberry, *382*, 383–84

Payard, François, 15, 19

Payard Patisserie, 15, 19

Peach(es)

Almond Panna Cotta with Stone Fruit Cocktail, *354*, 355–56

-Blueberry Cobbler, Summer, *360*, 361–62

Fresh, Crostatas, *258*, 259–60

-Ginger Crumb Cake, 306–7

ripe, for recipes, 36

Peanut–Brown Butter Rice Crispy Treats with Peanut Butter Ganache, *400*, 400–401

Peanut Butter

–Chocolate Buttercrunch, *424*, 425–26

Frosting, 288

Ganache, Brown Butter–Peanut Rice Crispy Treats with, *400*, 400–401

Pear(s)

ripe, for recipes, 36

Tarte Tatin, Autumn, 275–76, *277*

Pecan(s)

Apple Spice Muffins, Gluten-Free, 58–59, *59*

-Cranberry Bread, 146–48, *147*

Ginger-Peach Crumb Cake, 306–7

Hummingbird Cupcakes, 283–84, *285*

-Pumpkin Bread Pudding, 357–58, *359*

Sandies, 160–61, *161*

Sticky Bun Kouigns Amann, 99–102, *101*

Sticky Bun Popcorn, 394, *395*

Tassies, Maple, 398–99, *399*

Pepitas

Nutty Seedy Breakfast Cookies, 78–79, *79*

Peppermint

Kisses, 405–6, *407*

Vanilla-Mint Marshmallows, 408–9, *409*

Persian Love Cookies, 174–75, *175*

Pie dough. *See under* Dough

Pie plates, 31

Pies

Apple, Old-Fashioned Double-Crust, 273–74, *274*

Banana Cream, with Salted Caramel and Dark Chocolate, 264–66, *265*

blind baking shells for, 21

Cherry Crumb, *242*, 243–44

Country Feta, 40–41, *41*

Hand, Blueberry, 249–51, *250*

Lime Cream, with Brown Sugar Graham Crust, 236–38, *237*

Rhubarb Brown Sugar, 255–56, *257*

S'mores, 261–62, *263*

Spring Ricotta, with Fresh Berries, 227–28, *229*

Strawberry Slab, *252*, 253–54

Pie Shells
 Brown Sugar Graham Cracker, 238
 Gingerbread, 314–15
 Milk Chocolate Graham Cracker, 262
Pineapple
 Hummingbird Cupcakes, 283–84, *285*
Pistachio(s)
 Almond Cherry Honey Nougat, 427–28,
  429
 Mixed Nut and Honey Whole Grain Biscotti,
  180–81, *181*
 Persian Love Cookies, 174–75, *175*
Plum(s)
 Almond Panna Cotta with Stone Fruit Cocktail,
  354, 355–56
 -Frangipane Tart, 230–32, *231*
 ripe, for recipes, 36
 Upside-Down Cake, 303–5, *304*
Polenta-Lemon Cookies, *164*, 165
Pomegranate Glaze, *175*, 175
Popcorn
 Caramel, Cookies, Jessi's, 191–92, *193*
 Sticky Bun, 394, *395*
Potato chips
 Super Bowl Cupcakes, *286*, 287–88
Pound Cake, Apple-Vanilla, 62–63, *63*
Pretzel twists
 Super Bowl Cupcakes, *286*, 287–88
Profiteroles, Vietnamese Espresso, with Spicy
 Chocolate Ganache, *374*, 375–77
Pudding
 Bread, Pumpkin-Pecan, 357–58, *359*
 Cake, Orange-Almond, with Chocolate Ganache,
  316, 317–18
 Parfait, Rum Butterscotch, with Ginger-
  Molasses Crumble, 364–66, *365*
Puff Pastry
 in Autumn Pear Tarte Tatin, 275–76, *277*
 in Baby Palmiers, *214*, 215–16
 in Chaussons aux Pommes, *270*, 271–72
 Dough, Master, 442–43
 Dough, Quick Master, 440–41

 in Galette des Rois, 267–68, *269*
 in Swedish Napoleon, 388–91, *389*
Puffs
 Gluten-Free Ham and Cheese, 47–48, *48*
 Matcha Cream, *370*, 371–73
Pumpkin-Pecan Bread Pudding, 357–58, *359*

Q

Quarter-sheet rimmed pans, 31
Quick Puff Pastry Dough, Master, 440–41

R

Rainbow sprinkles
 Funfetti Angel Food Cake, 319–20, *321*
 Homemade Sprinkles, *346*, 347
Raisin(s)
 Anzacs, 182–84, *183*
 Apricot Walnut Loaf, Henry's, 123–24, *125*
 Flour Power Bars, *168*, 169–70
 Hot Cross Buns, *128*, 129–31
 Mixed Nut and Honey Whole Grain Biscotti,
  180–81, *181*
 Panettone, 139–40, *141*
 Vegan Carrot-Ginger Muffins, *54*, 55
Raspberry(ies)
 Coulis, 204
 Fresh Fruit Tart, *224*, 225–26
 Lamingtons, *322*, 323–24
 Lemon Chia Muffins, Gluten-Free, 56, *57*
 and Passion Fruit Pavlovas, *382*, 383–84
 Spring Ricotta Pie with Fresh Berries, 227–28, *229*
 Swirl Meringues, 202–4, *203*
Raspberry jam
 in Hazelnut-Raspberry Rugelach, 211–13, *212*
 in Swedish Napoleon, 388–91, *389*
Recipes
 adjusting to your liking, 19
 baking time guidelines, 19

Recipes (cont.)

    following, 19

    reading, 18

    tests for doneness, 19

Rhubarb

    Brown Sugar Pie, 255–56, *257*

    -Strawberry Jam-n-Butter Biscuits, 75–76, *77*

    -Strawberry Spoon Jam, Homemade, 76, *77*

Rialto, 14–15

Rice, Coconut Sticky, with Mango-Lime Curd and Mango Snow, *378,* 379–81

Rice Crispy Treats, Brown Butter–Peanut, with Peanut Butter Ganache, *400,* 400–401

Rick's Master Shortbread, 436

Ricotta

    -Cherry Scones, *72,* 73–74

    Country Feta Pies, 40–41, *41*

    Pie, Spring, with Fresh Berries, 227–28, *229*

Rolling pins, 33

Rolls

    Brown Butter Cinnamon, with Cream Cheese Frosting, *96,* 97–98

    Whole Grain Pull-Apart, *116,* 117–18

Rose water

    Persian Love Cookies, 174–75, *175*

Rotating cake stand, 33

Rugelach, Hazelnut-Raspberry, 211–13, *212*

Rum

    Butterscotch Pudding Parfait with Ginger-Molasses Crumble, 364–66, *365*

    Eggnog Cheesecake with Gingerbread People, 312–15, *313*

    Sarah's Adult Spice Cake, *332,* 333–36

    Syrup, Strong, 335

Rye flour

    about, 36

    Ashley's Birthday Cake, *342,* 343–47

    Double Chocolate Rye Cookies, 196–98, *197*

    Irish Soda Bread, 66–68, *67*

    Mixed Nut and Honey Whole Grain Biscotti, 180–81, *181*

Mocha Chip Cookies, 199–200, *201*

My Rye Bread, 114–15, *115*

S

Salt, 19, 37

Salted Almond English Toffee, *418,* 419–20

Salted Butter, 76

Salted Caramel

    Bittersweet Chocolate–Orange Truffle Tart with, 245–48, *247*

    and Dark Chocolate, Banana Cream Pie with, 264–66, *265*

    Sauce for Banana Cream Pie, 266

    Sauce for Truffle Tart, 246

Sandies, Pecan, 160–61, *161*

Scale, digital, 33

Scales, digital, 18

Scones

    Currant Spelt Oat, 64–65, *65*

    Parmesan-Chive, 45–46, *46*

    Ricotta-Cherry, *72,* 73–74

    Whole Wheat Maple-Blueberry, 69–70, *71*

Seeds

    Coconut Sticky Rice with Mango-Lime Curd and Mango Snow, *378,* 379–81

    Flour Power Bars, *168,* 169–70

    Nutty Seedy Breakfast Cookies, 78–79, *79*

    Tahini–Black Sesame Spiral Shortbreads, *218,* 219–21

Sesame seeds

    Coconut Sticky Rice with Mango-Lime Curd and Mango Snow, *378,* 379–81

    Tahini–Black Sesame Spiral Shortbreads, *218,* 219–21

Shire, Lydia, 14

Shortbread

    Billionaire's, 402–4, *403*

    Master, Rick's, 436

Shortbreads, Tahini–Black Sesame Spiral, *218,* 219–21

Sifter, 33

Silicone baking mats, 33–34

Single-Crust Pâte Brisée, Master, 438

S'mores Pie, 261–62, *263*

Soda Bread, Irish, 66–68, *67*

Soy Ganache, 295

Soy milk, for recipes, 37

Spatulas

    offset, spreading with, 28

    offset, uses for, 34

    rubber and/or silicone, 34

Speckle, Chocolate, 340

Spelt flour

    about, 36

    Currant Spelt Oat Scones, 64–65, *65*

    Spelt Croissants, *80*, 81–85

    Vinal Bakery Multigrain English Muffins, *142*, 143–45

Spice Cake, Sarah's Adult, *332*, 333–36

Spicy Ganache, 377

Spinach

    Country Feta Pies, 40–41, *41*

Sprinkles

    Funfetti Angel Food Cake, 319–20, *321*

    Homemade, *346*, 347

Stand mixer, 34

Sticky Bun Kouigns Amann, 99–102, *101*

Sticky Bun Popcorn, 394, *395*

Sticky Buns, Apple Cider, 93–94, *95*

Sticky Rice, Coconut, with Mango-Lime Curd and Mango Snow, *378*, 379–81

Strawberry(ies)

    and Cream Chiffon Cake, *328*, 329–31

    Fresh Fruit Tart, *224*, 225–26

    -Rhubarb Jam-n-Butter Biscuits, 75–76, *77*

    -Rhubarb Spoon Jam, Homemade, 76, *77*

    Slab Pie, *252*, 253–54

Sugar

    and butter, creaming, 23

    cooking, 21–23

    superfine, about, 37

    superfine, making your own, 37

    vanilla, preparing, 26

Sugar, brown. *See* Brown Sugar

Sunflower seeds

    Flour Power Bars, *168*, 169–70

    Nutty Seedy Breakfast Cookies, 78–79, *79*

Super Bowl Cupcakes, *286*, 287–88

Swedish Napoleon, 388–91, *389*

Sweets and confections

    Almond Pistachio Cherry Honey Nougat, 427–28, *429*

    Apple Cider–Miso Caramels, 416–17, *417*

    Billionaire's Shortbread, 402–4, *403*

    Brown Butter Caramels, 413–14, *415*

    Brown Butter–Peanut Rice Crispy Treats with Peanut Butter Ganache, *400*, 400–401

    Butter Mochi, 396–97, *397*

    Chocolate Almond Cocoa Nib Caramels, 421–22, *423*

    Chocolate–Peanut Butter Buttercrunch, *424*, 425–26

    Christopher's Honeycomb, *410*, 411–12

    Maple Pecan Tassies, 398–99, *399*

    Peppermint Kisses, 405–6, *407*

    Salted Almond English Toffee, *418*, 419–20

    Sticky Bun Popcorn, 394, *395*

    Vanilla-Mint Marshmallows, 408–9, *409*

Syrian Nutmeg Cake, 298, *299*

Syrup

    Coffee, 347

    Strong Rum, 335

T

Tahini–Black Sesame Spiral Shortbreads, *218*, 219–21

Tangzhong, 134

Tapioca flour

    Gluten-Free Ham and Cheese Puffs, 47–48, *48*

Tart pans, 31

Tart rings, 31

Tarts

    Almond Joy, 233–35, *234*

    Autumn Pear Tarte Tatin, 275–76, *277*

Tarts (cont.)

    Bittersweet Chocolate–Orange Truffle, with Salted Caramel, 245–48, *247*

    blind baking shells for, 21

    Double Lemon Cream, 239–40, *241*

    Fresh Fruit, *224*, 225–26

    Fresh Peach Crostatas, *258*, 259–60

    Galette des Rois, 267–68, *269*

    Plum-Frangipane, 230–32, *231*

Tassies, Maple Pecan, 398–99, *399*

Techniques

    blind baking shells, 21

    buttering and flouring pans, 21

    cooking sugar, 21–23

    creaming butter and sugar, 23

    crumb coating a cake, 23

    cutting a parchment circle, 23–24

    docking dough, 24

Tachniques (cont.)

    filling a pastry bag, 24

    flicking flour, 24

    folding ingredients, 24–25

    fraisage, 25

    making a cornet, 25–26

    making vanilla sugar, 26

    melting chocolate, 26

    piping with a pastry bag, 26

    rolling out pastry dough, 26–27

    rotating cake pans, baking sheets, and muffin tins, 27

    scalding milk and cream, 27

    scoring and slashing bread, 27–28

    splitting a cake into layers, 28

    splitting and scraping vanilla beans, 28

    spreading with an offset spatula, 28

    tempering chocolate, 28–29

    tempering ingredients, 29

    toasting nuts, 29

    whipping egg whites, 29–30

Tempering

    chocolate, 28–29

    ingredients, 29

Thermometer, candy, 32

Thyme and Mushroom Brioches, 49–51, *50*

Toffee, Salted Almond English, *418*, 419–20

Tube pans, 31

Turnovers

    Chaussons aux Pommes, *270*, 271–72

V

Vanilla

    Apple Butter, 272

    Caramel Cream, 386

    Caramel Merveilleux, Marvelous, 385–87, *387*

    extract, for recipes, 37

    extract, substituting, for vanilla beans, 37

    Frosting, Creamy, 210

    Genoise, 324

    -Mint Marshmallows, 408–9, *409*

Vanilla Bean(s)

    Cupcakes with Creamy Ginger Frosting, *280*, 281–82

    making vanilla sugar with, 26

    splitting and scraping, 28

    storing, 37

Vegan Almond Macaroons, 166, *167*

Vegan Carrot-Ginger Muffins, *54*, 55

Vegan Chocolate-Banana Muffins, 52, *53*

Vegan Hostess Cupcakes, *292*, 293–95

Vegan Marshmallow, 294

Vietnamese Espresso Ice Cream, *374*, 377

Vietnamese Espresso Profiteroles with Spicy Chocolate Ganache, *374*, 375–77

Vinal Bakery Multigrain English Muffins, *142*, 143–45

W

Walnut(s)

Apricot Raisin Loaf, Henry's, 123–24, *125*

–Double Chocolate Brownies, Gluten-Free, 171–72, *173*

Double Chocolate Rye Cookies, 196–98, *197*

–Fig Bread, 149–50

Meltaways, 162–63, *163*

Mixed Nut and Honey Whole Grain Biscotti, 180–81, *181*

Nutty Seedy Breakfast Cookies, 78–79, *79*

Syrian Nutmeg Cake, 298, *299*

Vegan Carrot-Ginger Muffins, *54*, 55

Whipped Cream

Vanilla Caramel Cream, 386

Whisks, 34

White chocolate, buying, 35

Whole Grain Pull-Apart Rolls, *116*, 117–18

Whole wheat flour

about, 36

Honey Whole Wheat Bread, 151–52, *153*

Mixed Nut and Honey Whole Grain Biscotti, 180–81, *181*

My Rye Bread, 114–15, *115*

Nutty Seedy Breakfast Cookies, 78–79, *79*

Stone Fruit and Berry Financier Cake with Toasted Meringue, 325–27, *326*

Syrian Nutmeg Cake, 298, *299*

Vegan Carrot-Ginger Muffins, *54*, 55

Vinal Bakery Multigrain English Muffins, *142*, 143–45

Whole Grain Pull-Apart Rolls, *116*, 117–18

Whole Wheat Brioches à Tête, 119–22, *120*

Whole Wheat Maple-Blueberry Scones, 69–70, *71*

Wire racks, 34

Z

Zester, Microplane, 32